ADIÓS TO MY PARENTS
A MEMOIR

HÉCTOR AGUILAR CAMÍN

schaffner
press
Tucson, Arizona

First English Language Edition
Trade Paperback Original
License to reprint granted by Schavelzon Graham
Agencia Literaria
Tel (34) 932 011 310 * Fax (34) 932 003 886 *
info@schavelzon.com

Cover Design: Dan Stiles
Interior Design: Darci Slaten

ISBN: 978-1-943156-62-7 (Paperback)
ISBN: 978-1-943156-63-4 (PDF)
ISBN: 978-1-943156-64-1 (EPUB)
ISBN: 978-1-943156-65-8 (Mobipocket)

For Library of Congress Cataloguing-in-Publication
Information contact the Publisher.

Printed in the United States

ADIÓS TO MY PARENTS

A MEMOIR

HÉCTOR AGUILAR CAMÍN

Mexico City, 2004

I've seen a photo of my father as a young man, his best photo. He's twenty-six and wearing a light-colored linen suit that billows in the wind. He's standing on a beach of sand and pebbles next to a tall, long-limbed girl. In a few years that girl will be my mother. The photo captures a July morning in 1944 at the yacht club in Campeche, a city on the Gulf of Mexico on the country's southeast coast. The day the photo was taken British and Canadian troops occupied Caen. A month before, 160,000 soldiers had come ashore in Normandy. Nothing could be more remote from the beach in Campeche, the beach in the picture where my recently wed father and mother are embarking on what they suppose will be the best years of their lives.

The lives of the people in that paradise are almost over. All that's left is the wreckage of the faces in their first photo as a couple, the juvenile wisp of a smile, the plain-spoken phrase issuing from the trembling oval of a pair of lips. The smiling girl in the photo is now eighty-four and can hardly walk. She's lost her hearing and her sight is gone in one eye. A mysterious strain of emphysema has invaded her lungs though she never smoked. The young man who will become my father is now eighty-seven. He spends his waning days in an apartment near the Forest of Chapultepec, Mexico City, retelling old stories and repeating old names, among them the name of the woman in the photo, now only a murmur sealed in the glow of forgetting. These days his memory specializes in forgetting.

Nearly half a century has gone by since the last time my

father and mother saw each other, since the morning in 1959 when my father packed his suitcase and left our house on Avenida Mexico across the street from the park with the same name. In time this will become my family's mythic homestead. In those days it was just a two-story house with a garage and a balcony, an art deco façade, ironwork over the windows, black granite baseboards, and cornices. I don't know the date of the morning my father left the house without saying goodbye to my mother or us or, in all likelihood, to himself. He put his suitcase at the foot of the black granite stairs, the one luxury of the house's interior, while my mother cooked or pretended to cook in the kitchen, pleading for the husband she'd lived with for fifteen years, and with whom she'd had five children, to go without trying to make a scene of his departure. My father hesitates to bid goodbye to the one woman he's ever loved and has now lost for good. He doesn't feel worthy or deserving of a farewell. He feels small in the eyes of a wife who now looks down on him after having once looked up to him. He doesn't want to face her or tell her goodbye because he doesn't want to see the look of relief in her eyes or hear the words of reproach on her lips. He won't tell her goodbye, he leaves the house in surrender that morning, fulfilling the last wish of a wife who has long since lost her respect though not her love for him. She's the kind of woman who loves a man long after she ceases to respect him. My father's departure is timid but decisive, by which I mean he'll never be back except for a night five years later when I come home to find him drunk with his forearm against the wrought-iron door and his forehead leaning against his forearm, waiting to be let in. My mother and my aunt look out at him from between the slats of the wooden blinds, shaken by this unexpected assault on the realm of their freedom, the cave where they walled themselves in and set to work after my father went away. I happen to be home at an unaccustomed time, and my presence solves the scene by inertia. I take my father's arm, move him away from the door where he's blubbering, flag down a taxi, and take him home. I ask if he has a wife, as if suggesting that it would be normal for him to have one, that we can speak as grownups, man to man, the two of us. He watches me stupidly and cries, leaving his face even wetter than it already was, dampened by shame and alcohol. I watch him stupidly and tell myself I should remember what I'm seeing so I can write about it some day.

I don't see my father again until his life is about over, the afternoon of the November day when he calls my office after thirty-six years of unbroken absence. He calls before lunch and says he wants to see me. That same night I go to see him in the place where he lives, an inn lost in the streets around the city's old jai alai frontón. It's a district of ancient buildings, fleabag hotels, and dry-cleaners that still use steam irons and obsolescent, semi-toxic chemicals. The inn where my father lives is called the Alcázar Arms. There's no light in the doorway because the bulbs have burnt out. I have no idea who this hunchbacked little man is when he greets me in the shadows of the entrance hall. I've lived a lifetime without seeing him, and he's spent a life not looking like the person I remember. He walks me through the shadows to his room, which deserves a story unto itself. He shows me some legal pleadings and asks me for money. The scene begins to fill the gaping hole his absence left in my life.

I'll leave for later the years I coexisted with that gaping hole and the meeting that began to fill it. Now, as I write in November of 2004, my parents are back together for the first time in half a century on the strength of a reunion forged by pneumonia and by me. Pneumonia specializes in the aged, and it went to work on the two of them in the weeks that followed. I played my part by finding them somewhere to be treated. It's called the Mexico City English Hospital. I hate the place. Here, fourteen years ago, my aunt Luisa Camín died the atrocious death of a terminal patient kept alive by machine, and my hatred is greatest on the well-lit, mercilessly bright third floor where the intensive and intermediate care units are. After months of not dying in intensive care, my intubated aunt was transported to a public hospital on a day in November, 1991. My mother is now in intermediate care. The month is also November, but the year is 2004. I situate myself in that time and look back from there to my parents' unlikely reencounter at the end of their lives.

How did we get here? How did these two bodies end up being treated for pneumonia on parallel floors half a century after the rupture of a union they couldn't leave in the past?

Emma, my mother, enters the hospital through the emergency room to be treated for advanced pneumonia. She can hardly breathe, her nails are beginning to turn blue, and her oxygen-starved eyes bulge from their sockets. After two days of fevers and phlegm, her young doctor decides to admit her. José Luís López is slight of build, his olive skin smooth and his chin beardless as Montezuma's. Like Anton Chekhov before him, he's a doctor with a taste for French literature. He believes in universal health care, is willing to settle for modest earnings, wears his hair slicked back from his forehead, and has an exquisitely diffident Mexican soul. From the first day of her internment, the veins and arteries of Emma's hands bristle with needles like purple pin cushions. I remember eating mouthfuls of rice and ground beef wrapped in corn tortillas from those hands, bite-size cones perfectly formed between her nimble fingers. Two days after she's admitted, not a single vein or artery in Emma's hands and arms remains un-martyred by the needles and tubes injecting her with analgesics and antibiotics. Under her age spots are blotches of discoloration, meadows of stagnant blood beneath the yellow skin of her hands. I stare at them while listening to the doctor. He tells me how weak her hands are and explains that they wouldn't tolerate another needle. They'll have to open a vein in her neck and insert a catheter to feed her. Sometimes my sisters spend the night with Emma, but the one who usually stays with her is Ceci. She's worked for Emma since arriving in Mexico City eighteen years ago, fresh off the bus from the mountain village of Ahuehuetitlán in the mountains of Oaxaca. Ceci has looked after Emma since Emma ceased to be an older woman and became an old lady of sixty-five. From that day to this she's kept house for Emma, who at eighty-four is fighting for breath in the hospital's intermediate care unit with Ceci at her bedside. Ceci grew up in Ahuehuetlán with the couple she calls her parents but are in reality her grandparents. Now eighty and ninety respectively, Socorrito and Rafael have raised ten children and seven grandchildren. I know nothing about this flood of offspring typical of the old towns in rural Mexico. The one who knows the whole story and tells it to me is my sister Emma, who has her mother's manic gift for recalling the details of stories, people, and how they got along with one another. Unlike my sister, my memory is less an archive than a series of insights, a migration of butterflies. Most of the time my memories come to me in dreams. They stick up like rocks in a river, stepping stones to the distant shore where Emma and Héctor used to live. I don't look up or ask where they lead because these stones help me cross the river of forgetting. Forgetting pulls everything into its placenta except the stones protruding from memory.

Héctor is admitted to the English Hospital when Emma has already spent three weeks there fighting for breath. He gets the same diagnosis of pneumonia from the same discrete Dr. López Zaragoza after house calls two days in a row. López held off admitting him because I made him promise not to subject Héctor to a long-drawn-out death in a hospital riddled with catheters. Héctor lives near my house in an eleven-story building on Gelati Street, so named for Colonel Gregorio Vicente Gelati, who died in the battle of Molina del Rey while resisting the American invasion of 1848. The building stands on the site of the battle, which at the time was a cornfield at the foot of the Castle of Chapultepec. From the balcony of his apartment Héctor can see the towers of the castle sticking up through the trees.

Héctor's guardian angel Rita Tenorio lives in the apartment. She was born in Zitátacuaro in the state of Michoacán and has two beautiful daughters who live with her: twenty-two-year-old Gabi and eight-year-old Lupita. Like me, they're the progeny of missing fathers. Gabi had a son named Diego at a very early age, and his father left for the United States four seasons ago. There's been no news of him since then. Gabi does housework for me just two blocks from Héctor's, but she sleeps with her mother, her sister Lupita, and her son Diego in my father's apartment where Rita rules the roost. Rita's sister Delia has also moved in after her husband left her in Zitátacuaro with four kids. Thus my father, the absent father par excellence, finds himself surrounded by women with missing husbands and young Diego. Fate has chosen to leave Héctor's sunset years in these tender and loving hands. He's become the surrogate head of a surrogate family that bears him no grudge and will keep him company until death.

Chance has decreed that when Héctor goes to the hospital he gets a room on the east corner of the third floor directly under the room where my mother lies in intermediate care one floor up. There's nothing magic or symbolic about this convergence because I was the one who put the two of them in the same place. But it wasn't my decision that consigned them to symmetrical rooms one on top of the other. This unexpected coincidence winks at my despondence.

Héctor has a young psychiatrist who for months has tried to help him deal with the cosmic anguish brought on by his failing memory. The solemn young psychiatrist has fought this war against time with battalions of medications whose proper doses and side effects are a matter of theory because the prescribing physician is too young to have tried them on very many patients. Along with his anxiety, the drugs have erased what remains of Héctor's memory. When Rita hands the doctors treating his pneumonia the list of drugs my father is supposed to take, they grimace respectfully and keep their opinion of such witchcraft to themselves. The mix of fever, hospital, and drugs produces visions that begin the day he's admitted, and my father's reaction to these treacherous apparitions is unforgettable. He raves and mutters in his delirium, then abruptly sits up. Supporting himself on one arm, he points a trembling index finger toward a spot on the diminished horizon of his room. His arm is shortened by arthritis and Parkinson's, but the dreams his arm pursues were once as limitless as the horizon he imagines. Those dreams are lost and shrunken now, and he longs for places that are no more than glimmering shadows in his receding memory.

I'll visit Emma every morning in the intermediate care unit, then I'll go down a floor to see Héctor. They haven't been this physically close since the day they broke up.

Emma suffers through the worst days of her respiratory crisis connected to a catheter that pumps antibiotics into her chest. The mask over her face supplies her with oxygen and expectorant. Her appetite is back, and she's begun to chatter incessantly, to complain and tell stories. She never forgets a story. My father on the other hand doesn't remember a thing. He just asks if I'm taking care of his properties in Chetumal, the land he deliriously assumes might be taken away from him.

Then he stares straight ahead, raises his finger, and asks if it's raining. He's looking at the vertical bars of the forlorn chart hanging on the wall in front of his bed.

I begin to joke with Emma, telling her that her husband is on the floor below and she's on the one above, that life is full of surprises. She doesn't find the fact that gives rise to my joke particularly amusing, but it doesn't keep her from repeating a sentence she used over and over for years: "Poor man." I also tell Héctor his wife is right over him in intermediate care. "Emma Camín?" he says. He nods his head and remembers: "She was a beautiful girl in Chetumal."

The pneumonia runs its course, and so do their hospital stays.

Ceci is radiant when Emma is released. She's slept at my mother's bedside for fourteen of the sixteen days she's been in intermediate care and ten of the eleven nights when she was allowed two visitors at once. On the floor below, Rita is happy because Héctor hasn't lost his memory and is asking for Diego.

Héctor leaves the hospital a day before Emma, accompanied by his new family of Rita, Delia, and me. My siblings can't get used to the resuscitated ghost he's become. Strictly speaking, our father, the father I speak of and remember, exists solely in my mind, my sister Emma's, and, to a lesser degree, in the memories of my younger siblings Pilar and Juan José. Luís Miguel, my youngest brother, has no independent recollection of Héctor, but he's visited him regularly since his reappearance. He wrote a poem that says it all. The first lines are:

> *Three times I wanted to embrace*
> *the shadow of my father*
> *who still lives in this world*

Emma gets out in the company of Ceci and Ceci's four children. She chatters away, issuing instructions for dinner, a meal it's still too early to be planning for.

In *The Woman of Andros*, Thorton Wilder recounts the fable of a man the King of the Underworld lets return to the world of the living on one condition. He must carry within him two beings: one who lives and one who watches. He sees his parents on an ordinary day and concludes they're the living dead because they can't see how lucky they are; the joy of being alive is more good fortune than humans can bear.

It's not like that for us right now, nor for Emma and Héctor when they get home and are surrounded by the things they love. Back in my own house, I sleep all night and don't wake up until dawn. Then, on a walk through the woods of Chapultepec, I feel grateful for the damp and invigorating mist under the eucalyptus and cypress trees, and an old thought comes back to me. It always seemed to me that the old must have a secret they keep from the young. I've often considered writing a novel with that secret as its guiding theme. Uncovering it has been my life's mission in a way: wanting to grow up and cease being the child forbidden to know the adult secret, the enviable secret of the grownups who rule the world. Now, as I walk through the woods, it occurs to me that the secret is obvious. The adults who guard it so zealously aren't trying to fool anybody. They act out of shame because their secret is as obvious as the years that are gone before we know it. In the end nothing is left but the years themselves and the dry-eyed gaze that looks back on them. Life rushes towards an unscalable wall and ends in death. It's the secret the old learn gradually, and there's no way for them to pass it on. Or to teach those unable to hear for the simple reason that we all must learn it on our own. Nobody learns to die from someone else.

That may be so, but in the meantime...

Chetumal, 1938

The place called Cimadevilla is the highest point on a peninsula with a 360-degree view of the world below. Whoever sits on this ancient rock sees the same horizon the Roman sentries did. It's where I sit as dawn comes up over Cimadevilla. The city of Gijón, birthplace of my maternal grandparents, lies below, out of sight and out of earshot. The only sound is the eternal wind, the wind that's blown since time began. The sun rises, and I lose myself in the horizon. For a moment I'm the Roman sentry watching the ocean from the heights above the yet to be born village of Gijón, now just a fortified way station on the road by the shore. The sentry squints at the blurred line between the sky and the North Sea. He's on the lookout for ships approaching the harbor to trade or wage war. But, like me, he sees only a bank of fog, a headland shrouded in mist. For a moment he stops being a sentry, forgets his name, and loses the sense of who he is. He melts into the shapeless horizon, the timeless fog, the gateway to whatever lies beyond. He thinks about the first man ever to climb this cliff. He imagines him reaching the summit with a stick in his hand: naked, restless, and on the run. The wind washes over him, invites him to sit down and look around. For a moment, the Roman sentry becomes the first man to see the sunrise from these heights over the North Sea. But at the time there was no North Sea and no horizon because there was no vocabulary with which to name them. There's only the fog bank and the timeless wind blowing across this highland before the dawn of history.

These are the thoughts that fill my head at dawn in Cimadevilla one morning in August, 1994. I've traveled to Asturias to see where my grandparents came from. I spent a few hours in Albandi where my grandmother Josefa García was born. By the alleyways and buildings—and by the wall along San Lorenzo Beach—I believe I found the place in Gijón where my grandfather, Manuel Camín, was born. He was single when he left his homeland for the first time in 1907; in 1914, when he left for the second time, he left as a married man never to return. For years, first in Cuba, then in Mexico my grandmother Josefa prepared her return to Asturias, collecting and sending dishes, tablecloths, curtains, bed sheets and pillowcases. There was a place and use for everything in the house she'd have in Asturias once her adventure in America was over. In 1955 Hurricane Janet devastated Chetumal, where I was born, and put an end to Josefa García's forty-year dream of going home. I later learned that her trousseau dwindled away as her family struggled to survive the lean years following the Spanish Civil War. Janet's destruction of her house in Chetumal broke Josefa's spirits for good and turned her into a kind of ghost, closemouthed and utterly detached from the world around her. I remember her staring for hours over the waters of the Bay of Chetumal with the breeze blowing through her uncombed gray hair.

When day has dawned and I descend to Cimadevilla, the first thing that comes to mind is my memory of Josefa gazing at the ocean from Chetumal and knowing she'd never see it again from the shores of Asturias, where I just watched the sun come up.

How is it that Josefa García of Albandi, Asturias, age fifty, lands with her daughters Luisa, 26, and Emma, 17, in a town on Mexico's Caribbean coast known until recently as Payo Obispo, but now known as Chetumal, a place so new it's not even sure of its name?

She's come from Havana with daughters Luisa and Emma in tow. They made the trip on one of the small freighters with makeshift cabins for travelers between Cuba and the coral coast of Yucatán. They disembark in the port of Progreso on the northern tip of the peninsula. From there they board a fishing boat that goes ashore on the islet of Isla Mujeres and the island of Cozumel ("land of swallows"). They sail past the pristine bays of Ascensión and Espíritu Santo to the fishing village of Xcalak at the mouth of Chetumal Bay. The land on the far side of the shallow bay belongs to England under a treaty that drew the line between Mexico and Belize in 1897. Forty-one years later, in the navigable month of June, the boat with Josefa and her daughters plows over dense growths of seaweed. From time to time it scrapes bottom as it heads towards a nondescript string of white houses on a shore whose only distinction is a few tall palm trees topped by fronds more ragged than elegant. Except for the odor of vegetation decaying in the tropical heat, the place is a far cry from the stately Cuban city Josefa and her daughters have come from. They used to live in Camagüey where they rode out the years since 1929 when the sugar market collapsed and the island's economy fell apart. Josefa's husband belonged to the legion of immigrants from Asturias and Galicia who, along with Cubans of Spanish descent, thrived from the excesses and spin-offs of the Cuban sugar industry. Manuel Camín had prospered as the manager of hotels or stores in the towns that grew up around the sugar mills, the small settlements Cubans call *quintas*. The *quintas* were a world apart from the cheerless landscape seen while crossing a bay redolent of mangroves and marshes. This was nothing like the white sand beaches and blue waters of the Caribbean along so much of the Yucatán shore. It bore no resemblance whatsoever to Cozumel, which in the morning light had made the girl named Emma think of an emerald set in platinum when she saw it from the unassuming prow of a fishing boat.

In 2004, from my house in Mexico City, I track the route of that journey in 1938. The satellite images bring me dazzlingly near the blue Caribbean that bathes the Yucatán Peninsula. I'm transfixed by these turquoise waters as seen from a satellite, the chlorophyll green of jungle, the blue of estuaries, the faded green of the shallow bay. The travelers whose steps I retrace must have felt something similar when they reminisced about this journey. True, they'd left everything they ever owned in their beloved Camagüey, their much loved Cuba, for a world echoing with threats of Indian wars and the scrapes among revolutionaries who only recently stopped shooting at each other. An aura of legends shimmered about the unknown and ominous land the sisters saw from their boat. They were leaving much behind, but they were on their way to making their dream aboard an orphan fishing vessel come true: the prospect of reuniting with their father, Manuel Camín.

The first time Camín left Gijón it was 1907, and he was twenty-seven. He left behind the green hills of his homeland and his fiance Josefa, who, belonging to a family of women who bled late, had yet to bleed. Though he leaves as a bachelor, he's committed. He's schooled in the secrets of carpentry and the construction trade, and he's a voluble talker disenchanted with socialism and Freemasonry. His chest swells with pride in the Spain he disavowed in the first flush of youth. He fell, as he would put it, under the curse of anarchism and the Jacobin fever sweeping the docks of Asturias. Manuel Camín clashes with his father, the harbor master in the port of Gijón. When the dock workers go on strike, Manuel is inflamed by the chimera of universal justice and joins the walkout. As the weeks go by, he comes to realize that among the things the protesters want to abolish is his father's job, a post that ends up in the hands of the leader who inspired Camín to go on strike for the first and last time. He sails for Cuba and comes ashore in Havana, where he works in exchange for food and a place to sleep. He gets help from an uncle and helps himself by rising before dawn and going to work. When told someone lucked out and got rich, he replies: "Luck is a gift that's given daily on jobs that start at five in the morning." Although the island is Spanish to the bone, new arrivals from the mother country lead a hard life. Their best hope for getting ahead is to find work with other Spaniards. Camín cleans and does odd jobs in a hotel, a rooming house with corridors of unpainted wooden planks. He joins construction crews on plantations in Oriente Province, then returns to Gijón to marry. He's been gone two years and hasn't gotten rich, but the warmth of Cuba has chased the chill of his native Asturias from his bones. He marries and goes back to Havana with his brother-in-law Valentín but without Josefa, who stays home in Albandi to await the birth of their first child, Luisa, who comes into the world on June 3, 1912. Four years later Camín returns for his wife Josefa but not his daughter whom he leaves in the safety of his in-laws' home. He travels from one sugar operation to another in rural Cuba on construction jobs while also acquiring concessions to oversee a store here, a hotel there until his first son, Raul, is born in Palma Soriano and, four years later, in 1920, his second daughter, Emma. That same year he sends for Luisa, and her arrival from Spain brings his whole family together for the first time. Cuba builds and grows, and he grows along with the country until the crisis of 1929 spoils everything. He takes several initiatives that lead nowhere before deciding to migrate yet again. In 1934, he leaves all his savings with his family and leaves Havana as he once left Gijón. With nothing but the clothes on his back he sets out across the Caribbean from Cuba to Panama where there are plenty of jobs for construction workers to help maintain the trans-isthmus canal. After a season in Panama, where, in his judgment, there are too many blacks and too few jobs, he moves on to La Guaira and the budding towns in

the oil fields of Venezuela, where unattached men and single
women predominate. He considers such places unsuitable for
his family and at odds with the austere monastic side of his
own temperament. Paying his way as a deck hand, he travels
by freighter to other ports of call. Without spending a cent on
cheap liquor or the black women he finds nearly irresistible—
especially the ones in La Guaira—he collects the stories he'll
tell he rest of his life. Once, he says, he gave in to temptation
in the Panamanian port of Colón. According to posthumous
gossip, he also slipped up with a shameless daughter of Belize
in 1937, when she was barely more than a girl and he was fifty-
five. That was the year of his second exploration of unknown
American shores, in search of a place to ply his multiple trades,
and provide his wife and daughters with the home he'd sought
since the day he left Asturias: a safe place to settle down, raise a
family, grow old with Josefa, and die in peace.

In a port in Honduras, Camín meets a Spanish trader from
Galicia who travels back and forth to the Yucatán Peninsula
and longs to build a fine stone-and-mortar house in the place
of his dreams. It's got a climate just like Cuba's, he says, at least
it's just as hot. And like any place just starting out, it's perfect
for someone wanting to live in peace. In the sweaty peace,
that is, of hard work in a well run new town with a fledgling
government and a case of construction fever. It's the kind
of place he, Pepe Garabana—prodigal son of a prosperous
family—aspires to be an exemplary part of. There's nothing
in my memory, family records, or elsewhere to confirm this
conversation or even this meeting, but something of the sort
must have happened because it produced a structure for all
to see. The two-story dwelling built by Manuel Camín looks
over the bay from behind a row of almond trees to this day.
The Garabana residence stands proudly between city hall and
the customs house in the heart of what is now Chetumal and

was once Payo Obispo, a village eight blocks long and seven wide hemmed in by jungle. In places it's still jungle though it's under constant pressure from settlers whose respect for native vegetation is limited to palm trees and the handsomely crowned elephant-ear trees known to local indigenes as pix. The grid of the town so neatly carved from the jungle is still discernible near some of the wooden houses that overlook the bay and where some of the almond trees that once lined the waterfront boulevard still stand. But the royal palms are gone, killed off by the same yellow frond disease that swept like wildfire through Caribbean coconut groves several years ago. Nothing documents the irrefutable fact that Garabana brings Manuel Camín to Yucatán on his sailboat. Among his passenger's belongings is a trove of books whose titles are subject to debate, unlike the lore Camín himself carries in his head, and that I will hear quoted or repeated like gospel: the history of Freemasonry in Gijón, the scourge for which he was, or thought he was, the scapegoat during the strike against his father. Throughout a life as long and vigorous as his wiry body with its sinewy, claw like hands and the missing tip of one middle finger, he railed against the evils of Freemasonry and anarchism, and I could never take my eyes off the crack that split his right thumbnail in two and made me think of a ravine. His fingers had the prehensile strength of an eagle's talons; their carpenter's sense of touch was uncannily precise; and they belonged to a pair of hands as inhumanly hard as pumice stone.

I like to think about the arrival of Josefa and her daughters in Chetumal. I like to imagine them stepping onto the cement pier that replaced a dock of loose planks the year before. They're careful to keep up appearances as they disembark in outfits from another world: delicate palm-leaf hats with blue and yellow ribbons; chiffon skirts that cleave to their thighs if they walk into the wind or to their young Cuban bottoms if the wind's at their backs. I imagine this dash of elegance tainted by a whiff of mudflats at low tide. It creates a stir among the onlookers who turn out not to welcome them specifically but to hail the arrival of whatever vessel happens by. I can imagine the bustle that accompanies the unloading of bundles and trunks crammed with what the women think are bare household necessities, but turn out to be the furnishings of dreams that have nothing to do with the essential nakedness of the place where they've come to live. In one of the trunks unloaded from the boat that brought them are tablecloths from the Philippines and linen sheets that Josefa bought in Cuba. She plans to take them home to Albandi someday. Her husband will buy her a house with a raised granary, and she'll live out her days, red and sedentary to the end, in the damp mists of the land where she was born. She'd always been ready to go wherever the man in her life hung his hat. She'd gone everywhere in pursuit of goals that for her never changed. All she wanted was a safe place to raise her children and gather the things she yearned to carry home with her. Josefa's lone reason for going away was to return. Only the thought of a peaceful, well provisioned return eased the misery of a departure she acquiesced to out of need.

I'm told Manuel and his son Raul, who moved to Chetumal a year before his sisters, were on the pier to meet them. There is no testimony about kisses and embraces at this long-awaited encounter because they're the kind of women and men who have no idea what to do when bursting with joy. I know this because it's no more in their blood than in mine to give in to emotion. Their gestures of welcome are restrained because the one thing they know about feelings is how to keep them in check. It's a family trademark.

Dumbstruck by all the trunks and suitcases the women brought from Cuba, perhaps embarrassed by the sheer volume of so much luggage on the pier of the humble town where it's come to stay, Manuel Camín commandeers two wheelbarrows from the *Flotilla del Sur* shipping company. Ordinarily, the dockworkers use the wheelbarrows for the fresh mortar they take to building sites where they lay cement, but Camín has them loaded with trunks too heavy and unwieldy for one man to handle. The dockworkers who assist him descend from the armada of sailors who built the dock and founded the town in the eponymous year of 1898.

Manuel Camín has half the baggage put in one wheelbarrow; following his father's lead, Raul has the other half piled into the second one. They walk through the town with all the trunks and suitcases, showing their lovely ladies the way. If you think of it as personal effects for a trip, the load is enormous. If you think of it as the sum total of its owners' worldly possessions, all the bedding, all the dry goods, all the tableware, all the housewares, all the clothes, shoes, jewelry, cosmetics and toiletries they deem essential to their well-being, it's the forlorn, almost microscopic remains of a life they'll never go back to.

Children have no way of knowing what their parents think, but they can imagine. In my imagination there can be no doubt that as Emma and her sister walk through Chetumal for the first time with their father and brother pushing their belongings ahead of them, they feel both elated and lost. The heat is as stifling and the sunlight as blinding as in Cuba. Though they're bathed in sweat, the caress of a passing breeze is reassuringly familiar. The town itself is disheartening, a jumble of buildings hastily thrown up on a damp riverbank. The houses are made of wood, the sidewalks are nothing but sand, and the green almond trees do little to enhance the appearance of either. In my retrospective fantasy, as they come to the first corner on the town's main street, Emma Camín's face is crisscrossed with shadows from sunlight filtered through the weave of her hat. She looks up at the sign of the biggest business on the block: Casa Aguilar. The sign means nothing to her at the time, but she'll remember it later in the stories she tells her children. It sets the scene for her first steps in this impossible place. Years later, the lives of these young ladies from Cuba will become inextricably bound to the scions of this establishment, unthinkable as that may seem in the heat of this June morning. They walk through Chetumal with visions of Cuba still fresh in their memories, but this is a different Cuba, a newborn, half-formed Cuba. At least it's on the water, and the breeze is laced with the breath of the sea. The sky may be the same diaphanous blue, and the trees may be similar, but other things are not: the deadly monotony of the coastline; this down-at-the-heels town whose one saving grace is the wide, ramrod straight streets butting up against the jungle.

Only a few of Chetumal's 7,900 residents were born here. The rest, like the Cuban girls and their parents, came from somewhere else. The town has no drinking water or electricity. Nor does the unpainted wooden house with a tin roof where the girls and their mother are obliged to settle in the day they arrive. No one protests or complains, but it's not hard to imagine the sinking feelings of these smartly dressed new arrivals who suddenly find themselves stuck in this Mecca of sweat and tin, this undersized barrack. In time the women will fill the place with flowers to delight the eye and stories to brighten their lives, but for the time being there are only cots, rooms without doors, boxes with crumbs of cement in them where the men keep their clothes and their tools. The house is on the street named after Othón P. Blanco, whose memory it preserves to this day.

A few words must be said about the man who gives the street its name. Ramón Othón Pompeyo Blanco Núñez de Cáceres was born in 1868, fourteen years before Manuel Camín, in Ciudad Victoria, Tamaulipas, the dusty metropolis named for Mexico's first president, Guadalupe Victoria. In 1885 at age seventeen Othón leaves Ciudad Victoria to enroll in the *Colegio Militar de Chapultepec* in Mexico City with the goal of becoming a naval officer. In 1890, at twenty-two, he's commissioned as an ensign. He serves on the gunboat *Libertad* and is an orderly in the delegation that oversees construction of a training ship in the French port of Le Havre. In 1893, at twenty-five, he's promoted to the rank of lieutenant, junior grade. In 1895, at twenty-seven, he joins the East Coast Command in Quintana Roo, a force with a decades-long record of setbacks during the Maya uprising known as the War of Castes. The British, having founded the colony of Belize on coastal territories abandoned by Mexico and Guatemala, side with the Maya. In exchange for rifles and liquor, the British gain access to Yucatan's abundant forest reserves of cedar, mahogany, and *palo de tinte*—a plant whose sap is prized as a dye for English textiles. Mexico suffers painful losses of blood and money while the British side prospers, leading the government in Mexico City to accept a pact with England recognizing the territorial limits claimed for Belize. After both countries sign the boundary treaty, the Mexican government orders its navy and army to colonize the newly defined territory. Nobody knows what to do with so much unowned land. Yet it's imperative to establish a presence on the Hondo River, which flows from the jungles of Guatemala to the marshes of Chetumal Bay and now marks the border between Mexico and Belize. It occurs to Othón Pompeyo Blanco that nothing can be gained by trying to build a border fort or lighthouse in the middle of a swamp. A pontoon boat moored where the river drains into the bay would, according to Blanco, do a much better job of stopping shipments—meaning arms, alcohol, logs and corpses—from going in and out. What's needed, he insists, is a pontoon boat, not a gunboat or a battleship but an armored barge with a roof, gun mounts, and wooden bunks serviced by a pair of tenders that can go back and forth from the mainland where barracks and shops can be put up.

Plans call for the pontoon boat to be built with a hull of pine, oak and cypress over an iron frame. It will be twenty meters long and six meters wide, rise nearly four meters above its waterline, and have a draft of sixty centimeters. Nobody visualizes the craft as clearly as Blanco himself, and he's dispatched to New Orleans to supervise its construction. The first timbers are laid on June 17, 1896, on the left bank of the Mississippi River in the yard of the Croatian shipbuilder Valerian Zuvic. After a final payment of ten thousand dollars, its first crew takes possession of the vessel in early April, 1897. It casts off from New Orleans a short time later in the tow of the Mexican steamer *Tabasqueño* and with Othón Pompeyo on board. It sails down the Gulf Coast to the port of Campeche, where Lieutenant Junior Grade Blanco is given command of his invention. He's ordered to assemble a crew and proceed south, but few sailors in Campeche are ready to venture to the Maya coast where the rebels lie in waiting. Lieutenant Junior Grade Blanco can fill only seven of the twenty-two slots he's assigned. He leaves Campeche on October 6 in the tow of the steamer *Ibero*. In early December 1897 he reaches the port of Belize where he advises the colony's English governor that henceforth all shipping in and out of the Hondo River must clear the Mexican floating customs station at its mouth. The vessel with *Pontón Chetumal* painted on its bow drops its strategically placed anchor on January 22, 1898. The crew hacks out a clearing on the jungle shore and fashions funnels to collect rainwater in cisterns. They use planks of balsa-wood for a roof, and declare the result a customs post. They then board their supply tenders and visit the towns on the English shore to tell Mexican refugees they can return home in safety. They add that each returnee will be granted title to as much land as he can clear by hand. On May 5, 1898, Othón Pompeyo Blanco gathers the residents of the resulting settlements together, raises the flag, leads them in singing the national anthem, and celebrates the founding of the riverfront village on which he bestows the area's old Spanish name of Payo Obispo. The first thing Othón Pompeyo Blanco builds on the mainland, after a customs shed, is a school whose real organizer is his wife, Manuela Peyrefitte. Othón Pompeyo meets her one night at a dance in a town on the English shore and convinces her to abscond with him to his pontoon boat. Legend has it that she has a suitor who raises a posse of relatives and goes to get her back. She's at least engaged, and according to some, she's already married. The sailors on the pontoon boat greet their visitors with rifles at the ready, and the would-be boarding party turns back. Manuela Peyrefitte's school opens under a giant almond tree on the day Payo Obispo is founded. A century later, Othón Pompeyo Blanco is a statue, and Payo Obispo is a city of one hundred thousand whose citizens gather on the pier to observe the hundredth anniversary of its founding with a morning mass. The crowd attracts a family of manatees. They swim towards the pier with bovine aplomb because manatees are friendly by nature. Their appearance is taken as a sign that they approve of the city's founding a hundred years ago, as if, judging by the present, the past is worth celebrating. I was there for the occasion though I had not yet begun learning about the century gone by, and I didn't see the manatees. Still, I consider myself forgiven for exhuming the memory of so many things past.

My paternal grandparents must be counted among the first settlers in the new Payo Obispo. Their history is lost in the mists of the islands. Families driven off the mainland by the Maya war took refuge on the eastern islands. By 1867, when the republic topples the emperor Maximilian, the permanent population on the island of Cozumel had reached a thousand.

One of this number, José Gil Aguilar, married Francisca López and had seven children with her, including José Aguilar López, who married three times. One of his wives, Natalia Carrasco, was the mother of six of his children, the first of whom was my paternal grandfather, José Guadalupe Aguilar Carrasco. He was born in 1891 on the island of Holbox by some accounts, and on Cape San Pedro, Belize, by others, making him a true child of the island mists. These are the Aguilars attracted to Payo Obispo by the founding of the new town in hopes of putting to good use business skills acquired running a bar. Tending bar as a child on Cozumel, José Guadalupe Aguilar Carrasco acquired the lore he would later draw upon for the stories that astonished his daughters-in-law. A childhood spent serving liquor to others and seeing what it did to them teaches him to shun alcohol. Being paid across a counter he can barely see over, he serves drinks while standing on a box and learns to add, subtract and, if possible, pad the bill. As a boy he learns to read and write with help from the local schoolmarm to whom he takes clandestine rations of aguardiente each afternoon. She teaches him the penmanship style of his choice, the no-frills script of the island's mayor, a man named Coldwell.

By the time the Camín sisters come ashore in Chetumal and Emma sees the sign she'll always remember on Casa Aguilar, José Guadalupe Aguilar Carrasco is the wealthiest young man in the region, a chicle and lumber contractor, president of the National Chamber of Commerce and Industry of Quintana Roo, owner of the most lucrative corner on the town's main street. He also owns the pool hall, the gas station, the soft drink bottling plant (called *La Vencedora*), and the only movie theater, a multipurpose facility that also serves for fiestas and meetings and which was named in honor of the composer Juventino Rosas.

In 1909, at age eighteen, five years after his arrival in Payo Obispo, José Guadalupe Aguilar Carrasco has a falling out with his father, José Guadalupe Aguilar López. The older man has broken up with his wife, Natalia Carrasco, who has become pregnant unusually late in life, and has taken up with a young black woman. José Guadalupe Aguilar Carrasco has also married, to the slighter and whiter Juana Escolástica Marrufo, a girl from Cozumel who is less rotund than her name. José Guadalupe and Juana have seven children: Ángel, the firstborn; María de la Luz, who dies in childhood; Efraín, who dies young; Jaime, who dies as a child; Perfecto, who doesn't live up to his name; Omar, who will marry four times; and Héctor, who will grow up to be my grandfather. A cloud of mourning still hangs over the family in 1938 due to the death of Efraín, my grandfather's favorite son, who died a heroic death in the hurricane that ravaged Belize in 1931. Seven years have gone by since the demise of Efraín, but his father's grief is as fierce as ever. Don Lupe, as his daughter-in-law Emma Camín always called him—and as he remains in my memory—demonstrates the extent of his power and the depths of his desolation by having the main street in Chetumal renamed for his late son. The street bears the name of Efraín Aguilar for years until an opposition government replaces it with the more generic: *Avenida de los Héroes.* There's no consoling Don Lupe for the loss of the son he loved most and tried hardest to please; his lucidly secular soul has no use for biblical bromides. My mother has described to me the episode that exposes his sense of loss most acutely, the tale she heard Don Lupe tell many times. It goes like this:

On a day in September 1931 a hurricane pounds Belize. It strikes hardest at the Jesuit-run College of Saint John where Efraín and his cousin Raúl are enrolled. The boys do what they can to rescue children and women from drowning in the surging tide. Exhausted by cold and fatigue, they drown after saving many others. The next day Don Lupe sets out from Payo Obispo in his boat to look for his son who is reported missing.

He rows through the wreckage left in the stagnant waters after the storm until he finds him flat on his face in the branches of a downed tree. He hauls the body out of the water with an oar, lays it face-up before him on the bottom of the boat, and rows back. He must have rowed quite a while because a breeze comes up and dries Efraín's hair until it begins to blow over his forehead. The way it brushes over the skin suggests the dead flesh is still alive and that Efraín has only fallen asleep and is having a bad dream that wrinkles his brow. As he rows, Don Lupe thinks that maybe Efraín really is just asleep and will open his eyes any minute and say: "Where am I, and what are you doing here, Dad?" Don Lupe buries him the next day in Payo Obispo, but he doesn't really stay buried. For years whenever his remaining offspring— particularly Adán, his firstborn, who is as stubborn as Don Lupe himself, and Perfecto, who is as headstrong, unyielding and frugal as his name—engage in the filial specialty of doing something their father disapproves of, the old man invariably, unfairly and unforgettably invokes his loss by saying:

"Why didn't you die in the hurricane instead of Efraín?"

There's something about the figure of Don Lupe that evokes the moments when time began. He left indelible stories in the memory of many who came later. In their recollections, Emma and Luisa Camín have polished some of these tales to a high gloss in their efforts to take the measure of this portentous animal who fascinates and repels them. There is, for example, the story of the Chinese man who incurs Don Lupe's contempt due to his binges of drinking and gambling in Payo Obispo. One morning the woman who does Don Lupe's laundry finds the Chinese man hacked to death in the garbage can by his house. The word among the town's drug addicts is that a black man from Belize is the murderer. He's said to have been with the Chinese man on the night of his death and to be on a wild spending spree in Consejo, the border town in Belize whose lights can be seen at night from the dock in Payo Obispo. The black man is drinking heavily and has all but confessed to the killing. He's boasting that the Mexican police cannot touch him. He scoffs at Mexican law enforcement and claims he's protected under English justice. No sooner has Don Lupe heard all this than he gets in his boat and rows to Consejo where he bribes the local bobbies to arrest the suspect and load him onto Don Lupe's boat. The bobbies comply and Don Lupe brings him back. The black man serves some years in the Payo Obispo jail, where there are no bars, and he becomes a familiar face around town. By agreement with his keepers, he gets up very early and sweeps the streets. He prefers the cool of morning in Payo Obispo to the sweltering boredom of a jail which, though once a cattle pen, now occupies the basement of the police station. The wooden bars through which itching and vegetating inmates peer out at the street from within that suffocating cellar make the place not only more like a jail, but at times downright infernal. You can see the bay through the bars, but for some reason a pall of immanent justice hangs in the air and keeps the breeze outside.

Another Don Lupe story:

In March, 1938, the assets of foreign oil companies in Mexico were nationalized. When Don Lupe hears about the expropriation, he immediately grasps that in this case "nationalized" means "government takeover," and that "government" in this case means Quintana Roo's longtime benefactor President Lázaro Cárdenas. Don Lupe wined and dined the Cárdenas team when the general-turned-politician stopped in Payo Obispo during his mythic 1934 election campaign and has since maintained distant but cordial relations with his erstwhile visitors. He catches the first plane to Mérida and from Mérida flies to either Villahermosa or Veracruz, then on to Mexico City, where he asks his acquaintances for the gasoline concession—up to then held by the British-run *Compañía El Águila*—in Chetumal. Don Lupe thus opens the way to building and becoming the owner of the first patriotic gas station in Payo Obispo.

What to say about Juana Escolástica Marrufo, the frail, white and placid wife of the imposing Don Lupe? Everyone speaks of her in the diminutive. In Chetumal she's called "Doña Juanita". Her daughter-in-law, Emma Camín, calls her "Mamá Juanita" on the afternoons when, after dressing us in our good clothes and brushing our hair, she takes us to visit our grandmother. Mamá Juanita greets us on the second floor of her cement house, one of only three or four such structures in a town where most houses are built of wood and roofed with sheets of corrugated zinc. Juana Marrufo is linked in my childhood memories to the asthmatic aroma of the English talcum that powders her cheeks. Sunken and untouched by sunshine, they have the malarial pallor that tends to afflict white skin in the tropics. In my recollections of these visits, she sits in her wicker rocking chair, slight, elegant, freshly bathed and powdered in mitigation of the afternoon heat. I see the golden frame of her glasses. Attached to them is the silver chain that hangs down around her bare, slender neck. A tortoiseshell comb keeps her hair firmly on her head and free from any possible entanglement with the chain. In my memory she's serene, superior, and impeccably groomed. Her husband comes and goes from other houses and other women, but she doesn't let it bother her anymore. When he comes home, she makes Don Lupe take a ritual bath to rid him of the burrs that stick to him in the forest or elsewhere, and lets it go at that. She is, in my memory as in life, the woman who looks tenderly after Héctor when old age deprives him of his rest. She's the apparition my fathers' overnight caregivers see when her son is on the threshold of sleep. She pads about on cat's paws, waiting to welcome him when he gets to the other side.

But this is 1938. Emma Camín turns eighteen in August and Héctor Aguilar Marrufo twenty-one in October. The town they live in is eight blocks long by seven wide. Everyone knows Héctor as the son of a prominent father and Emma because she and her sister Luisa have set the standard for local fashion ever since they stepped off the boat. The governor's wife invites them to all of her social gatherings because, cooped up in her wooden palace, she's bored and welcomes new people like a pedestrian finding shade from the sun. This is the town where six years later Héctor and Emma will marry, but it's not where they meet. Their first encounter takes place more than two thousand kilometers away in Mexico City, a distance best measured as: three-days by boat to Veracruz plus a day by train to the capital; or by the puddle-jumping planes that fly passengers and freight from Chetumal to Mérida, Mérida to Villahermosa, Villahermosa to Veracruz, and Veracruz to Mexico City. Though it seems unlikely, the fact is that Héctor and Emma meet not on the streets of old Payo Obispo but in Mexico City. The encounter occurs in a mansion, now torn down, whose turrets once rose above the bucolic *Avenida Mariano Escobedo*. The street named for the war hero who fought on the republican side in the nineteenth century has two lanes and very little traffic. The owner of the house, which has a racquetball court and a swimming pool, belongs to a man with the viceregal name of Pedro Hurtado de Mendoza. He went into government service as a very young man, and over the past fifteen years his family ties to Payo Obispo have afforded him a successful career in the bureaucracy. He's also the father of a daughter on whom he declines to bestow his name. Alicia is a wonderful young lady who was taken in by Casa Aguilar. More than anyone else in Chetumal she personifies the high spirits of the times. She's the daughter of Don Lupe's imposing, free-spirited and beautiful younger sister Natalia Aguilar Carrasco. Nobody mentions such things in Chetumal although everybody knows about them. The door of the Hurtado de Mendoza house in Mexico City is always open to people from Chetumal. Héctor and Emma meet there due to a stroke of geographic fate that can be summarized as follows:

Emma Camín is invited to the capital by her namesake Emma Wadgymar who married Federico Pérez Gómez in Chetumal. Pérez Gómez is a Yucatán lawyer charged by the socialist government of Rafael E. Melgar with organizing workers on the peninsula's chicle plantations. The two Emmas meet and become friends in the social circle that grows up around the governor's wife. Wadgymar invites the other Emma to come along with her on one of her trips to Mexico City. One evening they're invited, as is Héctor, to the Hurtado de Mendoza house, a veritable way station for visitors and pilgrims from Chetumal.

Héctor doesn't remember meeting Emma at the Hurtado de Mendoza house. He's spent two years studying law and administration in the capital. More book learning doesn't make sense to him, and he decides to return to Chetumal, work in the family business, and build a world of his own. Long afterward, in the small apartment in the Roma District where he moves after our reunion in the Alcázar rooming house, Héctor tells me what he recalls about his first meetings with Emma Camín in Chetumal. His version goes like this:

> I came back after three years of school in Mexico City because I wanted to work. My father disagreed, and my brother Ángel was against it. They refused to let me do the things I wanted to do with Casa Aguilar. Instead, they stuck me in the

storeroom stripping the husks off coconuts and shelving inventory. I learned how to run a movie projector in the Juventino Rosas theater: how to thread film from one sprocket to another, how to glue pieces of burnt film together, I'd learned to pay attention in school, and I was a quick study, so I said to the projectionist, "Let me try that." To which he replied, "Sure." I worked days in the storeroom and nights at Juventino Rosas. In those days a woman from Corozal named Francisca and nicknamed Chita helped around the house and did other tasks. One day she said, "The Cuban girl came around and asked for you." "The Cuban girl?" I said. "What Cuban girl?" "She's very pretty," Chita told me. "And what did she want?" I said. "Well, she wanted to know where you slept." "And what did you tell her?" I said. "I said over there and pointed to your room. Then she asked, 'So, where are his sneakers? The ones he plays in.' I used to play basketball on the walk on the breakwater, what they called the Esplanade. She went to see me play or to make sure I wasn't bow-legged. Finding out if I had good legs was her sister Luisa's idea. "So who's this girl from Cuba?" I insisted. "Well, she's Cuban," Chita told me. "And she's a very good looking girl. One day as I was leaving the Casa Aguilar storeroom, I saw two girls go by. One of them looked at me, and I looked right back at her. When she walked she swung her hips like a gazelle." "How beautiful," I said, and Chita, who never missed a thing, looked out the window and said. "That's the one!" "What one?" "The one who came to find out where you sleep!" So she's the Cuban, I said to myself, I've got to dance with her.

But running the projector at the movies would get in the way. I told the projectionist, "I'm not helping you Thursdays and Sundays. I'm going dancing on the Esplanade." "I'm telling your brother Ángel," the projectionist said. "So tell him." Thursday I put on my guayabera, splashed on some cologne and went dancing on the Esplanade. I got up the courage to ask the Cuban to dance twice, and we danced for quite a while. Later, after I found out where she lived, I went to ask her out one evening. It was already getting dark when I knocked. The door of her house was in the back so you had to go around to get in. She said, "Wait outside while I let my father know I'm going for a walk with you." "Why do you have to tell your father? I just came by to say hello and see if you need anything. I see you don't have electricity." Which was true. What electricity there was in Chetumal came from private generators, and where she lived it was very expensive if you could get it at all. I went to see Don Adolfo Pérez, a Spanish merchant who had a Westinghouse motor he wasn't using. "That motor could serve as a generator," I said. "If you don't need it, I'll buy it from you." "Give it to the Aguilar boy," he told his helpers. So I took it to the house of Don Manuel Camín. I told your mother—that is, the girl who would become your mother, but who could have known back then—I had something for her. "I brought you this pump," I said, "and here's the gasoline and the batteries to make it go. The tank holds just enough gas to run from seven to ten. It turns off at ten. If you need more power, just throw this switch, and it'll run on the battery for two more hours. If you need it to go longer for a party or something, call me, and I'll fill the fuel tank with enough gasoline to last six more hours." "Oooh, how sweet!" your mother said. "You really shouldn't have." When your mother's speechless, she says, "Oooh. Oooh." "You're welcome," I said. "I got it for you to use because your house is so far from any generator." They lived very close to the jungle, far from where Farah ran the generator supposed to supply their neighborhood. "All right, then," she told me. "Let me tell my father." At the time I had no idea who her father was. I left her with the generator, then we got to know and understand each other. And everything was fine. It was really beautiful until your aunt stepped in.

Chetumal, 1946

Exactly two years after a Catholic marriage, Emma Camín gives birth to a male child weighing four kilos, three-hundred-fifty grams. Within a few years that infant will be me. It's an easy birth. The contractions begin as the church bells call the faithful to eight o'clock mass on a stifling Tuesday. They're over by the time the bells ring out for nine o'clock mass. Emma gives birth under the philosophical gaze of the midwife, Doña Nila, and the clinical eye of Dr. Barocio, who waits for just the right moment to cut the perineum and facilitate the delivery. The pain of the incision gives way to the relief of delivery. The date is July 9, 1946, the year when the distance between the earth and the moon is measured for the first time. This same month the first two-piece swimsuits known as bikinis—an allusion to the nuclear bomb test on the islet of Bikini in the Marshall Islands—go on sale in Paris. The United Nations holds its first session. Hermann Göring commits suicide in Nuremberg. Miguel Alemán is elected president of Mexico; Juan Domingo Perón and Ho Chi Minh are elected president in Argentina and Vietnam respectively.

None of this exists in the thoughts of the mother or in the minuscule and magnificent world around her, her marvelous microcosm. She's having a baby in the sweltering town of Chetumal with its eight blocks by the bay of the same name, a place of wooden houses with pitched tin roofs, barefoot kids, and black dirt patios on the edge of the encroaching jungle. The birth of a boy is a victory for this girl over in-laws who scoffed when her first baby, a little girl named Emma, came into the world in this same house one year, one month, and four days ago. Nobody celebrates the arrival of a girl baby in Chetumal, least of all the striplings of Casa Aguilar, offspring of that man among men who is their father.

The light bulb Héctor, her husband, mounted in his workshop at the rear of the patio that same year burns throughout the night of the birth. Héctor has decided to sever his ties with Casa Aguilar and the domain of his father, the man called Don Lupe by everyone except his sons, who address him by the ill-suited diminutive of "*papacito*". The elated mother of long ago remembers being visited by her in-laws and hearing them whisper that her newborn looks "real dark." Ten days later Don Lupe, who has been out of town, comes to visit. When he peers into the cradle, he's shaken. "He looks like Efraín," he tells Héctor. "I hope things turn out better for him." Héctor hears Don Lupe's comment as recognition that the birth of a boy baby changes his status within the family; for the baby's mother it's a bad omen. She never met Efraín and, though she can respect his memory, his mention in the same breath with her son upsets her. The last thing she needs right now is talk of premature deaths. The physical pain and postpartum blues have abated. The angel of life sweetens her dreams, a strain of joy pervades her waking hours, she feels immortal.

Emma and Héctor married on July 9, as I said, two years ago to the day. My sister Pilar, who hasn't been born yet, will one day draw on her child's wisdom to conflate the two events: "When my mother was married and my brother was born." On their wedding day Emma and Héctor hold a large party in which their participation is limited because they must catch the noon flight to Mérida. From Mérida they'll go on to Campeche for a few days at the beach. The best of their beach photos is the one I found at the start of my research, the one that got me wondering about the intimate yet unknown links that bind me to them. There's a paradox here: parents can be both the people closest to you and, wrapped as they are in a fog of inaccessible centrality, the most enigmatic. We cannot get inside them. To us they are gods, giants when we're little, demiurges as we grow up, and essential once again as life comes to a close.

I digress in order to explain the break between Héctor and Casa Aguilar. It's less an uprooting than a process as he draws ever closer to Emma Camín. She wants a house of her own and a man of her own, not a spouse to be shared with her in-laws. Even before he met Emma, Héctor had begun to think about the dangers inherent in distancing himself from his family, and he'd stopped worrying very much about the laws of the kingdom from which he intended to free himself. It is, I suppose, the path any patriot follows on the way to independence. When Héctor finishes high school in Chetumal, Don Lupe decides he should continue his studies in Mexico City. Héctor wrongly perceives this decision as an attempt to keep him from getting what he wants most: an active role in the management of Casa Aguilar. He's spent two years studying law and administration in the capital and has learned to fatten his cash reserves by asking Don Lupe to pay for things he doesn't really need and has no intention of buying. He's invested the money in a small grocery store where he works more than he studies, and which he winds up buying at the prodding of the owner's young wife, who is fed up with having her husband behind the counter for hours on end. She wants to see him retire with money in his pocket. The relationship between the young owner who wants to sell and the precocious young man who wants to buy is not entirely clear. One night, come closing time, the owner's wife padlocks the door from the inside and approaches Héctor with the key dangling between her fingers. Héctor asks her for the key, but the owner's wife drops it into her cleavage and tells him to come look for it. It's unclear what happens next. What can't be doubted is that Hector decides to drop out of school in the capital and return home to make a place for himself in the realm ruled by his father. He sells the store in the capital and goes home to find himself frozen out by the icy glare of Don Lupe, who takes his time finding something for his son to do. When his father finally lets Héctor work as an apprentice bookkeeper and cashier, he doesn't complain. He invents tasks for himself as a stacker in the storeroom and as a projectionist at the movie house. He meets and courts Emma Camín, gets engaged to her, and plans to make her his wife. But first he makes her his accomplice because Héctor has hung onto the money he made from selling the store in the capital. He tells no one about this hidden treasure—the seed stock for his independence—except the labile Cuban he intends to marry and whom he makes his business partner before she becomes his conjugal partner. Héctor has lent his money to a friend who owns a lot on the corner of Othón P. Blanco and Avenida Héroes, one of the town's best business sites. The friend opens a bar there, and it goes broke. The only way he can repay Héctor is by deeding the property to him. Héctor agrees, but if this acquisition is made public, Casa Aguilar will find out he came back from Mexico City with more money than he took with him. Since he expects to marry Emma very soon, he suggests she ask her father to be the property's nominal owner in the eyes of the public and Casa Aguilar. Which is what they do. For his part, Manuel Camín builds a wooden house on the lot he owns at number 17 Othón P. Blanco to be occupied by his daughter and son-in-law and where his grandchildren are to be born.

At the time of these transactions, Manuel Camín is the owner of half a block on Othón P. Blanco. His properties begin several meters before the corner of Avenida Héroes that now belongs to Héctor. On the lot immediately before the corner he and his son Raúl have opened a grocery store with a patio in which a mango tree grows; on the lot next to it, where there's a guava tree, Manuel Camín has a shop where he does carpentry and makes ornamental cement blocks; on the next lot, where there's an almond tree, Camín has built a small wooden house for himself, Josefa, and their daughter Luisa, who has come home after a failed marriage; the next lot is where he's putting up the house he's agreed to build for Emma, the place where she'll spend the first years of her marriage to Héctor and raise her four children. At the back of this lot, which is enhanced by an almond tree, Héctor has gone into business as a mechanic with a shop where pumps and motors cough and sputter and electricity is generated for the couple's house in a town with no power grid.

The offspring of Don Lupe and Juana Marrufo—Ángel, Perfecto, Héctor, and Omar, plus an uncle named Eustaquio, who's like a bother to them—all go to work in Casa Aguilar as children. Juana Marrufo treats Eustaquio like her own son. Since he's the same age as Ángel, she's even nursed him. He's the child born late in life to Natalia Carrasco, Juana's mother-in-law, which makes him Don Lupe's baby brother. The whole brood works unsalaried and with no fixed duties at Casa Aguilar. They all do a bit of everything on orders from Don Lupe. When grown and with children of their own, they still dip into the till at Casa Aguilar and leave chits explaining the reason for their withdrawals. Don Lupe goes over the chits when he comes home from his travels and accepts or rejects them. In his absence Ángel, as the oldest son, metes out punishments and assigns tasks.

As the firstborn son, Ángel is Don Lupe's favorite. He regards Eustaquio as not quite grown up, Perfecto as a mule, Héctor as spoiled, and Omar as a danger to the family. Juana Marrufo's favorite is Héctor, whom she calls Tito. In her son Ángel she sees all the traits she adores and fears in Don Lupe, her husband. She finds Perfecto's animal simplicity endearing, the bonds between Ángel and Eustaquio upset her, and Omar keeps her up at night when he comes home late. Don Lupe travels a lot and isn't around very much. When he does come home, Ángel and Eustaquio meet him at the dock or the airport and update him on what's going on around the house. This frightens Juana Marrufo because Ángel and Eustaquio skew what they tell their father, making him ready to take his other sons to task and undermine his wife's attempts at arbitration before he walks in the door.

Ángel is the most conventionally masculine of the brothers, Eustaquio the most even-tempered, Perfecto the strongest, Héctor the most diligent, and Omar the wildest. Ángel dominates Eustaquio, fears Perfecto, harasses Héctor, and lets Omar have his way. Eustaquio obeys Ángel, avoids Perfecto, looks down on Héctor, and manipulates Omar. Perfecto teases Ángel, looks down on Eustaquio, protects Héctor, and adores Omar. Héctor fears Ángel, ignores Eustaquio, manipulates Perfecto, and scolds Omar. Omar sweet talks Ángel, misleads Eustaquio, manipulates Perfecto, and confides in Héctor.

There's no satisfactory explanation for Héctor's break with Casa Aguilar. According to Emma and her sister Luisa, his older brothers Ángel and Eustaquio deliberately freeze him out little by little. Their scheme consists of charging him with disloyalty before the court of Don Lupe. They claim he's grown too friendly with the new territorial governor who has had it in for Don Lupe and Casa Aguilar since the day he took office. The charge casts a pall over relations between Héctor and his older brother Ángel and chills his relations with his father. But when Héctor's and Emma's first daughter is born, Don Lupe is entranced. His warm feelings for Emma—the sense that he and his daughter-in-law are somehow in league with each other— are rekindled. He remembers the night he saw her dancing with Héctor on the *Retreta*, the esplanade by the shore where dances and civic celebrations are held as are the "socialist evenings" the government hopes will win it favor among the people of Chetumal. The scene Don Lupe recalls has Héctor asking the beautiful young Cuban to dance. She's the most sought after girl in town, and Héctor has her laughing until she must hold onto him to keep from falling down. Seeing the two of them together improves Don Lupe's opinion of his son. "If you can get the Cuban," he says to himself, "you can get anything." Don Lupe is delighted with the courtship, the wedding, and the birth of Héctor's and Emma's first daughter. The baby isn't his first grandchild, but she quickly becomes the apple of his eye. Héctor's envious brothers react by questioning his allegiance to the family.

The story must be told of the governor who heaps abuse on Don Lupe and whose shadow darkens the story of the families joined in the household of Emma and Héctor. His name is Margarito Ramírez, and he takes office as the appointed governor of Quintana Roo in April, 1944, shortly before Emma's and Héctor's wedding. He succeeds another appointed governor, a general named Gabriel Guevara who turns his administration into an alcoholic holiday and the alcoholic holiday into a prelude for depravity. Margarito and Guevara are friends of the sitting president and ex-general Manuel Ávila Camacho. In 1940, while running for president, Ávila Camacho makes a campaign stop in Chetumal and is stung by critics who speak up loudly and harshly against him at a rally. The candidate—and now president—blames then Governor Melgar for the uproar. He thinks Melgar planted hecklers in the crowd, then feigned indignation while sitting beside him on the platform throughout the disturbance. The candidate adds Governor Melgar to his enemies list and vows to make this ridiculous excuse for a town pay for its disrespect. The Camín sisters enjoyed a brief but agreeable interlude in Melgar's social circle, and their admiration for the man they consider a model governor is unwavering. The Camín sisters share their family's belief in memory as the highest virtue and are nothing if not loyal to their memories. They remember passionately and forget severely. They have, for example, dismissed Melgar's successor from memory, because in their opinion he's unworthy of mention. Governor Guevara cares about little except going after Melgar for putting bumps in Ávila Camacho's road to the presidency. Aside from stalking Melgar, nothing gets more attention from Guevara than "beer halls" and brothels. He's removed from office before he drowns the territory in alcohol, a task he leaves well under way.

Margarito is the exact opposite of Guevara. He's austere and as rigid as the bough of an old tree. He comes on the scene in 1944 and, contrary to all expectations including his own, remains in power for fourteen years. It's a time of dreary memory for many, including the members of Casa Aguilar.

Margarito is a story in his own right. In 1920, while working on the railroad, he saves the life of the military strongman of the moment, Álvaro Obregón. He disguises Obregón as a fireman and puts him on a train out of Mexico City before his rivals can shoot him. Obregón gains the presidency in the military uprising that flares when he's forced to flee. He repays Margarito for saving his life with a political career. First, he makes Margarito a superintendent with *Ferrocarriles de México*, the national railroad. Then he gets him a seat in the federal legislature, followed by appointment to governor of his native state of Jalisco. There, Margarito becomes the scourge of God and the Church during the so-called Cristero War against the revolutionary government by Catholic peasants in the western part of the country. The year is 1926.

As governor of Jalisco, while hanging priests and Cristero leaders from telegraph poles, Margarito marries and acquires a lover. With heavenly clairvoyance as her guide, the wife finds out about the lover, goes to her house, and dispatches her with her husband's revolver. I can see smoke curling up from the barrel of an old pistol and the burn marks around the bullet holes in the nightgown of the victim whom the murderess caught in bed before breakfast. Margarito faces up to the scandal by declaring his wife insane. Thanks to this diagnosis, she spends the years that follow in a psychiatric hospital on the outskirts of Guadalajara rather than in the prison similarly located on the city's outskirts. The finding of insanity dissolves Margarito's marriage in the eyes of the law. He's forty-eight at the time, and in the first months of his *de jure* widowhood he meets Marcela Ladewig. She's twenty years younger than he is, the beautiful daughter of a German couple that has taken up residence in Guadalajara. He marries her and starts a family. They have one son and then another while the husband's political career continues apace. Though the times are troubled, Margarito rolls with the punches. Then, in 1928, a conspiracy between a nun and a Catholic caricaturist leads to the assassination of Margarito's protector, Álvaro Obregón, who had prophetically remarked: "I will die when someone wants to trade his life for mine." The caricaturist who killed Obregón is executed, but not the nun. In 1929, Margarito is driven out of the Jalisco governorship. He returns to his old job as a supervisor with the national railway. He belongs to the revolutionary family now, and he's comfortably perched in the political tree. Whether he climbs up or down through its branches, he's not likely to fall out altogether. 1932 is a good year for him, he's made a senator. 1936 isn't so hot, he's made warden of the Islas Marías penal colony. He returns from the place that one illustrious guest, the writer José Revueltas, calls "a prison with water for walls," and with help from a new friend and protector becomes a deputy in the federal legislature once more. Manuel Ávila Camacho is Secretary of War, and his star burns brighter as the radicalizing ardor of the Lázaro Cárdenas government begins to fade. When

Ávila Camacho ascends to the presidency, Margarito becomes head of the National Railroad. He rules the organization where his career began until a strike forces him out of office on February 18, 1944. By then General Guevara has soaked half the territory of Quintana Roo in alcohol, and it's time for a change. Change comes in the abstemious person of Margarito, a gaunt and frugal man with a pistol on his hip and dark glasses to cover a bad eye. Margarito is sixty-three at the time. He puts his new constituents at ease with a ringing pronouncement: "Don't worry about me. I couldn't be worse than Guevara."

Margarito cares more about power than money, but his idea of power includes his assumption that he can control people with money. He offers the wealthy of Quintana Roo deals which, though mutually beneficial, keep them under his thumb. Those with most and those with least all come to some sort of arrangement with Margarito. Except Don Lupe. He snubs the governor because, to his way of thinking, deals with the government always turn out to be plots to cheat or let yourself be cheated. He wants nothing to do with such schemes.

Luisa Camín cites chapter and verse of the deals Margarito tries to make with Don Lupe. I don't know if Don Lupe has a soft spot for Luisa Camín. Her Spanish accent and pale white skin are traits he always admires in women, and it's hard not to wonder if his treatment of Luisa and Emma has something to do with his taste for white skin. He sometimes boasts to them, and most emphatically to Luisa, who was not so distant from him in age, that he was wise to marry Juana Marrufo. She's the daughter of immigrants from the northwest of Spain who happened to land on Cozumel. Juana is the one he chose to be the mother of his children and the keeper of his house while he sated his lust upon bodies of a darker and more common order. This is what I surmise, not what Luisa says she hears from Don Lupe, though the two of them are close enough to speak of such things. When Don Lupe explains what Margarito wants,

Luisa replies: "Let him have his way, Don Lupe." Lupe says:
"No, Luisa. How am I going to do business with a scoundrel
like that?" "Your company's plenty strong enough," Luisa tells
him. "It won't hurt Casa Aguilar to agree with him, and it will
be good for business. Do it, Don Lupe." "No, Luisa, I can't."
Don Lupe doubts Margarito will be around any longer than the
appointed governors before him; one way or another, he'll be
gone soon enough. "Deal with him, Don Lupe." Luisa insists.
"Don't muddy the waters. He's here to steal, and if you don't
let him, he will make trouble for you." "No, he won't," Don
Lupe says, and they both laugh, convinced they can look out
for themselves and each other. Luisa Camín is thirty-two at the
time and Don Lupe fifty-three.

According to Emma and Luisa, Margarito makes the
decision that will ruin their lives after a conversation with their
father, Manuel Camín, who is indignant about the plundering of
Quintana Roo's vast expanses of mahogany and cedar forests.
The trees are being cut down indiscriminately and shipped out
of the country as logs, leaving Mexico with nothing but dead
stumps and rutted logging roads. This outrage must be stopped,
Camín tells the governor. Foreign companies are determining
the size of each tree they cut down by measuring the diameter of
the trunk at its narrowest point, a practice known in the lumber
business as "cubication." Cubication seriously underestimates
the volume of finished lumber to be sawed from each tree. It
lets the companies get away with paying for much of the wood
they take out of the country as if it were a byproduct of little
value. "Forbid the sale of raw timber," Camín tells Margarito.
"If they have to saw it here, we get a share of the profits, and
the exploitation will end once lumber is selling for what it's
actually worth."

Camín's thinking is in tune with the times, and so is
Margarito's: they're out to save the country from the pillaging

of its natural resources. The pillaging is real, and the example of what to do about it is in plain sight after the expropriation of the oil industry in 1938: the concessions must be removed from foreign hands and given to Mexicans. And rules must be put in place to make sure the nation's wealth stays at home. Margarito trains his artillery on those who exploit Quintana Roo's forest resources of wood and chicle and whose abuses are rampant and unregulated.

Margarito talks like a nationalist, but he's a wily politician who knows perfectly well that the country is made up of webs of entrenched interests and a national economy beholden to private wealth. The weapons Margarito deploys on behalf of the nation are eminently political: he rewards allies and punishes critics. When the time comes to grant or deny lumber and chicle concessions, Margarito imposes conditions. He's not about to give anybody anything unless he gets something back, and that applies to the handful of local brokers of timber and chicle. First and foremost among them is Don Lupe. The clash between Margarito and Casa Aguilar is one of many skirmishes taking place in the nationwide fight for control of the country's natural resources. Margarito intends to put an end to the sacking of Quintana Roo. He pledges to rid the forgotten and defenseless territory he governs of misrule, misbehavior, and stray dogs. As a public health measure to combat rabies, he orders a mass slaughter of the animals in Chetumal. The nation's welfare depends on: killing dogs, shuttering saloons, canceling concessions, and forbidding the export of un-sawed timber, which is a mainstay of the local lumber business and the prosperity of Don Lupe.

When he marries in 1944, Héctor's status within Casa Aguilar is on the rise. As the store's cashier and bookkeeper, he uses a mix of geniality and irresistible good humor to get employees and suppliers alike to take orders from him. He's the smiling face of the formidable Casa Aguilar.

Upon return from his honeymoon, Héctor begins setting up a machine shop in back of the house where he lives and which belongs to his father-in-law. Emma and Luisa go about opening a dry goods store on the corner of Heroes and Othón P. Blanco owned by Héctor and registered in the name of Manuel Camín. While getting their new businesses afloat, the Camíns and Aguilars overlook the fact that property is not a thing to be trifled with.

When he gets home from his honeymoon with Emma in the summer of 1944, Héctor is greeted by what may be called Margarito's first attempt at collusion. He's approached by subordinates of the Dogslayer, as Margarito is now known in local slang. They've come to offer him a job in the government or, in the alternative, to go into partnership with the government in private business ventures. Héctor turns down both options. All he wants at the moment is to work for Casa Aguilar and set up his machine shop in back of the house where the newlyweds have taken up residence at number seventeen Othón P. Blanco. He's encouraged to look beyond Casa Aguilar by his young, radiant, and enviable wife, Emma, who had the fortitude to remain single to the age of twenty-four in a place where girls marry or move in with boyfriends and begin to wither in their teens. Emma blossoms in her mid-twenties. She opens up to the world where her husband is getting ahead on the strength of the same invincible smile that won her over.

Not much is left of the whimsical disposition that characterizes Emma between her arrival in Chetumal in 1938, and her marriage to Héctor in 1944. Years later she confesses to a courtship, or the start of a courtship, or perhaps just the dream of a courtship, with Adolfo Pérez Schofield, the brother of Aurora, a girl she first met in Chetumal and who will go on to be her lifelong friend. It's been said—and Emma confirms it—that she only turns her attention to Héctor after seeing his legs at a basketball game on the Esplanade. Héctor recalls watching the Cubans go by from the balcony of his house. They're on their way to an affair hosted by Governor Melgar in the palace of government, and Héctor says to his cousin Licha, the daughter of Don Lupe's sister Natalia: "If I jump from here, that's where I'll land." With "that" standing for the breathtaking haunches of Emma Camín.

Margarito and his aides toy with Héctor to make mischief but also for the simple and less perverse reason that Margarito likes him. He's a good dancer and storyteller who can break the ice with anyone. The governor figures out that Héctor's idea of independence amounts to little more than the dream of setting up a machine shop behind his house. Margarito's people offer to put him in charge of maintaining the eleven cars and three dump trucks that make up the government's motor pool in a town of 8,104 inhabitants, 37 private cars, and two taxis. An additional 47 boats have motors that must be taken in for repairs when they break down. The arrangement cements good relations between Margarito and Héctor, but it also nourishes the suspicions that doing business with an avowed enemy inevitably arise in his father's house. Years later, at an advanced age, Héctor recalls with childish glee the grand opening of his machine shop in the back yard of his house on Othón P. Blanco. Both Margarito and Don Lupe are on hand for the occasion. The two old men shake hands and go so far as to have a cognac together, though both are teetotalers and far from friends.

The clash between Margarito and Don Lupe soon reaches the point of no return. There's not room enough for the two of them in the small but enviable world of Chetumal. Margarito suspends Don Lupe's forest concessions and sets his sights on his other holdings, most notably the filling station licensed to him by the government. This takes us to what could be called

Margarito's second attempt at collusion: he has his cronies offer Héctor the chance to become the new owner of the filling station they're trying to seize from Don Lupe. Once again, Héctor turns them down. Margarito suspends all the government purchases he can from Casa Aguilar, and he curtails the use of Don Lupe's boats for government shipping by water. In a small place where the government is nearly everything and the town itself little more than an extension of the government, this is tantamount to depriving Don Lupe of a livelihood. Margarito then sends to Cozumel for a prosperous young businessman named Nasim Joaquín and asks him to open a movie house to compete with the one Don Lupe owns, the Juventino Rosas. Nasim Joaquín declines to become involved in a business he knows nothing about and comes up with an alternate investor who clashes with Margarito. So Margarito opens a movie theater of his own and names it after his friend, President Manuel Ávila Camacho. Shortly before Héctor's break with Casa Aguilar, in 1948, Margarito's hostility towards Don Lupe boils over. One of his confidants, the head of public health services in the territory, approaches Héctor. The man is a political professional whom Margarito uses to put space between himself and the backroom deals that are the essence of political loyalty, but which must never be talked about openly. This man tells Héctor that a decision has been made to put an end to Casa Aguilar. He says Governor Margarito wishes to offer Héctor the opportunity to rebuild the Aguilar business network on the terms Don Lupe refused. Margarito's emissary is named Inocencio Ramírez Padilla. In years to come he'll become a hit man, the killer of Pedro Pérez, a political crime that captures the history of Chetumal in a single snapshot. Inocencio doesn't know it, but at the time of his dealings with Héctor he already carries the seeds of crime within him. For the time being, he's a handsome, charming, and virulently anticlerical young doctor with a taste for intrigue and an active nightlife. He urges Héctor to turn on his family and help seize its assets:

"This is your chance to get back at them," he says.

"Get back at them for what?" Héctor asks.

"For preferring your brother Ángel," Ramírez Padilla tells him.

Héctor can't believe his ears. Though he says nothing, his silence signifies neither acceptance nor rejection. When he gets home, he relates what he's just heard to his wife Emma and his sister-in-law Luisa. The year must be 1948, and it's possible my sister Emma is scurrying among the grownups in search of attention while I nap in a cradle covered with mosquito netting. As an adult I miss my childhood specialty: deep, undisturbed sleep. Upon learning of the offer that weighs upon Héctor and makes Emma nervous, Luisa says something similar to what she once told Don Lupe:

"Accept the offer or there will be nothing left for any of us."

Which means: deal with the devil. If you want to keep anything for yourself and your family, preserve what you can of your father's wealth. You'll get it all back after Margarito's gone, Luisa suggests. Things will return to normal, and you'll have a fortune of your own. Luisa speaks with the conviction of someone who knew ahead of time what was likely to happen and had warned Don Lupe of just such an outcome long ago.

"Agree or lose everything," she repeats.

Héctor is scared. He closes his ears to what his sister-in-law is telling him. He's scandalized by the very idea of considering what he's been offered. Even the thought of being rejected by his father is bone-chilling. Nor could he ever endure estrangement from his siblings or his mother's sorrow at the least hint that her favorite son had betrayed Casa Aguilar.

The rumor of Padilla Ramírez's offer sweeps through the

town, kept alive by its creators who say Héctor is considering a deal with Margarito in exchange for the spoils of Casa Aguilar. Loose talk spreads bitterness and sets the stage for Héctor's break with Casa Aguilar. Héctor is well on his way to leaving of his own accord, but blame and suspicion supply the final push. Ángel believes Héctor really is plotting with the governor and tells anyone who will listen: "My brother has built a wall between us that even God couldn't take down." Don Lupe does nothing to settle the dispute between his sons and, by not intervening, appears to side with Ángel. Héctor is offended. It's a grudge assuaged only by his mother's soothing affection, and he carries it with him the rest of his life.

A minor incident causes the final split. A worker at the bottling plant cuts his finger, and Héctor sends him to the doctor who tells him: "Nobody gets treatment here without Don Ángel's signature. Don Héctor's won't do."

Héctor decides it's time for him to sever his ties with Casa Aguilar, to show his father they've been unfair to him and that he can do fine on his own. He's got the machine shop behind his house, a wife who works in a dry goods store with her sister, his charm and his eagerness to conquer the world, to leave his brothers in the shade, to make his mother proud. He'll win over Don Lupe with his exploits and compete with the old man by following his example. He'll buy gasoline wholesale in Belize and sell it from portable tanks in Mexico instead of a filling station like his father's. Years later he'll recall with touching pride how he hears from an old black man in customs that Don Lupe likes to boast about Héctor's initiative. "On the other hand," his father reportedly says, "Ángel talks a lot but does nothing."

Almost half a century later Héctor remembers while I take notes:

"I got Esso and Standard Oil competing with each other. I drive a blue stake truck to Subteniente López (the border crossing to Belize over the Río Hondo) and go looking for a place that sells oil by the drum. The quality and price were better than in Mexico. Then I find a source of gasoline, and everything falls into place. I set up an outlet complete with pumps that show the right price unlike your grandfather's that were always out of adjustment or broken and you had to pay whatever they said you owed."

This is how Héctor expects to show his father the family's not being fair with him and that he doesn't need Casa Aguilar to get ahead. He soon ventures into the lumber business from which Don Lupe was shut out in Quintana Roo. Rather than deal with Margarito, who controls access to Mexico's forest resources, he sets up in the Petén Jungle of Guatemala, just over the border from Belize, where Casa Aguilar will also try to get a foothold and build a sawmill.

By the time his third child and second son, Juan José, is born in 1949, Héctor has left Casa Aguilar. He has a promising machine shop and a wife who cares for his growing family while also working with her sister Luisa in the dry goods store on the corner of Othón P. Blanco and Avenida Héroes. Luisa draws on the classes in *haute couture* she attended in Camagüey to set up the dressmaking shop that turns out women's clothing of quality and style for the store. In 1950, the second daughter of Emma and Héctor, María Pilar, is born. By now Héctor's independence from Don Lupe is complete. He won't settle for equaling his father anymore; now he dreams of outdoing him. I know full well that feelings of affection and the urge to rebel are not mutually exclusive. They grow out of self-esteem and the innocent assumption that members of a single family must share similar tastes. Héctor thinks his cry of independence will inspire not jealousy and rivalry but his relatives' love and admiration. I don't mean to suggest that he's misunderstood, only that he's moved to strike out on his own less by ambition than by good intentions. He went forth clad in a child's armor of thinking no one could possibly dislike him. His sunny but mistaken take on life is second nature to him.

None of this happens suddenly or in any particular sequence. It happens in fits and starts according to the random ups and downs of his life. Nevertheless, by the summer of 1953, Héctor has acquired a timber concession in Guatemala and set up a base camp in the tiny settlement of Fallabón on the banks of the Mopán River.

If I were to pick a single scene to bring back the feel of those years in the lives of Emma and Héctor, it would have to be a fiesta at our house in Chetumal, a house much given to fiestas. It's a good metaphor, a vivid and precise rendering of those happy years when Emma and Héctor's first four children were born and the future was theirs for the taking on a tray of promises.

The party is held in the huge patio whose size I remember through the eyes of a small boy. Clusters of men in loose-fitting white guayaberas talk, laugh, trade jokes, and argue. In their hands are pale glasses of scotch and soda made with whiskey imported tax-free from the neighboring British colony. The women wear light-colored chiffon dresses that flutter in the breeze as they seat their children at the tables or chase after them across the patio. The boys have had their hair slicked down with scented Yardley brilliantine by their mothers; the girls, whose hair is kept firmly in place under butterfly bows, are dressed in organdy and poplin frocks. Luisa Camín's seamstresses and workers from Héctor's machine shop come and go from the kitchen where Angela—Emma's guardian angel, cook, and ally—has spent thirty hours preparing for this day. Last night, under her surgically precise instructions, the crew from the machine shop butchered a pig in the patio. While four men hold onto its trotters, its throat is slit over a washtub to save the blood for sausages. The animal's squeals pierce the clear air of the small-town night. Its thorax is cut open to remove the intestines and kidneys, and its skin is shaved smooth. The whole carcass is tenderized with spices and branches of achiote shrub on a brass baking pan. At dawn it's wrapped in banana leaves and buried over smoldering embers which by noon will yield roast suckling pig, the immortal *cochinito pibil*, canonical dish of the Yucatán. Angela herself dispatches the chickens she uses for consommé and whose meat she marinates in escabeche. She grabs the birds by the throat and spins them around like pinwheels until their necks are broken. Deprived of the salt in sea water, the lobsters our godfather Inés Valencia brings from Xcalak die painlessly in fresh water. My childhood eyes see all this killing in a golden glow. With its less savory aspects expunged from memory or reshaped by forgetting, the slaughter is transubstantiated as food on the table for the ensuing party. Platefuls of cochinito come and go together with reams of freshly made corn tortillas, refried beans, lobster salad, and marinated chicken breasts, while the women talk, the men drink, and the children scamper about the patio. A trio sings Emma's and Héctor's favorite song of the time, the lament of a traveling man that evokes Héctor's increasingly frequent trips to his lumber camp at Fallabón in the wilds of the border between Belize and Guatemala. It's where Héctor hopes to follow his father's example, win his approval, and show he can equal and even surpass his achievements. The song at this party is the one I heard through my window in the silver dawn of a morning when Héctor and a trio sing it to Emma. Her husband and the musicians are all a bit tipsy, and though she scolds them, she's flattered by this bit of excess and doesn't really mind. From her window she calls Héctor inside. The song imprints on me the lighthearted, nocturnal shimmer of Emma's and Héctor's love for one another, and ushers in the days when the lumber business puts its mark on our household. The song is *Little Star of the South*, and its ragged lyrics have the sweetness of a lover's promised return darkened by the sadness of going away:

No, I won't say goodbye,
Little star of the south,
Because soon
I'll be back by your side.
Once again I'll rejoice
In your soft sweet fragrance.
The sun will shine, and
Bells will ring in my heart.

The word Fallabón speaks to my memory of many things, among them a river, a bridge, a roof thatched with palm fronds, a horse, and the word itself on my mother's lips. The horse has a hernia as big as a fist on his side and cavorts in the field in front of us. It makes no sense for me to remember seeing him from a window because there were no windows in this log house with its guano and palm roof in this place called Fallabón. It's not even a real house, just a barrack with a dirt floor and rough-cut planks for walls on the edge of the encampment where Héctor spends his first logging season in the Petén jungle. The logs are piled by the sawmill, which is in Guatemala. It overlooks our house and the camp's mess hall which are on the Belize side of the Mopán River. The buildings sit in a high meadow above a bend in the river that forms a crystalline backwater on the shore below. Near our house on the Belize side is the town of Benque Viejo, a name which has a nice lilt in my memory because I hear it spoken by my mother. Across the river in Guatemala near the sawmill in Fallabón is another town called *Plancha de Piedra*, or Rock Flat. The phonetic rasp of its name matches its harsh surroundings.

Stories from the early days of Fallabón tell how the place got its name. It's a mysterious word born of a mysterious fire that in 1950 destroys all the timber piled outside the sawmill.

The encampment's American owners say the wood burst into flames with the intensity of a "firebomb". The local creole hears this as "*fayabóm*", the term from which Spanish-speaking Guatemalans derive the proper name of "Fallabón". Etymology aside, it's what the place is called when Héctor and Emma take their four children there for summer vacation in 1953.

We live in the cabaña beside the shed that serves as the encampment's mess hall. Before we can settle in fully, Emma must wage her secret war against iguanas. She comes from Cuba, where they're called caguayos. Along with the wasps called *jicoteas,* these creatures cohabit any Cuban house, and Emma invests them with some of the terrors that roil her imagination. She looks for geckos, the intruders that can make her life miserable at home in Chetumal. She pokes around the edges of the cabaña where she and her children are about to take up residence. Then she shakes the palm fronds in the low ceiling and the narrow slats that hold them up. She peers into corners, drawers and wardrobes, looks behind the griddles in the kitchen, and between the planks of the walls, making sure the house is free of reptiles and the flies and larvae that salamanders and lizards feast on. The inspection comes up clean. The majordomo explains how to use mosquito netting to keep insects and scorpions away. Emma breathes an audible sigh of relief and says, "Scorpions! God save us! At least there aren't any iguanas or lizards."

The majordomo smiles and invites her to step into the open patio shaded by the multi-layered canopies of two *guanacaste* trees. The majordomo claps his hands a couple of times, and the trees come alive. Boughs bend. Leaves and fronds start to rustle. Iguanas the color of tree bark rise to full alert on their Herculean forepaws and flick their tongues over prehistoric jaws.

"They don't come down unless you call them or forget to feed them," the majordomo consoles Emma. He adds that the cooks raise them like chickens in a coop because iguana is the loggers' favorite dish.

In my memory the world of Fallabón consists of proud guanacastes and the split personality of the Mopán River. When it rains, the river's a muddy torrent that growls about the frail wooden bridge standing on pilings pounded into the riverbed eight meters below the deck. In the absence of rain, it's the crystalline stream that feeds the backwater where we go swimming before breakfast, the pool where the scabs from my bout of chicken pox in Chetumal are washed away. In my memory there can be no skin smoother and less wrinkled than the skin of my own body after immersion in the Mopán River.

The other thing I cannot help but associate with Fallabón is that's where the lumber business took its initial toll on my family. Héctor's first bid for wealth goes badly awry. His ambition is unrealistic in many ways, but it's enormously real in the memory of my family. Time adds shades of inevitability to the loss. History and fact put less blame on the way the stars happen to align.

Chetumal, 1955

The University of Florida weather service keeps records of Caribbean hurricanes that go back to 1871. Its graphs show that most hurricanes live and die over the ocean. They're like oceanic temper tantrums; they heat up, explode and dissipate in the huge masses of water they themselves suck up from the ocean. Only a few follow paths that reach land, and it's usually uninhabited land because population centers along the shores of the Caribbean are relatively few and far between. Janet, the one that strikes the town of Chetumal on September 27, 1955, is the most powerful hurricane in the region's recorded history.

For three days local radio stations have been warning that Janet could make landfall in Chetumal. Either nobody believes it or everybody half believes it. The most recent hurricane alert was in 1942. People remember that, after all the warnings, the storm produced only high winds and heavy rains. Thirteen years have gone by with no new warnings, but the warnings are back in late September thirteen years later. Throughout the morning of the 27th the airwaves are full of precautions and warnings. In the afternoon Luisa Camín goes to the waterfront for a look at the bay. She's surprised to see how far the sea has pulled back from the shore. Below the modest seawall is a band of coarse green sand with clumps of seaweed and starfish. It smells awful. Small, newly-hatched crabs scurry over the debris. The sky is leaden, and a breeze from the north brings the first drops of rain. Luisa has goosebumps and can hardly believe her eyes. "It looks as if the sea has deserted us," she tells her sister. Emma is folding the children's laundry on the dining room table. "It'll be back," she says. They talk about the weather, but they're actually wondering if they should pack a few blankets and take the children to higher ground away from the waterfront. A sound truck has been going through the streets of Chetumal since morning urging everyone to take shelter. Look out for your lives, leave your houses, seek refuge from the hurricane. The Camín sisters decide not to evacuate. Hurricanes don't scare them. They've weathered them in Cuba: great gusts of waterlogged wind that uproot palm trees and can blow away nearly anything that's not tied down. They particularly remember watching a dog and the doghouse to which it was chained fly through the air. The terrified animal looked like the hound of heaven with its legs akimbo and the doghouse flapping about like loose canvas. They'd also lost a parrot in a Cuban hurricane. The bird spent its days in an orange tree next to the house and sang along with Emma, who was always singing. When the hurricane passed, the parrot was gone. They mourned it like a dead relative for days, after which a creature that looked like a bandy-legged bat with a beak staggered into the yard. It was the plucked and mute parrot, and it refused to make a sound until its feathers grew back.

It rains all afternoon in Chetumal, but at seven in the evening the deluge begins in earnest. By ten the wind is ripping leaves off the trees, shredding bushes, and rattling windows. At eleven Emma and Luisa begin praying to the strains of a choir made up of: Angela, the cook; Dulce María, the nanny; and four half-awake, frightened children. The oldest sibling is my ten-year-old sister, and our father is away. We miss our father, who from now on will be going away too often or staying away too long. At midnight a lightning bolt of biblical proportions strikes the front of the house, a simple wooden structure with a pitched roof. Emma tries to hold up the front wall. I remember her pushing at it as if she has the strength to hold it in place; it's a scene that's a measure of her inner fortitude. She defends her world against the world outside with all her heart. Her convictions are rock-solid, invincible. At twelve thirty the wall gives way, taking the front half of the house down with it. We cower within the cement walls of the bathroom, but it's too close to the rain barrel. If it bursts we'd be drenched, so we retreat to the kitchen. It's the last safe place in the house. Luisa distracts us by making us sing. Damp, trembling from fear and cold, we sing interminably, song after song.

At daybreak the hurricane recedes. The air's as calm as the seventh day of creation, and you can hear your heart beat. First, my grandfather Camín appears in the back yard. He's come from the house next door where he lives with his wife Josefa. Then my uncle Raúl comes to take us to his house, a two-story cement structure thirty meters beyond a vacant lot and the shop where Emma's and Luisa's seamstresses make dresses. Those thirty meters appear in my memory as an expanse too vast to see across. We decide to make a dash for my uncle's house. We form a line with Raúl and me in the lead. We're barely at the edge of the vacant lot when the wind begins to blow with renewed intensity. A sheet of roofing breaks loose from the roof of the shop and gyrates through the pallid dawn air like the blade of a propeller. We retreat from the vacant lot to the narrow passage between the enclosure that houses the rain barrel and the wall of the dressmaking shop. The loose roofing flies past my uncle just below his chin and crashes into the wall of the shop. He crouches down beside me. The wind begins to whistle, and it starts to rain again. We withdraw in defeat to the kitchen we came from. We've missed our chance to reach safety during the lull at the eye of the hurricane. Janet's tail lashes the sea over the low-lying sections of Chetumal where we live. The next thing I remember is the gush of water pouring though the gap between the floor and the bottom of the kitchen door as if from a fire hose.

"The sea's coming right in the door," Emma says.

The grownups hoist the children onto the kitchen table, then stand next to us with their feet on the floor. The water is still coming in under the door. It washes over the grownups' ankles, then their knees. When it reaches their waists, they too climb on the table and take us in their arms. There are no prayers, no hymns, just the splashing of water as it rises towards their waists once again. It wets our ankles, then our knees. It's nearing our chests when it desists.

"It's stopped," Emma says.

"Right," says my Uncle Raúl.

At that moment the water begins to recede. It reverses its flow, splashing and gurgling its way back to where it came from.

When it's daylight, we make our way to Raúl's store through a layer of mud a foot thick. The town looks like a derelict shipyard. All we can see sticking up from the mud are off-kilter power poles, downed trees, and the remains of furniture and houses. The streets are choked with mud and uprooted shrubbery.

A day later my foot starts to hurt from a cut so deep it nearly severed my big toe. It's taken twenty-four hours for me to feel it, but now it really hurts. I get a tetanus shot at the hospital. The place is inundated with patients awaiting treatment, and mud. There's mud everywhere.

Journalists from the nation's capital arrive on special flights to cover the disaster. "Hurricane Janet flattened Quintano Roo, leaving a wake of death and destruction," says one paper. Another says, "The city of Chetumal looks bombed out." A third concluded, "Chetumal is a graveyard." The official death toll is 87, according to Francisco Bautista Pérez, author of the best account of the storm. Before battering Chetumal, Janet took two hundred lives and downed a hurricane-tracking plane with a crew of eleven on board.

Janet lasts seven days from its September 22 birth near the island of St. Vincent, south of Martinique, to September 29 when it peters out after crossing the Yucatán Peninsula and the Gulf of Mexico and making landfall once again between Veracruz and Punta Delgado. It devastates the towns of El Viejón, Palma de Abajo, Palma de Arriba, Palma Sola, Villa Rica, and La Antigua. It changes the course of the stream that runs through Barranca Fernández, a verdant canyon where, as I recall from visits years later, howler monkeys race through the trees. All these things are vividly imprinted on my memory, which proves nothing. I also recall with absolute clarity a sheltered childhood of edenic bliss, blue almonds, and, in the fragrant night air, ecstatic dragons that couldn't possibly be real.

Where's Héctor the day the hurricane flattens Chetumal, destroys his house, almost drowns his family, and leaves the whole city caked in mud? He's at the encampment in Fallabón on the border between Belize and Guatemala, harvesting logs, taking his first steps towards glory.

He began traveling to the timberland of Petén four years ago to seek his fortune. He wants to emulate his father and win his praise. In the Chetumal of those years, as in Yucatán, Belize and Guatemala, the lust for lumber resembles a gold rush. It lasts a few decades until the big trees and big profits are just a memory. Héctor is no longer content with his modest income in Chetumal and wants to disentangle himself from the intrigues that are beginning to ensnare him. He quits Casa Aguilar and sets out on a path blazed by his father. He's less interested in competing with Don Lupe than in making him realize that letting Héctor leave Casa Aguilar was a mistake. Don Lupe's greatest setback seems to have come when he tried to go into the lumber business. His fight with Margarito puts Quintana Roo out of reach, and he fails to acquire the generous logging rights that would let him prosper in Belize or Guatemala. So Héctor decides to try his own luck in the lumber trade. Years later Pedro Martínez, his second in command in the repair shop, will remember a moment when Héctor thinks his dreams are about to come true. "We're going into the lumber business," he declares. Pedro is caught off guard. "Héctor," he says, "we don't know a thing about the lumber business." To which Héctor replies, "Tomorrow I'm on my way to Guatemala."

Emma remembers packing her husband's suitcase for these trips to Guatemala. Héctor has made friends with a lawyer named Toledo who has close ties to the government of Jacobo Arbenz, and he goes to see him. He's sure he can acquire the kind of logging concessions that escaped his father's grasp. Emma goes along with his enthusiasm without sharing it. The day before one trip they have a mild falling out. Emma tells Héctor that if he wants to go into a new business, he should try something simple. For example: turn the dry goods store on the corner into a market: "We bring in things from Mexico, from Belize," Emma suggests, "from England, and we don't try to do too much. You make sales and pay your bills every day. And every day you know how you're doing. Lumber may have big payoffs on big investments, but when it doesn't pay off you're left with nothing." Héctor gives her the same answer he gave Pedro Martínez: "We're going into the lumber business," and that means he's going to Guatemala.

He comes home two weeks later with a concession under his arm. Though the Arbenz government is loath to grant foreigners anything, Héctor's charm offensive scores a small triumph within its labyrinthine bureaucracy. He's given a modest logging quota in the rain forests around Petén's capital of Flores. By the end of the 1953 logging season, the timber Héctor has waiting outside the sawmill at Fallabón is worth two-hundred-thousand dollars, my mother will always insist. He's cut the trunks into logs and hauls them down from the mountainous jungle with his own equipment: a tractor and two trucks big enough for three logs to be chained to their trailers. Or just one the size of the freshly cut mahogany trunk that dwarfs 1.6-meter Héctor as he poses for a photo beside it. He wears the smile of a hunter showing off his prey, and the prey is a tree trunk a meter thicker than he is tall.

Something must be said about the Petén in those years, about this virgin expanse of cedar and mahogany and the Mayan temples and kingdoms swallowed up by the jungle. When we go on vacation there in the summer of 1953, a coup against Jacobo Arbenz is already brewing. Stirring the pot are the CIA, the United Fruit Company, the archbishop of Guatemala, and Carlos Castillo Armas, a colonel with a sprig of mustache like Hitler's. The coup is consummated on July 8, 1954. That same month Castillo Armas repeals the Arbenz land reforms, creates Latin America's first death squads, purges communists from the government and the unions, and bans anyone unable to read and write from voting. On July 26, 1957, a few days after my eleventh birthday and two days before an earthquake topples the Angel of Independence in Mexico City, Castillo Armas is shot in the back by a member of his own security detail. The two events serve as a metaphor writ large for the travails Janet and Fallabón inflict on my family.

Forty years later my father recalls: "The one thing I didn't learn back then was how to die an easy death, but I came close more than once." For my benefit he recapitulates what he remembers about Fallabón, including the time he went to jail.

A tractor he used while logging levels a mound in the jungle, and the mound turns out to be a pre-Hispanic shrine. This desecration of a Mayan ruin triggers a burst of local anger. The police inspector in Plancha de Piedra comes to investigate and demands to know who's the responsible party. Héctor says he is though his nephew Pepe, his brother Ángel's son who spends vacations at the lumber camp, was driving the tractor at the time. Héctor agrees to accompany the inspector to Plancha de Piedra and wait with him while his driver Encalada calls Guatemala City to explain what happened and request instructions on how to proceed. The inspector has Héctor walk through town behind him as if he's under arrest, and an irate mob gathers at his back.

Plancha de Piedra is a boomtown whose main street is lined with bars and brothels. It's the only street where loggers, peons, crew chiefs and the owners of logging camps are welcome. They're welcome because they have money and are sneered at for the same reason. Loggers are the scourge of the town, its enemy. The denizens of the Petén—meaning the inhabitants of the municipality of Plancha de Piedra— are jealous guardians of their forests. The nationalism of the Arbenz years, when land was redistributed and logging in the Petén was curtailed, has taught them to be wary of outsiders ready to chop down the jungle of the ancient Mayas. These interlopers come to be hated after the 1954 coup overthrows Arbenz and the restrictions on logging are lifted.

In the barrack where Héctor is jailed, a fellow Mexican with a stump instead of a foot sits on something resembling a pillow. Héctor greets him with his family's trademark smile. His countryman smiles back. A while later he limps up to Héctor and says: "If I may, let me ask which side of the orange you're on?" "Orange? What orange?" Héctor inquires. "The orange you live on," says his countryman. "The world is a spinning orange, and you need to be damn sure you know which side of it you're on. If you're on top, fine, but if you're on one side or the other, if you're on the way down or the way up, you better be careful and hang on with all your fingers and toenails unless you're ready for a hell of a clobbering. So, where are you? Are you on the way up or the way down?"

He's on the way up, and he's not holding on very tightly.

But he doesn't know it.

In order to buy or rent the equipment needed for the lumbering season in Fallabón, Héctor has mortgaged everything he owns in Chetumal: the house where he lives with his family, which is registered in the name of Manuel Camín; the shop where he still repairs cars; the corner lot where his wife's and sister-in-law's store is located. Emma and Luisa sign mortgages and promissory notes and get their father—my grandfather Camín—to do likewise despite his fierce dislike of lumbermen. He repeats ad nauseum the words of Constancio C. Vigil, the Uruguayan whose writing looms large in a library assembled to suit his highly personal preferences and prejudices: "Damned be the man who builds his fortune on a fallen tree."

By pledging these properties, Héctor raises the money to meet his equipment needs from his maternal uncle, Goyo Marrufo. Then with the equipment and the concession in hand, he acquires from an American company called Robinson Lumber the funding to cover his overhead for the 1954 timber harvest: hiring lumberjacks and loggers; setting up camp in Fallabón; exploring the forest and marking trees to be felled. His unwritten agreement with the Robinson Company obliges him to repay his debt in finished lumber worth more than the un-sawed wood. Half way through the season Héctor has plenty of logs, but his money has run low. This sets the scene for his first setback in Fallabón, or perhaps the first time Héctor lets opportunity slip away. He underplays the cards in his hand and ends up losing the whole deck.

The Robinson representative, an Austrian named Mishner, comes to dinner. When the meal is over, as my mother recalls, Mishner explains the bargain the company proposes to strike with Héctor:

"Look, Héctor, the Robinson people consider themselves your partner in the lumber business. They've authorized me to propose that in exchange for a lien on your equipment, they'll lend you what you need to saw the lumber already at the mill and continue operations without seeking further financing. The partnership will make you stronger and give Robinson the assurances it needs to cover your expenses for the rest of the harvesting season provided you agree not to sell your timber to another buyer. As the lien-holder on your equipment, the Robinson Company will be at your service for whatever you need."

Emma senses that her husband's being lured into a trap and decides to intervene:

"See here, Mishner, why is Robinson demanding more collateral when there's two-hundred-thousand dollars' worth of timber sitting at the mill? Nobody's arguing it isn't yours, so why is the company demanding a lien on the equipment Héctor needs for his work? Robinson has the timber Héctor's delivered for less than it's worth. What more collateral does it need?"

"Doña Emma," Mishner says. "Business is done by building trust among partners who protect their interests with ironclad agreements. I promise you Héctor will profit more from a deal like this than the Robinson Company. All we need is his signature on the contract because up to now everything's been done on a handshake."

The following day Héctor goes to Belize for talks with the Robinson people. Emma will remember for the rest of her life what she told her husband while packing his overnight bag that day:

"Whatever you do, don't sign their proposal. All the collateral they need is sitting outside the sawmill, and that's all you have to give them. Any other buyer would pay twice as much for what you've cut already, knowing that what you still have in the forest is worth twice that. Don't sign anything. Don't even think of signing."

This is what happens as the day breaks. At eleven in Belize,

Héctor is deaf to his wife's forebodings as he signs the contract set before him.

Why he signs I don't know. His seemingly gratuitous decision is beyond understanding. I could never get him to give me his version of what happened. While I had him in my charge in his old age, he never spoke of his losses in detail. He lapses into circumlocution and silence rather than talk about them. By contrast, my mother's version is crystal clear, too transparent to embody the whole truth.

"You father was born to be cheated," she says, "and because he was born to be cheated, he never listened."

The Robinson Company ends up demanding more wood than first agreed upon, and Héctor is forced to hand over what he's delivered to the mill to get his equipment back and harvest the wood he has left in the forest. He's rushing to meet his obligations before the rains come in early summer 1954. But at that exact moment, in July 1954, the Castillo Armas coup against Jacobo Arbenz seals the border, and Héctor's equipment is confiscated, along with everybody else's.

He has no choice but to start all over again.

Héctor explains how he got out of this jam in the course of my efforts to retrieve what's left of his memory in 1997: He's having a drink at the bar of a club in Belize, undoubtedly the Pickwick since it's the only bar worthy of such a name in that stagnant tropical city that stinks of sewage and the fumes from its sluggish river. At the bar Héctor runs into a lawyer named Luis Ortiz Sandoval, who will serve as his new key to the Petén.

"A visibly shaken Sandoval was drinking whiskey at the bar," Héctor recalls. "I smiled and asked if he'd mind my sitting next to him. 'Far from it,' he replied. 'Have a seat and talk to me. Maybe it'll help calm me down.' He was a government lawyer and, following the recent coup, he'd been put in charge of the

Petén by the Castillo Armas regime. He was in Belize because it was faster to fly to the British colony and travel by road to Flores than to make the whole trip overland from Guatemala City. 'I need to go to the Petén, but I have no idea how to get there,' he told me. I said, 'I'm headed that way, you can come with me.' We'd become good friends, so he agreed, and on the road I told him about the troubles I was facing. We crossed the border at Benque Viejo near my encampment at Fallabón. From there I took him into the Petén, and he never forgot the favor. When a bulldozer of ours ran over some ruins and we were jailed on I don't know how many charges, I sent him a message, and he radioed back orders for some soldiers to go to the jail. They grabbed our captors by the scruff of their necks and let us out. Ortiz Sandoval's nephew was Mario Sandoval, the private secretary of the new President, Colonel Castillo Armas."

In the eyes of the Castillo Armas government, the Petén region was a hotbed of pro-Arbenz zealots. To celebrate the ex-president's overthrow a pilgrimage blessed by Archbishop Mario Rossell sets out for the capital from the Basilica in the city of Esquipulas. A North American plane leaflets Guatemala City with a pastoral letter from the archbishop, and anyone who had anything to do with Arbenz is suspected of communist sympathies. Héctor, Emma and Luisa know right away what they must do to allay such suspicions. They write Monsignor Alberto Mendoza y Bedolla, Bishop of Campeche, a regular guest in the home of Emma and Héctor during his annual pastoral visits to the domain of the stridently Jacobin executioner of Cristeros, Margarito Ramírez.

I remember the odor of mothballs in the clerical garb of Bishop Mendoza, who on one occasion puts his arm around me. Mendoza is a longtime friend of Archbishop Rossell. They both joined the front ranks of the church in 1939 when Mendoza became bishop of Campeche and Rossell archbishop of Guatemala, positions they'll each hold for life, until Rossell's death in 1964 and Mendoza's in 1967. In a letter to Rossell, Mendoza praises Emma's and Héctor's hospitality despite the Jacobin atmosphere that prevails in Chetumal. He speaks of them as an honorable couple planning to visit Guatemala in hopes of resolving certain matters they have pending with the government. Rossell replies that they'll receive a warm welcome, and Emma is sure to ask what the archbishop of Guatemala would like them to bring him from Mexico. Mendoza says he'd like a Vatican flag, and Emma and Luisa have some nuns in Mérida make a silk flag in the Vatican colors and embroidered with the shield and keys on the Holy See.

I hasten to note that neither Emma nor Héctor ever committed the sin of piety. Their dealings with the unknown take another form. They keep their lukewarm convictions to themselves and at the risk of God's punishment for their charade simply play the part of believing Catholics while in Guatemala. Forty years later my father looks back on the trip in delicious detail:

"They drove us to the presidential palace in a large car as guests of the government. We were greeted by Mario Sandoval, the private secretary of Castillo Armas and the nephew of the lawyer I'd taken to the Petén. We had the Vatican flag for the archbishop with us. It has a hand-sewn border, half yellow and half white with the shield in the middle. When we arrived at the archbishop's residence, an usher ran out to our car: 'Please come in. Come right in.' When we meet the archbishop, I bend down and kiss his hand. I think the gesture pleases him. 'We have a present for you in the car,' I say. 'If you want to see it, I'll have it brought in.' 'Please do,' he says. An aide and the driver go to get it, and when they return they set the package on the table. As soon as it's opened, you can see the cloth. The aide steps back and crosses himself. The archbishop gets up to see what's in the package, and I say to the aide, 'Let's unfold it.' When the flag is spread over the table it's huge. It's so big there's hardly room for it in the small office. By the mist in his glasses, I can see the archbishop is touched. He slips his left hand under the fabric and lets it slide between his fingers. With his right hand he feels the weight of the embroidery around the edges. He knows its worth and treats it gently. 'I want you to know that, starting from now on, you'll be considered a friend of the Guatemalan church and its hierarchy,' he tells me. 'How can we help you?'"

Years later Emma recalls:

"The doors to the president's office open automatically. Your father meets with Castillo Armas, and Guatemala opens up to us. The next day we see the flag in the cathedral. They have it under glass right next to the altar. It must be there still."

This is how Héctor finds his way to a second lumbering concession in Guatemala. The news comes from Minister of Agriculture Lázaro Chacón in words Emma purports to remember exactly as he'd said them: "We know there have been problems with your prior concession, but we're going to give you something to make up for your many losses. Look, in the *Aguas Turbias* preserve Guatemala has timber resources that haven't been granted to any North American company. It's been a struggle to hold onto them because large companies have pressured us to open them up. But we know that if we do, a big company will level them. We're going to give you logging rights in Aguas Turbias for two years. There's no bad wood in Aguas Turbias, and your concession's for two years. Keep in mind it's for two years, and that's that."

Don Goyo Marrufo, Héctor's uncle and partner, is the first to hear about the concession in Chetumal. He tells Héctor:

"You have no idea what you've been given, kid. In two years I'll make you a millionaire."

Don Goyo says he's willing to absorb the debts from the

prior season into a new partnership to exploit the woodlands of Aguas Turbias, so named for the abundance of silt in its rivers and marshes.   It's spring 1955. Héctor seems to be over his losses to the Robinson Company: he has his own equipment in the Petén; he has the lumber he rescued from the first concession in Flores; he has his encampment in Fallabón up and running; he's got the new concession in Aguas Turbias; and his partner is an eager millionaire to be. He has everything sitting on the border and ready to go in late September 1955 when Hurricane Janet lays waste to Chetumal. Hence his absence on the night disaster strikes. He's back the next day. He arrives by private plane from Belize. He remembers bursting into tears upon seeing the splintered remains of the city sticking out of the mud. He remembers shoveling mud out of his house and going to ask Don Lupe for wood to rebuild his house. At the time Don Lupe's the only one in town with unused lumber, leftover output from his sawmill at Santa Elena on the Río Hondó the preceding summer. He gives Héctor permission to take whatever he needs. Héctor gets to work rebuilding his house.

I remember Don Lupe in the days after the hurricane. I remember him barefoot, seated on the second floor of his big cement house. The storm has blown the glass out of all the windows. He has his legs crossed like a Buddha before an open safe, and his elbows are resting on his knees. He's flattening and stacking bills wrinkled and dirtied by the flood. The hurricane has blown in through the broken windows and drenched everything. Don Lupe smooths the bills and places them in piles like fruit in a market stall. He's in his shirtsleeves, unkempt with his hair uncombed. Without his gold-rimmed glasses, his linen suits and the inevitable necktie, bereft of his alligator shoes and Panama hat, he has the unwashed look of a true peasant. There are corns on his feet, and his thick fingers hover over the bills with a sadness that exposes the roots of avarice in its most primitive form: want.

Three days after the hurricane, Chetumal reeks of death. The townspeople live in fear of sickness and disease. My family's first major decision at the time is to send the children away. My siblings and I mustn't remain in the open-air morgue that the ruined and the germ-infested city has become. The emergency forces us to live in adversity—no more the dream Emma and Luisa had long wished would come true in prosperity: to move to the metropolis where there are Jesuit schools for boys and schools run by nuns for girls. Emma and Luisa always counted on wealth from the lumber business to enable the whole family to move in style, but they now settle for doing so piecemeal and on a shoestring. The children would go to Mexico City with Luisa while Emma would stay behind with Héctor until the lumber business changed their fortunes for the better.

It's not the family but the governor who makes the second key decision at the time. Using the emergency as his justification, Margarito seizes by decree the lumber Don Lupe has accumulated at his sawmill in Santa Elena. The wood—which Margarito promises to pay for—is all that's left of Don Lupe's properties and his earnings during the past year. The hurricane has sunk his boats, paralyzed his store, and devastated his bottling plant; the Juventino Rosas theater is destroyed together with his children's houses across the street. For a time Casa Aguilar's sole income is from its pool hall while its expenses remain unchanged. The government uses Don Lupe's lumber to build houses for victims of the storm but doesn't pay him for it. In 1956, the year after the hurricane, Margarito leaves Don Lupe on the verge of bankruptcy. It's the year Héctor begins lumbering in Aguas Turbias in partnership with Don Goyo. It's also the year Don Lupe learns of his son's logging concession in Aguas Turbias. When Héctor's in town Don Lupe goes to his house to talk business. When Héctor's gone, he chats with his daughter-in-law Emma over cups of her delicious coffee which he insists is the best in all the Caribbean.

In late September Luisa departs Chetumal with the four siblings in tow. Emma's ten; I'm nine; Juan José's six; and Pilar's five. We travel on the floor of a cargo plane that spends a hot, humid, and unbearable night on the ground in Villahermosa, the first of two stops on the way to Mexico City. The four of us make up the cast of Luisa Camín's greatest adventure, a production driven by her unshakable belief that we must be rescued from Chetumal at all costs. The local schools only go to the eighth grade, she'll say later, and lack of education leads men to a life of carousing, and women to one of putting up with drunken husbands.

I don't know who decides to flee, to convert the hurricane's wrath into opportunity, but I'm willing to bet it's Luisa who convinces Emma and Héctor it's time to move on. She's also the one who volunteers to act: to leave town with her nieces and nephews under her wing and the unspoken but evident intention of never returning. Luisa's never lived in Mexico City, she's never even been there. No job awaits her, no money, no family. In my memories of childhood, though, she's less adventurous than cautious. She thinks of Mexico City as a place without a soul, a gigantic den of thieves, kidnappers, and purse snatchers where life must be lived behind barred doors and dealings with outsiders kept to a minimum.

Luisa knows no one in Mexico City except the family of Federico Pérez Gómez and his wife, Emma Wadgymar, known to us children as "the lady with the same first name as our mother". Emma and Luisa made friends with Señora Wadgymar twenty years ago when her lawyer husband was an aide to Quintana Roo governor Rafael Melgar. The Pérez Gómez family lives at 67 Manzanillo Street in the Roma district. It's a pleasant, middle-class neighborhood on the Piedad River whose waters were diverted through a culvert just two years before. Until recently, the stream marked the city's southeast boundary. Beyond it lay the orchards and fields of alfalfa that gave way to the district of Del Valle. In the years I speak of, the meadows and hay fields of a few farms are still visible, and you can see the green slopes of the majestic Sierra del Ajusco in the distance.

The Pérez Gómez residence is a one-story structure with three bedrooms, a two-car garage, and a garage in the rear with a room above it. Señor Pérez Gómez is the owner of a Nash automobile that smells of leather, fresh paint, and the allure of sweet, vanilla-infused tobacco, a mix of scents imprinted on my memory with Proustian indelibility. The living room has a high window that looks over a small garden to the street beyond. A low ivy-covered wall is all that separates the house from the street.

There are three children in the Pérez Gómez family. Federico is the oldest; Emma, age fifteen, is nicknamed the Doll; and Fernando is the same age as my sister Emma. To make room for us Fernando must give up his bedroom. I recall many uneventful days in the shadowy confines of the house, where we were strictly forbidden to leave even in the company of the maid on her trips to the corner bakery. In the enchanted penumbra of that house I discover television, the jumble of images from a set mysteriously and luxuriously housed in the wooden cabinet we open each day to watch black-and-white cartoons on *Club Quintito*. I become accustomed to the maid's efforts to rein in my excess energy. In her Nahuatl-accented Spanish, "Quiet there" equates to "Calm down." I'm not sure how long we stayed at Manzanillo 67, but, for reasons I'll explain later, I know it wasn't too long. Before the year is out we move to the country house in Cuautla where the Pérez Gómez family spends its weekends.

With help from our mother's namesake, Luisa satisfies her

obsession by enrolling me and my brother in Jesuit school. She puts my sister Emma in Helen Herly Hall, the bilingual school the Doll attends. This leaves Luisa in a cultural bind since she rejects English as the tongue of the British, a people her father has taught her to shun. Her anguish is increased by a clash with the Jesuits who consider me too young for fifth grade. The average age of fifth graders is eleven, and I'm nine. Luisa agrees to let the wily Jesuits test me and determine my grade level by results, not age. When I pass, they let me into fifth grade, a decision that will haunt me as long as I'm in school. I'll always be younger than my classmates and forced to pretend I'm older than I am. The discrepancy between outward appearance and inner reality will follow me all my life. Once she has us in school, Luisa sets about finding us a a place to live. She rents an apartment in a three-story building on Medellín Street in the Roma district that runs beside what had been the Piedad River, but now borders a stretch of the first viaduct to circle the whole city.

In our eyes the city is huge and grim, an endless expanse of concrete and asphalt. It's full of lights, and come Christmas, there are even more lights on the major thoroughfares. Cars race through the streets, and menacing shadows infest corners where the light grows dim. A smiling man blows smoke rings from a giant billboard above a movie theater that looks like a palace to us. It's called the *Insurgentes*, and it dominates an intersection on the boulevard of the same name, then as now the longest thoroughfare in the city. It is and isn't the street it once was. Five million people live in the city it traverses in the days when we first set eyes on it. At the time five million feels no different to us than twenty million today. We are what's changed. We've adapted to the walled-in life of an anonymous city. We go from a place where everybody knows everybody and nobody locks their doors to a place where everyone's a stranger. It's the most drastic change we'll ever undergo. Except for the hurricane. Change on top of change.

October is when a parent or guardian must fill out the paperwork required to enroll you in school for the coming year. Classes begin in February. October's also when it becomes clear we can't go on living with the Pérez Gómez family. Nor can we afford to set up housekeeping in a city where the cost of living far exceeds the remittances we get from Chetumal. My thoughts turn to Luisa as I write. She must have been terrified at the idea of having to look after four dumbstruck children in a city whose gods write the rules in hieroglyphics she doesn't understand. The four of us really are speechless, at least I am. Not a single syllable can escape the hornets' nest of emotions inside my head and find its way to my mouth. We're wearing out our welcome with the Pérez Gómez family, and the city is too overwhelming for us to grapple with on our own. Sra. Pérez Gómez comes up with the ideal solution during a weekend at her country house in Cuautla. We can spend the winter there, she tells Luisa. She says winters in Mexico City are cold and damp, but they're mild and sunny in Cuautla. We can stay in Cuautla until school starts in February. She adds that our fears will be gone by then, and we'll be able to find a house of our own in the city. The country house turns out to be the aforementioned apartment on Medellín where the renowned actress Sara Montes lives on the first floor and Tere and Lorena Velázquez, two sisters who must be actresses, live on the second. The three stories of the San Antonio Building are still standing, and it may still have an elevator.

I remember the weeks in Cuautla as a time of delicious idleness. The days we spend waiting for school to begin are long and happy. The meals Luisa serves us each evening come with mugs of hot chocolate and slices of toast to dip in the intensely sweet liquid as we listen to soap operas on the radio.

While we revel in the therapeutic pleasures of being left

on our own, something both similar and better is happening 750 miles to the south in Chetumal. Mired in the wreckage of Janet and with their children gone, Emma and Héctor might as well have been newlyweds. Sometime in December they jointly create the fertilized egg that will become their final offspring, Luis Miguel. He's not the child of Janet and fright, as Luis Miguel will one day assert in a poem about a woman of Chetumal. He's the child of Janet and the hope glimpsed by Héctor and Emma as the couple's gaze comes to rest on the logging season about to begin in Aguas Turbias. Emma has turned thirty-six in August and Héctor thirty-nine in October. They're still able to believe in a future together. Youth may be that and nothing more: a delirium of believing, a future agreed upon before the world molds it into reality.

Aguas Turbias—muddy waters indeed!

In February we start school in the city. The winter cold splits our lips and dries our skin. We return to the country house in Cuautla for the May vacation. In November my sister Emma completes sixth grade, and I finish fifth. My brother Juan José finishes second and my sister Emma first. My brother and I go to *Instituto Patria*, a Jesuit school; my sisters study with the Mexican nuns at the French-run Colegio Pasteur. The two schools are in one of the city's wealthiest and most prestigious neighborhoods. In *Colonia Polanco*, the houses are well built, and the street names are as dignified as the houses. In *Colonia Roma*, where we live, the streets are named for the cities and regions of Mexico: Manzanillo and Monterrey; Yucatán and Coahuila; Bajío or Tehuantepec. The streets of *Colonia Escandón*, where the school bus picks us up each day, bear the names of such secular faiths as Agriculture and Mining, Labor or Progress. By contrast, the streets of Polanco resonate with the names of Homer and Horace, Socrates and Plato (located in back of my school), Hegel and Schiller (on the same corner as my sisters' school). Here is where Emma and Luisa want to live, and it's where we will end up living though all we can afford for the time being is a two-bedroom apartment in *Colonia Roma*, an hour's ride on the school bus that takes us from the corner of Medellín and Bajío to the districts of Escandón and Condesa, strongholds of the emergent middle class that will march the city headlong into the future.

While Mexico City captivates us with the new and unexpected, Héctor confronts other changes in Chetumal. Two births at once are almost more than his nerves can stand. His wife gives birth to the couple's fifth child, and the lumber business comes to life in the jungle. His wife's pregnancy becomes evident within a few months of its December inception. Emma spend the days of her final pregnancy in a state of bliss, according to Rosemary Pérez, her friend since adolescence. Long after the hurricane the smell of burnt bodies hangs over the town, Rosemary says. She visits Emma often at the house on Othón P. Blanco in the space now occupied by the Quintana Roo Women's Institute where Rosemary works.

"Even now in 2005," Rosemary says. "I look out my office window and remember the sounds from the car repair shop Don Héctor had in the back yard. When I visited Emma in the months after the hurricane, she was always well scrubbed and very beautiful in the flower prints of her loose maternity clothes. She had the soft hair of a young girl, and she emerged from her afternoon baths in a fragrant cloud of talcum powder and lotion, in stockings and high heels. When we sat down to talk I sensed she was worried but at peace with herself. Her smile was as warm as ever. Sometimes I'd find her sketching dress patterns on tracing paper with the kind of drawing instruments I always associated with astronomical calculations. It fascinated me to watch her manipulate the wooden brackets with a metal blade. When she was through, she'd serve us glasses of the most delicious lemonade I ever tasted. She never talked to me about you children or Héctor or Luisa. We talked about other things." "Aye, Rosa María," Emma would say, "imagine how hard it must have been for your grandfather Adolfo to approach your grandmother Rosa. He must have said, 'Señora, is it all right if I touch your hand here? She was so English and stuck up!' My grandmother Schofield was very English, and it made Emma wonder. 'When they kissed, Rosa's phlegm turned into saliva,' I'd say, and we'd laugh our heads of."

Sometime during Emma's pregnancy she writes Luisa: "Don Lupe wants to talk with Héctor." The next letter adds: "Héctor's thinking of going into business with Don Lupe." The one that follows says: "Héctor's breaking his ties with Don Goyo so he can form a partnership with his father." Luisa plays the Cassandra as usual and writes Héctor: "Don't be ungrateful, don't break with Don Goyo. Ingratitude will cost you."

The only account of what happens next is a conversational duet I recorded between my mother and my aunt twenty-five years after the fact:

Emma: Don Lupe comes to the door and starts sweet-talking your father.

Luisa: He just barges in and tries to make amends.

Emma: He begins to win over your father.

Luisa: Nobody can resist Don Lupe. He has a way with people, like a snake with birds.

Emma: When Héctor sees his father trying to make up with him, he gives in. He snubs Don Goyo and sides with his father instead.

Luisa: How sad!

Emma: Everything in life has its price. I write Luisa: "Can you believe what's happening? Don Lupe's asking Héctor for help."

Luisa: The one who helped Héctor and gave him money is Don Goyo.

Emma: Luisa tells Héctor: "If you give in to your father, he'll ruin you."

Luisa: That's right.

Emma: But Héctor will do anything to get back in his father's good graces.

Luisa: He snubs Don Goyo and joins forces with Don Lupe.

Emma: When the first raft is loaded with lumber and ready to leave Aguas Turbias, Don Lupe goes to get it. He sells it, pockets the money, and refuses to give us a cent for our expenses.

Luisa: Casa Aguilar gives nothing away.

Emma: We had to cover all those costs ourselves.

Luisa: Harvesting timber and shipping it downriver costs a bundle, and if you want to stay in business, the workers must be paid every two weeks.

Emma: Then there are the taxes. You have to pay the central government for the permits to work in the forests of Guatemala. And then there are local taxes. If you don't pay them, you can't work.

Luisa: And they won't let you export a thing.

Emma: You have to pay, and that's that.

Luisa: Getting behind on your taxes is no joke.

Emma: The first load of lumber is allowed to leave Aguas Turbias before the taxes are paid. That's four thousand dollars, or six thousand quetzals, that we owe. So your father says to Don Lupe: "Dad, it's important for us to pay those taxes." Don Lupe replies: "I already told your brother Ángel to pay them."

Luisa: By then the old man had made friends with everybody in Guatemala.

Emma: Your father introduced him to all the local officials, but he still won't do anything about the four thousand dollars.

Luisa: The tax question dragged on and on, but the lumber rafts were still allowed to leave Aguas Turbias without paying as a favor to your father.

Emma: The local tax collectors finally ran out of patience and demanded that your father pay up. They wouldn't let us go on working. So you know what your grandfather did?

Luisa: The creep.

Emma: Instead of paying the four-thousand dollars we owed, he offered the Guatemalans thirty thousand to buy out your father's concession.

Luisa: And the Guatemalans agreed.

Emma: They withdrew the concession, and that was the end of your father's year in Aguas Turbias.

Luisa: He paid to harvest and market the timber, but the old man got the money.

Emma: And Aguas Turbias isn't all he got. They also let him begin operating around Flores in the Petén.

Luisa: Your father lost everything, including his reputation.

Emma: He was completely ruined.

Me: Why did my father let that happen?

Emma: Because he was born to lose whatever he earned.

Luisa: He was a better man than his father or his brother.

Emma: But he was born to be swindled.

Luisa: To give away what was rightfully his.

Emma is harder on Héctor than Luisa, who reacts with a sister-in-law's discretion. Emma is full of spousal reproach. I venture to say there's a masculine side to this setback that neither Emma nor Luisa grasp. There's something enigmatic about Héctor's ambitions and inclinations. His inner fears make him susceptible to the demands of others, especially but not only to his father's. And now he's failed to stand up to Mishner and the Robinson Company. It may be that for Héctor being well liked is a handicap. He's lived a charmed life, and he aims to please. Faced with conflict, he's at a loss to defend himself. His eagerness to make friends is an obsession that must have begun in early childhood. His takes the good intentions of others for granted and assumes that misfortune can never last long because he doesn't really believe he can fall victim to ruin and disgrace. The world, his mother, his family will always give him a second chance to seize or, as he's just done, turn his back on opportunity. His guardian angel is always ready to step in and set things right. Come what may, he can bide his time.

As Luisa says, how sad.

How sad indeed says the angel who watches him win and lose, then win and lose again, then win and lose once and for all.

It's also the rule rather than the exception for the timid to go down to defeat. They give up without a fight, they're unwilling to offend, and they let others reap the benefits of their success. And they're crippled by fear of failure. It's the best kept secret of men who are tested. It snatches defeat from the hands of victory.

All these hypotheses tend to explain Héctor, but they don't apply to Don Lupe. Why does Don Lupe take what is rightfully his son's rather than applaud his son's achievements? Maybe he can't get used to the idea of his son as a grown man, a competitor or successor, the possible founder of a new Casa Aguilar. Maybe he's unable to see his son as more than a part of Casa Aguilar. It may be normal for Héctor to want to strike out on his own, but he's not up to doing so and doesn't really need to. The desire to leave Casa Aguilar is just a childish whim he needs to get over. The Aguas Turbias venture puts everything back in place: The Father runs the business and gives the orders, the Son takes comfort in being part of the Father's business.

I theorize without knowing the truth. With one exception: the Son has something the Father needs. The Father takes it from the Son, and the Son lets him. They both regret it to the end of their days.

Mexico City, 1959

I shake flies and mosquitoes away from my head, but there are no flies or mosquitoes. At school they've taken to calling me crazy. I have photos that show me as I was then. My narrow forehead is about to burst into the predictable scowl of a juvenile delinquent, into the glare of a child who's left childhood behind. I'm not myself in that photo. Though it's an embarrassment, it's one of the truest and perhaps the most genuine representation of the battlefield in my mind, the battlefield that sprung from the heads of my parents, Héctor and Emma, and my aunt Luisa, after the losses we suffered. Héctor, Emma and Luisa are aware of these losses as they happen, but for me they're only the din that fills my head. My parents and my aunt understand its origins, but I don't. They suffer its every detail as it happens but will only come to see its true size as the whole story emerges in the fullness of time.

I return to Héctor in the years of his downfall. His downfall as seen with the excruciating clarity of hindsight. Like an animal run to ground for the first time, he's determined to regain his feet. His dreams of grandeur remain intact. He continues to charge like a wounded bull on weakened legs. He still believes in a way to safety, a way out of the ring if only he can make the right moves with the full fury of his waning youth. He personifies the metaphysics of philosopher George Santayana's raging bull, a metaphor that may be too big for what happens to Héctor, to his wife Emma, and his sister-in-law Luisa. And too big for the children who go with them to the city. We're less visible and less vulnerable here than in the town we came from where our losses are on display for all to see. In the enormous city we've moved to these losses exist only in the memories of Héctor, Emma, Luisa, and the children they care for. Years later I learn a line from Bertolt Brecht: "I came to the city in my mother's stomach." I take pleasure in applying this line to the tale of our lost world though, unlike my brother Luis Miguel, this isn't the way I come to the city. Not for nothing has Luis Miguel always been better than I at deciphering the enigmas of Emma's slender, magnificent and melancholy gut.

My brother Luis Miguel doesn't come to the city in my mother's belly either, but he almost did. He's born in Chetumal in the month of September the year after Hurricane Janet uproots his siblings and transplants them to Mexico City in the care of their Aunt Luisa. I remember the frown on her face in the days leading up to the birth of Luis Miguel and how she jumped for joy when a telegram brought news that all was well. I know she had forebodings about her sister's fifth pregnancy, and she's elated by the better than expected outcome. My next memory of our new sibling is as a bundle in my mother's arms at the door of the apartment in *Colonia Roma* where we've spent a whole year as orphans from Chetumal with no mother, no father and only an aunt to look after us. It must be December 1956. My mother has the roundness of a woman who has recently given birth and the glow of a person who has made up her mind to do what she has to do. She's pleased to see to her children, to embrace her sister, to be in the city. She has the air of a person ready to make a fresh start in life. We know there are no fresh starts. Time marches on, and memory adds the punctuation that gives it order and makes sense of what makes no sense. Someone said that about the writing of history. Though it's true, it doesn't make it any easier to explain how certain moments become so vivid in retrospect.

There's no telling what makes feelings wax or wane, but they turn our recollections of daily life into indelible memories. I have many such memories. The time that begins with the arrival of my swaddled brother and our gradual reacquaintance with the woman who was lost to us for a whole year seems to last forever. I remember the nights when Luisa and Emma sit down to talk while we sleep or pretend to sleep. My brother Luis Miguel is just a bundle of no particular age sleeping undisturbed between my mother and aunt as they reminisce about his recent birth, about the slumbering children who keep them up at night, about the dispute with the children's father over their leaving for Mexico City, about the money left over from the lumbering venture, about the children's schools, about the shameless young ladies downstairs who, like them, chatter day and night. What did father say when you told him you were leaving, what frightens you about the city, how does it feel to have a baby, where are we, what do we do now?

They're sitting together in the apartment where we live on Medellín Street in *Colonia Roma*, Mexico City. With an infant at their side and four children who pretend to sleep but are really listening as children always have to when in the middle of a conversation between women that goes on forever.

These are difficult days for the sisters, but they're happy to be together again. They've finally settled down in the city, and they have the children in schools they approve of. I remember the time as a season of cold weather and gray skies, which makes it hard to remember exactly when the scene I'm about to describe took place. On a Sunday morning under a brilliant highland sun, the sisters take us to see the house they're about to buy in *Colonia Roma*. It's on Tlacotalpan Street near the corner of Campeche in the district called Rome though nearly all its streets bear the names of Mexican provinces and cities. At the time Tlacotalpan runs along one bank of the Papaloapan

River, a watercourse with sidewalks on either shore and, like the Nile, a tendency to flood every few years. Those who live along Tlacotalpan sing the praises of their neighborhood despite this inconvenience.

That Sunday the sisters walk us through the sun-drenched streets of *Colonia Roma*. The house they're taking us to see is well away from the part of Tlacotalpan prone to floods. It's also far from the place called Chetumal, a town blown away by the fury of Hurricane Janet. It's a two-story house with an art deco facade, three bedrooms, a dining room, a sala, a garage, and a wrought-iron fence that can be scaled one leg after the other. Behind the fence and its gate is a small yard, and in the yard a planter with two dead rose bushes. They're not dead, they just need water, Emma says, as ready as ever to ignore life's darker sides. She's come to see her dream house in a state of euphoria as sparkling as the morning and as ready as the morning to banish any dark cloud from her sight. I suppose this is why this scene with my mother and aunt is engraved in my memory as the clearest expression of the life we ought to have, the life they want for us and which they pursue under the impression that it's theirs for the taking.

All this happens months before a serious loss that has already occurred in a way but which doesn't become evident to us until after we see the house, until after we move from our modest quarters on Medellín Street in Colonia Roma to the lush environs of Avenida *Moliére* in *Colonia Polanco*, the street where my school, Instituto Patria is located. The French-run *Colegio Pasteur* where my sisters are enrolled is nearby on the corner of Schiller and Homer. The building we move into is half a block from my school. It has eight stories and a Schindler elevator that never loses its allure of plastic, iron and aluminum-infused newness. The number of each floor is displayed in green as the elevator goes up and down. The building is next to the Polanco Cinema, one of fifteen large movie houses in a city of five million, the acromegalic head of a nation of twenty-five million. The country is too small for its territory; it has more land than it can use productively and a capital with an overdose of asphalt. There's something both mad and liberating about this enormous city where frightened newcomers must get by on their wits. The year we came so did two-hundred thousand others. The figure jumped to three-hundred thousand the following year and reached an estimated peak of five-hundred thousand in 1960. Something is happening, and it's happening fast. Millions are forced from their homes as the country rushes ahead, and, like us, they strive to make a place for themselves in this quiet city that's not as quiet as it used to be. Small towns are emptied, and the story of families like ours is repeated time after time. We're all refugees forced to plod on as best we can, unfazed by the fate of so many others who set out on the same solipsistic trek. We see only what happens to us while something similar is happening to everyone around us.

The apartment on Moliére Street in Polanco is the place I think of most when I remember those days. The sunny streets of Tlacotalpan, where we go to see the house we're due to move into, pale next to the night when I'm shaken from my bed by the earthquake of 1957. I have no idea what an earthquake is. The word is more formidable than the facts it seeks to describe. I wake up with my shoulders in the grasp of someone trying to throttle me. I feel as if I'm being punished for failing to explain something I know nothing about, as if my room is being attacked by giants bent on turning it upside down. Héctor comes to my bedside and hugs me as we rock back and forth in the darkness. It's nothing, he tells me, nothing to be afraid of. But something is happening, the tremors are bouncing the bed up and down. Héctor keeps his arms around me, protecting me from whatever it is that he fears. But his efforts to calm my fears are the measure of his own. He's in the grip of forces that defy protection, reduced to a diminished body quivering with fright. I don't know why, but at that moment I'm suddenly aware that he can never be counted on for solid support. The earth has crumbled beneath his feet, and he can't regain his balance. I don't know how I know that. I only know it's the knowledge of irretrievable loss.

What's this loss all about? How does it make its presence felt in our life? It's the rude awakening from the dream of prospering in the lumber business. The dream ends when Héctor loses a fortune at the hands of his own father. Don Lupe has made himself a partner in Héctor's lumber venture and at a key moment reneges on his promise to give Héctor the money he must have to hold onto the concession, four thousand dollars, six thousand quetzals. Then Don Lupe takes the concession for himself.

This is the story I've heard at home from Emma and Luisa all my life, and so far as I'm concerned it's true. Half a century later I get Héctor's version of what happened. According to him, he went to his father for the six thousand quetzals and was refused. He never implies that his father did him wrong. He says he's partly to blame, that he's a less than perfect son for going to his father for the six thousand quetzals he can't raise on his own. To which his father replies with undisguised paternalism:

"You're all the same. You all come to me when you're out of your depth."

In the days when I write these lines, I'm reading what Gibbon wrote about Roman law in his history. I read that deep within its deftly balanced rules and regulations Roman law incorporates at least one instance of rank inequality: it gives the father unconditional dominion over the son. The exalted status of the Roman father, Gibbon says, grants the father the power of life and death over his progeny. Neither age nor high office nor victory in war bestows on even the most illustrious citizen immunity from the will of the father. The adult son of a Roman citizen may win praise in the forum or the senate or glory on the battlefield, but at home he's simply a possession like furniture, cattle, or slaves. Wealth gained by the son whether by luck or hard work belongs, like the son himself, to the father and may be used and disposed of as the father sees fit.

An echo of Roman paternalism pervades the story of my father and my father's father. I hear its archaic ring in the recriminations that distinguish Emma's version of what happened from the one Héctor struggles to recite many years later. It always revolves around the same sum of money, six thousand quetzals. Emma sees betrayal on a biblical scale in the tale of a son ruined by a father's greed; Héctor paints a more prosaic picture of a father berating his sons for their shortcomings. In Emma's version Héctor gives his father what the older man must have in order to save Casa Aguilar and gets nothing in return. In Héctor's version he gives Don Lupe what he needs to keep Casa Aguilar afloat after the hurricane; it amounts to very little compared to what Casa Aguilar has given him over the years. I think that in an adversarial way both versions are true. They clash only in the fog of the impenetrable past from which they arose; they're woven together in a present that suggests to me that they're both right. The truth is derived from the sum of the contradictions, an opaque relic we can never fully unearth.

The family's loss permeates every aspect of daily life except the occasional scene that doesn't end peacefully. The loss isn't spoken of directly, it just is, and, as I've said, it sets the swarm of mosquitoes buzzing in my head. The silence in my house is deafening, and I suppose it imprints itself on me as mosquitoes. Children know only what they glean from the world around them, but at eleven I'm not exactly a child.

I know my family's dark secrets not from listening behind the door but because they hang in the air like an invisible cloud that penetrates everything I do. The cloud is with me wherever I go, but I feel it most at home where the mosquitoes buzz and the sense of loss is suffocating. Each day is worse and more enigmatic than the one before, weighed down by an unspoken message: Back home you were someone. Here you're nobody. So who are you?

The turmoil in my head is cushioned by the sonorous rumble of things that make no sense to me. What's going on in my father's head? I can't see inside his head, but on the outside he's acquired a tic that makes his neck twitch as if his shirt collar is too tight or his back hurts, and his jaw drops as if he's about to yawn. But a yawn doesn't happen so fast. It's a grimace, not the languid "crocodile yawn" of Lezama Lima. What is my father thinking when his neck and his jaw contort like that? I don't know, but it makes him look like a condemned man feeling the first snap of the rope as he drops from the gallows.

I remember him coming through the door of the apartment where we live in Polanco. It's late, and he's clearly upset about something. Whatever business he conducts must be strange and mysterious. Sometimes, he leaves early the next morning, before we have breakfast and leave for school. He comes home late, flushed from whatever he's done all day. He asks to be fed and makes vague promises about tomorrow. I imagine he's still expecting great news from the logging camp in Guatemala. He must think of his father's takeover of the lumber concession as a simple change of owners, not an expropriation. There must be something left for him in the form of property or money. But he's the one saddled with debt, and he's liable for everything his father and partner hasn't paid or refuses to pay plus the debts to his uncle Goyo Marrufo, the partner he spurned when he let himself be drawn into the embrace of his paternally arrogant and all too Roman father.

In 1957, soon after the earthquake, Emma goes to Chetumal to salvage what she can. My father is trying to arrange for the shipment of three trucks and a tractor to Mexico City. Emma is trying to rent the house she never expects to return to and the corner lot where she'll never open a store. The house and the store secure the debts to Don Goyo Marrufo, but the loans haven't come due yet and there are no liens on the property. During her stay Emma attempts to put her affairs in order; she sees people, renews old friendships, and puts up with gossip about her husband. She hears that Don Lupe and Ángel blame Héctor for all their troubles. They gave him millions, they say, and he squandered them. Manuel Camín shares this opinion of his son-in-law and says he's to blame for not living up to expectations. He absolves Casa Aguilar of all blame and incurs Emma's indignation by claiming that Héctor is solely responsible for everything that went wrong. Manuel Camín thinks the hurricane cost him more than money. In its wake he's also lost his daughters because they desert him when he's on the verge of bankruptcy and side with the man who is their undoing. He calls their decision a betrayal, a sign of weakness he considers unworthy of them, and he resents it. The truth is there's no way his son-in-law and his daughters Luisa and Emma can meet expectations. He doesn't want them to go away, he wants them with him. He's very hard on them. When they move to the city he says, "You're too small to be buried in such a big cemetery." The loss is simply too much for him. He's begun investing in Héctor's ventures, and he's building a house for Raúl. He's bought a roaster and thinks he'll make windfall profits selling coffee, but now he's drowning in debt, his daughters are gone, and he's forced to start over. Héctor's mired in scandal and lawsuits. He's facing charges of forgery, and there's a warrant out for his arrest. With a judge and creditors on his trail, it will be years before he can come back to Chetumal. He's no longer the pride of his hometown and family. But he wants the trucks back and asks Emma to get them.

While in Chetumal, Emma sleeps alone in her house for the first time ever. Her world is in ruins. Rather than a place of prosperity and hope, it's become a maelstrom of uncertainty and debt. She stays awake at night, and when she dozes off she awakens to a recurring nightmare. Later she says, "I'd think it was all a bad dream." But the nightmare is real. To help her sleep, Laureano Pérez, the father of Rose Mary and husband of Aurora, gives her a pill called Ecuanil that's now off the market. It keeps the nightmare at bay but only for an hour or so, which is the most she's able to sleep. She's smothered in debt, her children are in Mexico City, her husband faces criminal charges, she's tried her luck and lost. Each of these things swirls about her and breaks the fragile silence of her rest. All she can do is rent the house, get the trucks, and leave.

The trucks she must get out of Chetumal are the ones Héctor hauls timber with. He wants them in hopes of turning a profit on the schemes of a friend. Each truck has a hitch that hooks up to a flatbed logging trailer. Every day Emma asks customs for clearance to take the truck out of Quintana Roo. When her brother-in-law Ángel hears about this, he sends word that she can have the trucks but not the hitches. He has Héctor's driver Alfonso Encalada tell Emma, "She better let me have the hitches or else I'll have the law on her, and right now she's in no position to deal with the law." I don't know what right Ángel has to the hitches on Héctor's trucks, but he's right: this is no time for Emma Camín to run afoul of the law. Leaving the hitches just adds insult to injury. The day of her departure is full of sorrow and grief. The cook Ángela, her daughter La Chata, and Valentina Mena, who was our nanny forever, try not to cry when Emma's around, but she hears their sobs. In her presence they choke back tears and dry their cheeks. La Chata's husband José Sosa cries openly. He rests his arm on the edge of the rain barrel and repeats over and over, "It just not fair."

When Emma tells Luisa about the hitches, Luisa pledges to go to Chetumal and kill Ángel. Every day for months she renews this vow in her heart. She's relieved of it when chance, in her case providence, confronts her with the disappearance of my brother Juan. On an afternoon like any other Juan doesn't come home from school. He's supposed to be back by five, and it's now seven o'clock. Emma begins to fear the worst and starts to cry. Her children share her grief. Our imaginations fill with all the terrible things that could happen to Juan in the city. Emma cries more than she did after the hurricane, as if she were about to drown in her tears. Luisa fears her sister will lose her mind, that she may have lost it already. She sidles up to the Sacred Heart of Jesus on the apartment wall. It's the same smoke-stained effigy of a handsome bearded Christ that's been in every home I've ever had—before, during, and after the hurricane. Luisa looks at it out of the corner of her eye and says:

"All right, you win. If Juan comes back, I won't go to Chetumal and kill Ángel."

At seven thirty, Juan appears on Moliére Street, cheerful as can be with his book bag dragging on the ground. He's been at the house of some friends, and he lost track of the time. I remember running towards him in tears under the marquee of the Polanco cinema. From then on I can't get over the thought that my brother Juan is my mother's favorite child. Perhaps it's just because she feels he's the one she came closest to losing.

Once more I imagine myself inside Héctor's head looking for tremors that resonate in mine: the clouds that blur his thinking; the wounded animal struggling to break free. At forty-two he's lost two fortunes. He's in a bind that won't let him be himself but doesn't keep him from thinking about who he's been or shield him from the mad idea of becoming someone else. There are three trucks left from the debacle in Guatemala. Three tractor cabs that can't be hitched to a load, to be exact. He's brought one of the cabs to Mexico City, but everything else is lost. He offers his services as a long-haul shipper. I remember a conversation he had with one of his drivers in the kitchen of the apartment in Polanco. Later, I remember his anguish when he hears that one of the trucks has rolled over and its driver has fled the scene. Finally, I remember the scene when the driver comes to our house pleading for help for his family and himself. He's limping due to injuries suffered in the accident, and he can't work until his leg heals. And I remember how my father sympathized with him. He gave the man a few of the bills he still had and begged his pardon for a predicament that wasn't Héctor's fault.

That, according to Emma and Luisa, is all Héctor's done with what's left after Don Lupe pockets the profits from the Aguas Turbias episode. By the time the concession ends, Héctor has nothing but a load of lumber encircled by the fence his creditors have put up around it. He recovers only fifteen-thousand-eight-hundred dollars from the entire venture. That's what he tells Emma in a telegram from Guatemala City in early 1957 after she arrives in Mexico City to visit her children and introduce them to their new brother, Luis Miguel. And those dollars are what we're counting on that morning of brilliant sunshine when we go to see the house in the Roma district that's supposed to be our home in the city.

My mother tells how those dollars went up in smoke before she can get to the notary's office and buy the house on Tlacotalpan. Héctor has lavished the money on whoever happened to cross his path. He gives five thousand to Sr. Toledo, the lawyer who helped him when the socialist Arbenz government ruled Guatemala. He gives another five thousand to one Tony Chacón, a relative of the secretary of forest resources who granted him the Aguas Turbias concession during the anticommunist Castillo Armas regime. The rest goes to the frenetic Dr. Luis Sandoval, who has heart trouble and is determined to travel to Mexico City for treatment by Ignacio Chávez, the nation's preeminent cardiologist and founder of the Mexican Heart Institute.

Luisa paints a picture of her brother-in-law's prodigiously spendthrift ways in a scene that involves fewer dollars but is equally senseless. In the days prior to our removal to Mexico City, Luisa says, Emma goes to Belize with Héctor to shop for blankets to protect us from the chill of the capital. Héctor goes to the bank in Belize to withdraw three-hundred dollars for blankets while Emma waits in the car. When Héctor exits the bank, the local chief of police is walking right next to him as they cross a street with no sidewalks. The chief talks and talks, Héctor nods and nods. Finally, he extracts the cash from his pocket and hands it all to the chief. He doesn't even take the time to ask if he can please keep half of it. Emma is watching from the car. When he gets in, she asks about the money for blankets. Héctor says he gave it to the chief, but he'll get more. Luisa goes into less detail than I do here about what happens next, but what she does say is this: Héctor's a guy who will pay to keep on the good side of anyone who asks him for money; he'll even relinquish the little he has left for his family.

I see my spendthrift father in a different light: he's paying for services rendered. He's a compulsive deal-maker, but he lacks the guile of a swindler. It's the deficiency that leads to his undoing. He's a rich man's son who thinks he'll always find enough money in the depths of his pockets to win the praise of others and keep them from calling him selfish. He thinks generosity will turn enemies into friends and rebuff charges of greed. He's the polar opposite of Don Lupe.

Even when he has nothing to gain from the affection of

others, Héctor still wants to be loved. He's magnanimously blind. His handouts to the needy and not so needy are rapidly depleting his wealth. I'm touched by my father's singular weakness, but he pays a terrible price for it as long as he lives. From now on he'll be the victim of his own largesse.

So we're settled in Polanco, and our schools are nearby. Héctor's trying to get a foothold in the trucking business.

One afternoon Emma and Luisa notice the for-rent sign just placed in the window of an empty storefront by the door of the building where we live. They're practical and enterprising enough to take the place and get to work. They buy sewing machines on credit and set up shop as *Mom's Fashions and Mine*. The name embodies its business model: dresses for mothers and school uniforms and communion gowns for their daughters. Business is slow at first, but then it begins to pick up. It replaces income the head of household doesn't provide and covers the children's inevitable expenses. But sad to say, it also leads to despair. One December morning in 1958, just as the shop is beginning to prosper, it's broken into, and the burglars leave nothing behind. They steal the sewing machines that aren't yet paid off along with every thread of inventory: all the finished dresses, all the bulk fabric, all the mannequins. Adding insult to injury, they smash the display cases and anything else they can't carry off.

The burglary hits our family like a second hurricane though the blame is apportioned differently. There's no one to blame for the hurricane, but someone's responsible for making their business a total loss. When Emma and Luisa go to look for their insurance policy, they can't find it. They're left with no sewing machines, no store and no insurance. Why is there no insurance? I find out years later when Luisa and Emma deem it too late for the truth to do any harm. Telling it won't be disloyal, and it's won't spoil the lingering aura of our childhood innocence. They give Héctor the money for the insurance, but he spends it on fees and permits for his trucking business instead. For months while Héctor comes and goes on his quest for a kingdom to conquer, Emma and Luisa demand that he put his dreams aside for a while and settle for a modest but secure job in an office while they get on with reviving *Mom's Fashions and Mine*. But Héctor's not about to take a desk job. His head is full of dreams of a trucking empire that will let him pay off his debts and recoup his losses in the lumber business. He's bound to show his father and his brothers that far from being a failure, he's succeeded on a grand scale. Or something like that.

In time I come to realize that by ignoring the need to insure the store and indulging his obsessive, even pathological urge to misspend money, he's wearing away the bonds of mutual support and companionship that should underpin a marriage. Héctor's recklessness poisons his marriage to Emma and his standing in the eyes of Luisa. In writing about this period, I can see it must be the time when they begin to attribute his setbacks less to weakness than betrayal. The sisters learn they can't depend on the man of the house. They must set to sea in their own ship whether Héctor comes aboard or not. They press on knowing he'll always be less an asset than a liability.

My memories of those days are linked to the fortunes of Raúl Macías, a Mexican boxer whose ring name was *El Ratón*. The Rat is about to fight the Frenchman Alphonse Halimi for the world flyweight title. I don't know what divine attributes I've bestowed on this symbol of the nation's pride, what religious yearnings make me want to share his fate, to be him and measure the stature of my country and myself by his exploits. After spending a whole night trying and failing to tune in the fight on the radio, I braved the predawn chill of the following morning. I set out for the newsstands on Moliére Street to learn the outcome of the contest my soul depends upon. Who won? Not even the newsstand on the corner of Moliére and Ejército Nacional was open yet. The sepia morning had barely begun to shed the damp of night, and ghosts hung in the fog thirsting for the same news I hungered for. I looked up at the eucalyptus trees lining Ejército Nacional, green and remote with white streaks of dew trickling down their trunks and an Olympian indifference to ghosts. I wandered about in search of newsstands I knew didn't exist, hoping to run into someone with a newspaper to tell me how the fight had ended. At last my fruitless quest brought me back to where it began on Moliére Street, and I came across the neighborhood baker cranking up the metal curtain of his bakery. It was he who told me, "The fight wasn't yesterday, son. It's tonight."

I felt truly lost, though not so devastated as I was that night when I finally got the fight on the radio and could listen to it through the static. Raúl Macías was robbed when the judges at the Los Angeles Coliseum awarded Halimi a spit decision. Raúl had obviously won as everybody who followed the battle over the air knew perfectly well. Round by round, the announcer had reported his every blow with little mention of those thrown by his opponent. That night I didn't sleep, I cried as if I myself were being washed away in a tidal wave of gloom I could share with no one any more than I could share with myself or anybody else the wreck of my family.

The burglary of the store brings down on the family two mountains of debt: the ones Héctor's piled up in Chetumal and those that plague the shop in Polanco for want of insurance on the lost sewing machines. The combined obligations plant a wild idea in the minds of Luisa and Emma: they'll rent a house like the one they were unable to buy in *Colonia Roma* and turn it into a boarding house. They'll keep the family afloat while they win back their customers in Polanco and put Héctor to work. But Héctor refuses to work. What's more, he disapproves of providing shelter for strangers because in those days the whole city regarded "boarding house" as a a polite way to say "brothel". The idea that their plan would fill his head with such distasteful thoughts bolsters the sisters' suspicion that Héctor's lost his mind.

Emma and Luisa are so young to be burdened with five children and so afire with ambition. It staggers me to think of the enormous challenge they face with few resources and little to rely on except the force of their wills. They take on the city with the blind determination of fighting bulls at a time when the man they've cast their lot with is falling apart. He's about to desert them, and his florid dreams have them on the edge of ruin.

A stroke of urban luck comes to the sisters' rescue when they find a beautiful house they can afford to rent on *Avenida México*. The house overlooks one of the city's few large parks. Known as *Parque México* in popular parlance, it's officially dubbed Parque *San Martín*, and it lies at the heart of one of the city's smartest and greenest neighborhoods. *Colonia Condesa* is the site of the old racetrack, an oval now planted with a handsome stand of trees. The re-baptized *Avenida Amsterdam* forms the district's outer perimeter and encloses, in turn, the lesser ovals of México Avenue and San Martín Park. This arpeggio of ovals linked by cross streets every couple of blocks and dotted with roundabouts full of flowers is a true maze in a city of mazes, barrios that the sprawling city swallows whole. Though the distinguishing features of many mazes are blurred, their boundaries remain outlined by small, zealously preserved ovals. In Mexico City urban sprawl has entangled but not obliterated this archipelago of what were once farms and small towns— settlements that live on in the districts we now call *colonias*. It's possible to traverse the whole city on its major avenues, beltways and cross streets without seeing how these barrios have resisted absorption into the surrounding metropolis by turning in on themselves. Their flight from creditors in both Chetumal and Polanco lands Emma and Luisa in the diaphanous refuge of Avenida México 15, where they'll spend the rest of their lives.

My father and I move to México Avenue under protest. He is vexed because to his ear "boardinghouse" sounds like "whorehouse" while I, as his sidekick, am similarly bothered. He hasn't said a word about his displeasure in front of me, but his silence is deafening. We both regard the move as shameful. I live many of the best years following our change of address under a burden of humiliation while Luisa and Emma live out the small, stubborn, humble and proud epic they've chosen for themselves. They take in boarders, sew, work and raise the children in their care. It's the life they choose, the life they never stop talking about together. My mother sings whenever the spirit moves her. My aunt sews at her sister's side and holds forth on whatever subjects draw her attention. Her tone of voice turns melancholy at times, but her bursts of resonantly Iberian rhetoric always suggest that she knows more than she's ready to disclose. My father thinks the way of life the sisters have chosen is demeaning, and though I keep my feelings to myself, I'm as insulted as he is. All my schizophrenic tendencies stem, I believe, from this split, the second expulsion from paradise that comes with the move from Polanco to Condesa. In some all too discomfiting way we're fugitives too embarrassed to admit where we live. There's a stigma attached to the notion of a boardinghouse that takes root in my imagination, and it's exacerbated at the rich kids' school where I study. My classmates have nothing to hide except perhaps the size of their fortunes. The fact is I'm telepathically infected with my father's misgivings, and I spend a year and a half hiding from my friends the shameful fact that I live in a boardinghouse.

In the first chapter of this book I tell how Emma and

Héctor's life together comes to an end shortly before Christmas 1959. But that's not the exact moment of the sisters' permanent break with the man from whom they've expected so much. The moment that convinces them their loss is irretrievable comes when Don Lupe unexpectedly appears in Mexico City. He's come to see his son Héctor. The Aguas Turbias concession expired two years earlier in 1957, and Don Lupe has been unable to renew it. He has permission to log only in the much smaller concession around Petén-Flores. Casa Aguilar is facing the same dilemma Héctor faced when he logged Plancha de Piedra and Fallabón. To profit from the lumber they continue to take out of Guatemala after the hurricane and Margarito's seizures, Don Lupe and his son Ángel have moved their sawmill to Belize. They're not doing badly, but Don Lupe has savored the quality of the timber in Aguas Turbias, and the taste of the wood in Petén-Flores is nowhere near so sweet. He's come to Mexico City to talk Héctor into traveling to Guatemala with him and helping him resume operations in Aguas Turbias. Héctor has kept in touch with his brother Omar, and it's through Omar that Don Lupe communicates his wish to see his estranged son. Héctor agrees. Don Lupe proposes that Héctor accompany him to Guatemala. He wants timber from Aguas Turbias, and he wants to make amends with his son. He also wants to burnish his image, which has lost its luster in the eyes of those who saw firsthand what he did to Héctor in Guatemala and in those who visit us from Chetumal and hear the tale of his misdeeds as told by the formidably articulate Camín sisters. One day Emma's namesake, the wife of ex-governor Melgar, pays the sisters a visit. She's been to Chetumal and she's seen Don Lupe. She says he's sorry to have put the Cubans (meaning Emma and Luisa) and their children (meaning my siblings and me) in such a terrible bind. Thirty years later, Luisa recalls her reaction to what their friend tells them about Don Lupe: "Emma, you can visit that man and listen to his yarns to your heart's content, but don't repeat them to me because I have to sit here and sew just to earn our daily bread. I don't have time to go and kick him where he deserves to be kicked. He's a criminal, a thief with no scruples." In the course of these acerbic days, Luisa puts hexes on Ángel and Don Lupe: Let their burials be a blessing to those they leave behind, she decrees, but, first, let her stand by and gloat as Don Lupe becomes a penniless old man and dies in a house he doesn't own. The years make good on her curses with stunning precision.

Don Lupe's reason for coming to the city is to get Héctor to go to Guatemala with him. Either he wants to use him as he's done before or he wants to lure him back to Casa Aguilar, which is where he thinks his sons belong. Héctor doesn't react as if he'd been wronged. To him the idea of bearing a grudge against his father sounds like blasphemy, and that makes him a slave to his father's wishes. Or maybe he has his back to the wall and is just too worn down to feel offended. Don Lupe says he wants to see his grandchildren and daughter-in-law, he wants to pay them a visit, to be reunited with them. Luisa speaks for both the Camín women, and her reply is scathing: "Tell your old man to stay away from this house unless he wants to be branded with the scar of the vermin he is."

For Emma and Luisa this exchange is final confirmation that Héctor has gone to pieces. You don't have to look very hard to see that the cheerful, self-assured person who used to make everyone laugh is now a self-absorbed and lugubrious drunk, a timid introvert with a tic that makes his neck twitch and twists one side of his face—normally the right side—into a grimace from his mouth to his cheek.

This may be when—given his symptoms and the obsequious way he parrots Don Lupe's request—Emma and Luisa begin to suspect their broken man is bewitched. He's been turned into a weakling, and the change can only be attributed to some potion he drank or herb that he ate in the logging camps of Guatemala, in some filthy bar in Belize, or in the all-too-notorious dives of Chetumal. Some foreign spirit or substance must have come over Héctor and made him a shadow of the man he used to be, turning his smile into a grimace, his head into a hornets' nest, his look into a stare, and his life into an unbearable ordeal. These odd and disturbing tendencies may be what plant in the sisters' pagan and credulous minds the idea that Héctor has fallen under a spell that calls for a cure also born of superstition, a homeopathic vaccination to pit magic against magic, herb against herb, witch against witch. Acting on this hypothesis, the sisters seek and find a possible cure in the person of a palm reader named Nelly Mulley, who advertises in the newspaper and in a straight-laced humor magazine called *Ha-Ha*. Nelly Mulley is a celebrity in the shadowy but vibrant world of soothsayers and exorcists, specialists in cures for spiritual ailments, lost souls, bad luck, adversity, lives with no meaning, and cosmic dissonance. Her renown is so great that she has a contract with a company that puts her name and image on its chewing gum. The outer wrapper of each stick features the countenance of Nelly wearing a gypsy bandana on her head and gazing into a crystal ball. When the wax is rubbed off the inner wrapper and the wrapper is warmed by the flame of a match, the chewer's fortune appears followed by words of wisdom written in Palmer script: *A stranger will make you happy. Don't be afraid of good luck. Seize it.* We'll burn hundreds of wrappers and read hundreds of fortunes without knowing if any of them play a part in our life.

The two final scenes in Héctor's breakup with Emma—at least the ones I know about—stem from, one, lack of money and, two, amorous advances gone awry. The scene that results from lack of money also entails the humiliation of the father as breadwinner. My brother Juan José is a stubborn child who for the umpteenth time asks for money to buy shoes. Our shoes wear out quickly. The soles split, and they soon begin to smell bad. Juan goes through shoes in no time and needs new ones. Emma hasn't got the money to replace them, and she's tired of saying no, so she says go ask your father instead. Juan does as he's told, Héctor bristles at the child's wheedling and accuses his wife of foul play. He's stung by the request because there's no money in his pocket to buy the shoes his son is demanding. Juan glowers at him as only a small boy with a shaved head can. We're accustomed to being bald because it cuts down on trips to the barber shop. We're shorn like sheep. Our ears stick out from our naked pates in mute testimony to our frugal ways. Héctor can't give Juan the money he wants and tells him to wait until tomorrow. The next morning Juan is at it again. Day after day the scene repeats itself until Héctor begins to fear it will get out of hand. He starts to wait until everyone's asleep before coming home at night and leaves before anyone is up in the morning.

One night Héctor tries to make a pass at his wife. Though what follows is unrelated to the struggle over the shoes, it fits here because it's of a piece with all the other crossed wires that entangle our family. I don't know how intimate Héctor and Emma have been since he came to the city. But the apartment in Polanco was full of children, the house on Avenida México is full of boarders, and there's never a time when Luisa isn't around. I know my mother once confided to her friend Rosemary in Chetumal that she was always happy in her husband's arms. And I know what my mother told me when my first marriage broke up: that before he disappeared my father was always satisfied, "at home and in bed." Many years later she also told Rosemary that as long as they were together Héctor always appreciated her as a woman, which is how he meant to approach her on the night I speak of. I have the story as told by my father as an old man. To keep from disturbing the sleeping household he slips furtively in the door at México15, without turning on the lights. He goes to the bedroom where he sleeps with Emma, and half undressed, he reaches for her body under the covers. Which is when he discovers the bed is occupied not by his wife but by his daughter, Emma. He's horrified when he realizes the wrong he's committed, and he's overcome with shame. He decides there's no place for him here anymore, that it's time for him to go.

The next day or several days later in a chain of events whose continuity is obvious regardless of the time between them, Héctor acts on his decision. He departs at mid-morning when the children are gone and the boarders are out of the house. Emma, Luisa, and Luis Miguel, who's three at the time, are alone in the house. Héctor packs his bag in the upstairs room where he's slept with Emma and has now slept with his daughter of the same name. He comes silently down the stairs. His sister-in-law Luisa is taking a bath. In the kitchen his wife Emma is singing to herself as she always does. At the foot of the stairs his son Luis Miguel is playing with a wooden boat Héctor remembers giving him. He tells the little boy not to make noise. He places his suitcase on the floor, then takes a few steps down the hall towards the kitchen. From the hall he sees his wife facing the stove with her back to him. He takes two steps forward, then stops and goes back for his suitcase. His son Luis Miguel has stopped playing with the wooden boat and is watching him. He again tells the child not to talk and puts a finger to his lips. He picks up the suitcase, walks noiselessly to the door, and steps out to the park.

Emma has known for days that it's only a matter of time before her husband goes away. She sings and listens to the silence by the stairs where her youngest son isn't making a sound. Perhaps she listens for her husband's footsteps coming, going, hesitating. She wants to stop him but can't bring herself to go after him. She stops singing without turning around, she continues to cook, listening for the door to shut. The door shuts with the muffled rattle of the beveled glass against its frame, of the wrought iron grill and the heavy wooden door swollen by humidity. It's kept out of balance by its weight. On the way out you have to pull it to open and pull it to close. When Emma hears the door, she breathes a huge sigh of relief as if an elephant has been removed from her house. Then she's seized by a sense of utter desolation. Her marriage has come to an end.

Where does Héctor go when he leaves the house in Condesa in the month of December 1959? He goes to his therapist, spiritual adviser and seer Nelly Mulley, who lives on Bucareli Street in the old center of Mexico City. Nelly has cured him of his demons or at least of his marriage. Héctor will spend the next forty years of his life in the city where Nelly lives, the ghost of a city that will exist mainly in my head.

Mexico City, 1964

When I think about Emma Camín, when Emma Camín appears unbidden in my memory, she's takes the form of a young girl singing in Cuba. She's washing dishes in the kitchen of the country house where her family lives on a sugar plantation in Palma Soriano. She has the windows open to let in the breeze that mitigates the island's ubiquitous heat. She sings a parody of the tango that's all the rage on the radio. Her mother Josefa makes her quit. The window looks out on a hollow where the tracks of carts and wagons have worn a trail in the grass. Where the trail slopes to the left there are two carob trees and another house with a porch. A woman on the porch is getting over a fever. The voice of the girl singing in her kitchen, the voice in the wind, helps cool the fever. We know this because a day after her mother stifles Emma's singing, the peasant woman who cares for the invalid comes up the trail on her way home. She stops next to the porch where mother and daughters are relaxing in the evening breeze. She wants to know why the singing has stopped because it makes her patient feel better.

This is the first image of Emma Camín that comes to me, an image drawn from a family anecdote. If memory serves, I heard it in the house where Emma Camín lives at Avenida Mexico 15, where she must make a life for herself with her sister Luisa as a partner after her husband leaves forever in 1959. As I said before, the house sits on a tree-lined street in Colonia Condesa across from the officially named San Martín

Park that everyone calls Mexico Park. Left on their own, the sisters do all they can to ward off hopelessness and boredom. There are lots of things that can be done without in this house, but conversation and humor are not among them. The sisters are running a business and a boardinghouse, and there's never a dull moment. As seamstresses they're not just free to talk; they must talk to stay alert. They laugh at each other's stories and whatever else happens to amuse them.

Over time I come to suspect that losing the man of the house is a relief for the sisters. Except for the bother of having to explain his absence to the children, they seem perfectly happy to have him gone. Nobody misses him very much. In recent years, the ups and downs of the lumber business have kept Héctor away from his family for months at a time. In Mexico City he's been out more than in. Even his presence is a kind of absence that weighs on the minds of his older children. My sister Emma is fourteen when he goes away, and I'm thirteen. He doesn't leave much of an impression on Juan José and Pilar, who barely remember life in Chetumal, and Luis Miguel is just a baby. I have few memories of Héctor before he leaves, and many of the ones I do have are bolstered by hearsay. In many ways the story of Héctor that I'm at pains to tell is a ghost story made up of bits and pieces floating in the ether. By contrast Emma and Luisa loom large and formidable. They turn up everywhere and shine their light into the darkest of corners.

The history of our house after my father leaves isn't always clear to me. It's too full of twists and turns, and it's too long. One thread is the sentimental education of siblings minus a father, a void to be filled by dissembling. Another is the boardinghouse at Mexico 15 with its throng of legendary personalities: a carnival of characters; myriad lessons learned; and episodes not to be recounted beyond its walls. Another is the endless squabbles of a dysfunctional family: Héctor against Emma and Luisa; Emma and Luisa against Héctor; Héctor against his brother Ángel and his father Don Lupe; Emma and Luisa against Don Lupe and Ángel; Manuel Camín against Luisa and Emma and Luisa and Emma against Manuel Camín and their brother Raúl, who sides with his father in his struggles with Emma and Luisa. There's also the thread of redemption through work: of Mexico 15 as the cave where the sisters toil, where they gather their forces and gain the strength to do battle with the world outside.

Let us take a closer look: Héctor abandons my house late in 1959. There comes a night when I make an effort to mourn his absence. It's Christmastime, and Emma and Luisa celebrate the season with a roast chicken dinner, a meal very much a fad at the time. It's served in our frugally lit dining room where we always eat alone and, to the best of my recollection, never invite outsiders. That night is the one time I try really hard to miss my father. His absence may later gnaw at my insides, but I'll pay no attention. I'll pretend my insides don't exist and keep hurt feelings to myself except when I'm drunk. Naturally, those feelings will come to the surface in any number of ways though they'll be unrecognizable to anyone not in on my secrets. But I'm the only one who's in on my secrets. Nobody else can account for the sadness, anger or indignation that I parade about for years. Or the charade of self-sufficiency which is a sign not of vanity but of having been abandoned, a fact I'll staunchly refuse to admit to myself and to friends and foes alike the rest of my life. I suppose that in the days immediately following my father's desertion I thought he was being unfair and I'd been inexplicably cheated. It feels like the last link in a chain of raw deals: what Margarito did to Don Lupe, what Don Lupe did to Héctor, and Héctor to me. Margarito Ramírez cheated Don Lupe out of his lumber, Don Lupe cheated Héctor out of his lumber, and Héctor deprived me of a father. Héctor and I suffered reciprocal damages: he was oppressed by his father and I by the hole he left in my life. The truth is I could never stop obsessing about this gap. Years later a friend summed it all up in a joke. He said Mexicans always blame the victim, not the perpetrator, and that's exactly what I do when wires get crossed. When the place where I live becomes a boardinghouse, I spend years hiding the fact from my friends.

The house has an art deco facade, a wrought-iron front door and a garage door with a torsion spring. On the ground floor there's a sala, a vestibule, a dining room, a half bath, a breakfast nook, and the kitchen. The doors to the sala and dining room have wood frames, glass knobs and windows. The floor in the entry and vestibule is made of rhomboid slabs of white granite. From the ground fleet a flight of black granite stairs with an iron banister goes upstairs. At the foot of the stairs is the dining room with its ceiling-height window of frosted glass in the far wall. The breakfast nook and kitchen are next to the dining room, and the maid's quarters are behind the kitchen. The bath in the maid's quarters is so cramped that the stream from the shower soaks the commode with water from a crude iron water heater that you light with oily packets of metal shavings. There are two porches with red tile floors. The one behind the maid's quarters has an asbestos sink and a tin roof. The other produces the chink of light between the garage and the breakfast nook. The chink of light shines on the gas water heater, a white tank warmed by a pilot light.

The granite stairway opens onto a second vestibule with a floor of white granite rhombuses smaller than the ones downstairs. The upstairs vestibule leads to four bedrooms and two full baths. One has blue and white tiles and a tub with a force-fed shower. The other has yellow tiles and is so small that boiling water from the shower quickly makes it a virtual steam bath. A second stairway, also of black granite but not as wide, rises to a single bedroom that overlooks the corrugated cement roof, an asbestos washtub, a sagging clothesline, and the park across the street. Some years later the wobbly wooden structure we call the Pigeon Roost will be added in front of the washtub and become the bedroom where Luis Miguel grows up.

To make room for boarders and accommodations for ourselves we turn the sala into a ground-floor bedroom for three and sometimes four guests. The dining room becomes the sewing room where Emma, Luisa and Luis Miguel also sleep. For a while Juan and I sleep in the garage. The cook and the servant who cleans house and makes the beds sleep in the maid's quarters. Upstairs five guests sleep in the bedrooms that overlook the park and five more in the bedrooms at the back of the house. The two back bedrooms look down on the turrets of the house next to ours. It has a patio paved with checkerboard tiles and bougainvillea climbing the walls. It also has a balcony occupied for days, months, years—in any event an eternity—by a nymphet who likes to be looked at and commands the attention of our randy boarders at all hours. Our sisters Pilar and Emma have the lone bedroom on the topmost level. Sometimes they share it with Emma or Luisa and Luis Miguel when one of the women doesn't sleep downstairs in the dining room, the domain where my memory always pictures them sewing and talking until the break of dawn.

Long afterwards I can still see Luis and Emma next to their sewing box at the back of the sala, sewing away amid a prodigious uproar. The house is overrun with youthful boarders. Their families send them to study in Mexico City, but what they really are is a band of marauders bent on making their mark in the world. They're all from the hinterlands, from Apizaco or Los Mochis, Acapulco or Xalapa, and they belong to a faded cast of legendary characters in my memory. But, first, there's Hortensia, the guest who moves in before all the others. She sells cosmetics, and invites me into her room while she puts on her makeup. The place is fragrant with scents and perfumes, and I'm free to enter whenever I want. I watch Hortensia powder her cheeks, wield her eyebrow pencil, and dab eye shadow on her lashes. After Hortensia, the house and my memory fill with males, whose nicknames say more about them than their names. *El Caballo*, the Horse, studies architecture at UNAM, the National University; *El Monkey* drops out of engineering at UNAM; *El Cachorro*, the Cub, sells patent medicines for a living and for drink; *La Perica*, the Chatterbox, is a born comedian; *El Tronco* really does sleep like a log; *El Chamaco de las Cejas Depiladas*, the Kid with Plucked Eyebrows, likes to cut morning classes at the Polytechnic Institute; *El Gacelo*, the Gazelle, blares the horn of his Fiat to wake up *El Tronco* and drag him off to the recently founded communications school where they're in the second class to enroll and I'll be in the fourth; *El Grillo*, the Cricket, fills out accounting sheets by day and empties glasses of rum and Coca Cola by night; *El Caimán*, the Crocodile, ravishes his hapless girlfriends then quaffs bottles of tequila all by himself; *El Trucutrú* is the anthropological pride and latest link in a family that breeds fighting bulls; *El Asqueroso*, is the Depraved, the inheritor of a genital endowment that, when measured, proves to exceed that of *El Coliñón*, the Dangler (whose nickname actually derives from his surname of Colignon).

As the years go by we have other boarders. There's the card sharp from Coatepec, Veracruz, who plucks the wallet of the Kid with Plucked Eyebrows. The Cuban painter and his Ecuadoran wife who appear mysteriously in Mexico City. We later learn she blew the arm off a comrade in Quito with a homemade bomb. There's a doctor from Monterrey who has a wife and two children and is gay. A forty-something court clerk with bottle-thick glasses, and a wife who's hardly more than a girl but, despite her plain face and startled look, is smarter than he is. An ex-captain in the Guatemalan army who has joined the resistance and after a few months in Mexico will return to die in the jungles of Petén. An engineer with a walrus mustache whom I envy to this day for the privileges lavished upon him by my mother. An ultra-fastidious homosexual who wears brand-name clothes and sells them in a brand-name store. A captivating homosexual whose face is the mirror image of the actress María Félix. A full-blooded Indian from Xochimilco who studies economics, wears a necktie, and confides to me one night that his goal is to get rich and rule his people with an iron hand. A ruddy pair of brothers from a farm in Sinaloa, one of whom will become a soldier and the other a drug trafficker. *El Man* of the north is a learned barbarian from Torreón who suffers from epilepsy, and *El Man* from the south is a grandchild of the Valencias, my godparents from Xalak. He's in love with a black girl from Belize and is sent to the city to get over her. He arranges for her to follow him unobserved, then makes her his wife.

I return to the tale of the sisters and their far-away family in Chetumal.

I've spoken of Emma's and Luisa's falling out with Manuel Camín and of his falling out with them. Their troubles stem from Héctor's downfall, but the ire of a father who refuses to forgive his daughters' absence also plays a part. Manuel Camín and his son Raúl never stop talking about how Héctor deserted Emma and Luisa and abandoned them to their fate in the city. They won't admit their plight out of pride, Manuel Camín says, but they're dying of hunger. Nobody fumes over these assertions more than my grandmother, whom time and disillusion have reduced to a shadow of her former self. Before the 1955 hurricane that ravages Chetumal, Josefa's dreams of returning to Spain were shattered by upheavals in her family. In the euphoria that preceded the crash of the timber market, the Camín family had planned a voyage to Spain. They hadn't been back since leaving in 1919. It's now 1952, and they're making plans to return for the first time. Josefa and Manuel are going, as is their daughter Emma and possibly Héctor. They announce their intentions to Josefa's family in Asturias. Or at least to what's left of the family. Her sister Pilar has clung to what she has through two wars—the Spanish Civil War and World War Two—plus the dreary aftermath of both conflicts. Josefa has kept her dream alive in the form of an inventory that includes her bridal trousseau, everything else left behind when she sailed for Cuba, and all the things she sent from Cuba to Spain over the years. Her daughters recall her frequent soliloquies about the treasures that await them in Spain: "You have no idea of all the quilts and blankets, all the bedspreads, all the handkerchiefs and tableware I have in Spain." Emma especially remembers an ivory-handled carving knife and lots and lots of bed sheets. As the time to travel nears, Josefa begins to receive letters of forewarning from her relatives in Spain. Her trousseau has fallen victim to moths and had to be burned. Her apartment is unavailable because Pilar temporarily rented it to meet her living expenses, and now her adoptive daughter, who regards the place as her own, lives there. The news goes from bad to worse. There was no place to store everything Josefa sent from Cuba, and some items have been sold. The last letter makes it clear that nearly everything has either been sold or given away. If the Camíns are coming to Spain, they need to understand that Josefa's inventory is gone. This is when she realizes—because Pilar reminds her—that upon leaving Spain, she told Pilar to take whatever she needed from Josefa's trousseau for her wedding. Confronted with scarcity, Pilar needed it all. And none of the things Josefa sent from overseas are left either. Need and the grueling postwar years took everything. Nothing is left of Josefa's inventory in Spain. And her emotional inventory, the dream that shielded her from the privations of exile, has vanished.

According to Luisa and Emma, this is the blow their mother will never recover from. She loses her love of conversation and the pleasure of being with others. She shuts herself up in the little house next to where Emma used to live on Othón P. Blanco and speaks to no one except Angela, the cook. Angela is of African and Chinese descent, a quiet companion with a soft step. Her eyes seem to know all there is to know about how cruel and unfair life can be. Their whites are brown, and the black of her corneas glistens as if she cries a lot. She either goes from the kitchen of Emma's old house to visit Josefa or Josefa comes to the kitchen of the larger house to commiserate with her. "I never dreamed my family would treat me like this," Josefa says. The disappearance of her inventory is a death blow to her family pride. She's always thought she married down, and her family accuses Manuel's father, Anselmo, of squandering the wealth of his daughter-in-law. It's a grievance Josefa doesn't share, but she does hold Manuel responsible for not making her dream of a triumphant return to Spain come true. The story of her letdown matches what Emma goes through with Héctor, and Manuel Camín must see the promise he never fulfilled reflected in Héctor's failure, which may be why he's so hard on him. Manuel's world has crumbled; he can no more rebuild his world than Josefa can hers. Perhaps a morass of disillusion like the one I describe explains why Manuel Camín is so angry at the son-in-law from whom he expected so much and at the daughters whose desertion he can neither understand or forgive. He watches his fondest dreams being destroyed by the obstinance of his daughters, the descent of his wife into old age and depression, and the inability of his son, Raúl, to bear up under the burden of children and be the master of his own fate. Manuel needs his daughters to hold onto in his declining years, but Luisa and Emma have gone to Mexico City with Héctor.

Manuel Camín's rage lasts for years, and he swears he'll never forgive his daughter Emma for getting him involved in

Héctor's business dealings which, among other things, put his house and grocery store at risk. People get tired of listening to him, and one acquaintance, a Doctor Montemayor, tells him to quit complaining. Emma and Luisa think Raúl is to blame for much of their father's hostility towards Héctor because he echoes local gossip about Héctor's excesses, about how Héctor wastes, gives away, and mismanages money. Luisa and Emma accuse Manuel Camín of refusing to admit that the real culprit is Don Lupe. When Don Lupe goes into business with his son Héctor, Luisa says, the Camíns in Chetumal are delighted, and they're just as blind as Héctor to the dangers involved. Luisa writes two letters of warning before disaster strikes, one to Emma and another to her parents. It's fall 1956, and the logging season has just begun in Aguas Turbias. Héctor has backed out of his partnership with Don Goyo Marrufo and has put up the Camíns' house and grocery store as security for the debts he ran up to Don Goyo the year before. Luisa writes her relatives to say: You'll be sorry if you get mixed up with Don Lupe, he'll drown you. In a letter to Héctor she writes: If you let yourself fall into your father's clutches, he'll destroy you. Nobody pays attention. Héctor and the Camíns both ignore her. When her prophecy comes true, the Camíns don't point the finger at either themselves or Don Lupe. It's all Héctor's fault, and Emma is a weakling for standing by her husband come what may. Nobody sees the loving wife who's just had a baby with a man on the verge of drowning. Nobody sees the mother who accepts her husband's misfortune and is ready to make herself and her children part of a solution to his problems. They only see a woman who's thrown family money out the window and has compounded the Camíns' losses with Héctor's. To Emma's and Luisa's way of thinking, they're the only ones in the family, including Héctor, with a clear understanding of what went wrong. They look reality in the face then and forever after. At first they see themselves as victims of a tragedy brought down on them by the villainous Don Lupe, but a time comes when Luisa's savage sense of humor alters their attitude. In the year before her unexpected death, she's in high spirits, and when I put the tape recorder on the table in front of her, she says: "I'm not going to heaven, you can be sure of that. I'm going to hell because I still need to give Don Lupe a good kick in the pants."

Everything Josefa knows about the life of her daughters in Mexico City she gets from her husband and their son, Raúl. What she hears is grim and sad, even catastrophic at times. It's all she wants to talk about at first. She asks for news about her daughters in Mexico City. She remembers what her daughters did in Camaguey. She talks about what they'll do when they're back in Albandi, Asturias. She slips a cog and remarks she doesn't hear Emma singing in the morning anymore. Why doesn't she hear Emma sing every morning? Where is her daughter Emma? She's stopped bringing her coffee with an egg yolk the way she used to. Or her elastic stockings. And what about Héctor, her son-in-law, where is he? Why has he stopped coming by to ask if she'd like to go for an afternoon ride around town in his car? Héctor owns a gray Packard, and he drives Josefa past the military compound all the way to the Chetumal lighthouse where she can enjoy the breeze off the bay. It's the cleanest part of the bay where you don't smell the mangrove swamps or the sewage at the mouth of the river where the town was founded. Where's Héctor's car? Why doesn't he take her to the lighthouse? When is he coming back from Cuba to take her to Spain as he promised? Josefa's obsessive questioning about her daughters and son-in-law drives everyone crazy until the family decides she should visit her daughters in Mexico City. The decision breaks the silence between the Chetumal Camíns and Emma and Luisa, who agree to a visit from their mother. Justa Quivén, a Spanish neighbor who lives on the same block of Othón P. Blanco—the mother of Araceli, La Gallega, and my boyhood friend Moncho—volunteers to accompany Josefa to Mexico City. Justa and Josefa set out overland. Ahead lies the twelve-hundred kilometer journey to Mexico City. The road traverses the flats along the Gulf coast, where the waterways must be crossed in small but rugged boats called *pangas*, then goes up the hairpin curves to the Peaks of Acultzingo before descending onto the plateau of Mexico City. Obviously, the trip from Chetumal to the capital must be made in stages. The first is the half day to Mérida followed by 400 kilometers up the Yucatán Peninsula. Then come six hours and 500 kilometers to Villahermosa in southeast Mexico, four hours to Coatzacualcos on the Gulf, five to Puebla at the east end of the plateau, and three or four more to the diaphanous heart of the republic at 2,300 meters above sea level.

Josefa falls completely apart in Coatzacoalcos. She arrives at the home of the Peyrefitte family, former neighbors in Chetumal. But she's forgotten them and can't recall who they are. She also ceases to recognize her traveling companion, Justa Quivén. She feels surrounded by strangers. She grows arrogant, then frightened, then overcome with terror.

Emma goes to get her mother. A woman she sews for offers to have her husband fly Josefa to Mexico City on an emergency basis. He's the celebrated airman and fighter pilot Radamés Gaxiola, whose Squadron 201 was the only Mexican military unit to see combat in World War Two. "If Radamés can fly in the war, of course he can get Josefa," the wife declares. Emma laughs. Though the offer is tempting, she decides to get her mother on her own. Josefa calms down the minute she sees Emma and continues on to the capital without trepidation. Her faculties are clearly diminished, and she's lost ground. She has a suitcase full of ragged clothes and seven hundred pesos which she presses into Emma's hand. With the urgency of a benefactor who has no time for explanations, she says, "Take it, and buy whatever you need." Emma concludes that her mother thinks she's in dire straits.

Josefa's days in Mexico City aren't the happiest of her life. As already noted, the few memories I have of her amount to little more than pebbles from a lost civilization. I've said I remember her old lady's acid breath in the tender but hasty words that fell from her lips. I remember those lips because there were no teeth in back of them. I don't know when my grandmother Josefa lost her real teeth, but a set of false ones lingers in my memory. There was humor in the way she took them out and put them in, something I can vouch for only insofar as it lays to rest any hint that she's grown old without pretension or elegance. Nobody ages without pretension and with elegance, least of all my grandmother Josefa. In my memory she appears inelegant and feeble. Her most vivid trait is the palette of colors in her face and the glint of her pale eyes, which I speak of elsewhere. What I left out before were the hairs on her chin and the plain brown stockings over her bent legs.

Emma looks upon Josefa with pity and is annoyed to discover the contents of the suitcase that comes with her from Chetumal. Her self-respect is gone, and she hasn't taken care of her clothes. Her concerns are her own and no one else's: I have six dresses I haven't worn yet. I have six boxes of stockings that I put away. I have four tablecloths, four sets of sheets. And in Asturias I have so many sheets, so many bedspreads. Lost in the realm of her possessions, she's forgotten all about the trip from Coatzacoalcos to Mexico City. Luisa will always blame her mother's troubles on her father and brother. She says they neglected the old lady and plied her with exaggerated accounts of her daughters' travails in Mexico City. Josefa is upset about Héctor's misfeasance because he's always been a favorite of hers and has always been fond of her. "He was so good to me," she says. But she's not in a position to refute charges that he cost the Camíns money, that he deserted her daughters, that he left his poverty-stricken children in Mexico City without enough to eat. The Josefa García that Emma finds in Coatzalcoacos doesn't ask about Héctor. She knows he's gone. It's obvious he's not around. Talking about his disappearance is painful for the sisters and, I suppose, for Josefa.

Through Justa Quivén, her mother's traveling companion, Emma learns that Josefa had an operation on her uterus in Mérida, and it wasn't a success. The first thing Emma and Luisa do is have her examined at the then new and gleaming Neurological Hospital founded and directed by Dr. Manuel Velasco Suárez, the husband of one of the sisters' clients. The diagnoses are that Josefa suffers from a senile atrophic uterus and cognitive impairment, which explains her extreme self-absorption, her lapses of memory, her absentmindedness. And diabetes.

Josefa García suffers from migraines and has ever since her first contact with the heat of Cuba. It's because of the migraines that she orders her daughter Emma to quit singing. Emma and Luisa remember tiptoeing about the house to keep from being scolded by their mother. "Stop that bellyaching," Josefa shouts at her daughter, meaning, in the speech of her native Asturias, "Shut your beak." The memory brings a smile to the faces of her daughters as they baste slices of canned ham with powdered sugar in the kitchen. The ham arrives in care packages together with the Spanish and Catalan sausages that Josefa would kill for and which may be the source of her migraines.

Luis Miguel recalls a childish threat from this woman in her second childhood. When she's upset with him, she says: "I'm going to crack you one." By which she means she'll slap him, but to Luis Miguel this sounds like sugar cracker, and he replies: "So let me have it." Luis Miguel is her confidant and chronicler.

He barely understands that she's his grandmother or what makes her his grandmother. He doesn't know a thing about our family or the clashes between parents and grandparents. What Luis Miguel remembers is the time when someone in the house sees sugar ants crawling all over the excrement in Josefa's chamber pot. He also recalls her confusion of Gargarin, our tiger cat at Mexico 15, with a cat from her Asturian childhood. "That kitty was very small when I was little," Josefa says, pointing at Gargarin. "And his name was Oviedo." On another day she accuses Luis Miguel of stealing her "farm in La Viña" (her grandfather's homestead). She also complains, "You won't let me play with your cat Oviedo." At the time she talks about them the farm and the cat exist only in her head. She also talks about another little boy and another childhood. Josefa never tires of having her hair brushed by her granddaughter Emma. She sits for hours beside her daughters while they sew, listening to them chat as they work, soothed perhaps by the invisible bonds that unite the sisters. One day she says she's going to see her son Raúl. She gets up and walks towards the door. Raúl's in Chetumal, Luisa tells her. Raúl's in the store, I'm going to see him, Josefa replies. It's the start of an obsession. Josefa thinks she can step outside and walk down the street as if she's in Chetumal. Or else get on a bus and visit her son Raúl, who's minding the store on Othón P. Blanco 1,200, kilometers away. "I'll catch a bus here and go to my son's house," Josefa says. "Raúl's just around the corner." Then she lapses into a daze or eyes her daughters with a suspicious scowl: "You're trying to fool me, but after I finish breakfast, I'm going to see Raúl." After breakfast she goes to the door. Some days, she's bound she'll see her son Raúl, others not. But the thought of their mother's slipping out of the house and going adrift in the city haunts Emma and Luisa every day. They can't help imagining terrifying scenes of her being robbed, taunted, harassed, run over. Nothing worries Emma and Luisa more than the impossibility of being at their mother's side every second, caring for her, standing by her in the days of her decline. One afternoon they find her at the corner of the park somnambulantly dithering about which way to turn.

One Sunday afternoon a very nice-looking elderly woman who appears to be Spanish comes to the door at Mexico 15. She inquires for the lady of the house, and when Emma asks what she wants, she replies: "My dear lady, let's see if you can help me. I'm looking for some seamstresses who used to make clothes for my dolls and lived around here. But no matter what I said, my chauffeur refused to let me out at their house. He drove me back to where I live."

"And where do you live?" Emma asks.

"By the Madero brandy bottle. I live with my son, but I have an awful daughter-in-law who won't let me pick flowers."

"So what's your son's name?"

"Fernandito Gargallo."

Emma lets her in the house, gives her a glass of water, and listens to her rant while looking up Fernando Gargallo in the phone book. The name and surname belong to a number in Las Lomas. Emma calls and explains the situation to the maid who answers the phone. Just a moment, the maid says. Her footsteps are audible as she hurries off. Different footsteps near the phone, and a woman's voice says: "Ay, señora, what a relief. She's my mother-in-law. Keep here there for me." When the daughter-in-law comes for her, she explains that her mother-in-law has a nurse who looks after her but is off on Sundays. The boy who waters the yard left the gate open, and the mother-in-law got out. While listening to this, it strikes Emma that there's no one to stop Josefa if she wanders into the street looking for Raúl's store. The sisters can't shake the idea of their own mother going up to people in the street and telling them her daughters won't let her see her son. They realize they can't keep

Josefa in Mexico City anymore. Not while continuing to work, not with people going in and out of the boarding house at all hours, not with Josefa prone to marching out the door to see her son Raúl from one moment to the next. They don't decide on their own. They go over their decision with Valentín, a younger brother of Josefa's whom I've only mentioned in passing before now. Valentín is ten years younger than Josefa and has also come from Asturias to Mexico via Cuba. Like Josefa he has pale eyes, red cheeks, and graying chestnut hair. He's raised a family and owns a parking lot and repair shop near La Villa in an area where all the streets are named for minerals. He's the only family Emma and Luisa have in the city, for years the one family we're sure to visit Christmas and New Years. Valentín has room for Josefa in the big house where he lives on the same lot as his business, which is located in a poor neighborhood on a corner of Copper Street. Recalling it fills me with yuletide nostalgia, a mix of roasted chestnuts and an urban landscape that couldn't have been as cold and desolate during our first winters in Mexico City as it is now in memory. The experiment with Valentín doesn't last long. While at his house Josefa still wants to go see her son Raúl who, she insists, lives just around the corner. And there soon comes a day when she sets out through Copper, Aluminum, Tin and similarly named streets of the neighborhood where Valentín is settled and will die without ever returning to Asturias. Recreating these scenes reminds me that the Camíns belong to the diaspora of luckless Asturians who will never go home with the wealth they dream of from America. They'll never be like the Spaniards who return home to build large houses and proudly plant palm trees to show the world their fortunes were made in America.

Josefa will go back to Chetumal in a fog of senile dementia shortly after being diagnosed with an advanced case of diabetes. The year is 1961, and she's 73. She's rapidly losing her grip on life, and the one good thing about her condition is that she feels no pain in either body or soul.

Luis Miguel remembers a night when Luisa goes to the door for a telegram that's addressed to her. He remembers the way she whimpers, puts her hand to her forehead, and rushes through the vestibule where the guests and his siblings are crowded in front of the Motorola television. Sobs from the sewing room interrupt the television program and draw the siblings' attention. The telegram announces the death of Josefa García. It's September 18, 1963. At the time Emma's and Luisa's relations with their father and brother in Chetumal are close to the breaking point. They've had next to no news from them and nothing about Josefa. Luisa's still furious with them. She decides to stay and run the house while Emma makes the trip to Chetumal. Emma arrives unannounced and shows up at the burial unexpectedly. When she goes to Raúl's house for an account of the death, her brother and father ask if she plans to spend the night. They can prepare a room for her. She haughtily replies that she'll be staying with Justa Quivén, the woman who two years ago took Josefa to Coatzalcoalcos on the trip to her daughters. It's a particularly painful moment for the family. In recent years they seem to have lost their bearings. They're at cross purposes with one another, and they clash because they don't stop to think before acting. From Angela the cook, Emma learns that her father, Manuel Camín, has taken his wife's death especially hard. She's comforted by the old cook's version of her mother's passing. Angela describes how Manuel Camín sat on the dying woman's bed clasping her hand as the life drained out of her and for a long time after she dies. Angela herself went to him and said: Don Manuel, let her go, she's gone. Meanwhile, Raúl is disconsolate. He bursts into tears whenever and wherever his grief catches up with him.

Emma returns from Chetumal saddened but relieved. Reconciliation with her father and brother after Josefa's death eases her guilt for sending her mother off to die. The father-and-son grocery store is doing well. Thanks as much to what the Camíns have to say as to what they have for sale, it's among the most popular places in town. Old Manuel is a kind of local prophet, his son is a wellspring of gossip and lore, and the counter is as busy as an anthill. Raúl's and Carmen's flock—eight children born one after the other in perfect lockstep—is irresistible. Their house is like a rudderless ship with the wind briefly at its back. Shortly after Josefa's demise, Manuel Camín begins to lose his eyesight to glaucoma that nobody notices until it's too late to treat. There are no signs of the disease when Emma returns two weeks after her mother's death. Once they're over the pain of losing Josefa, her father and brother are content to look after their store and their progeny. Everyone turns a new page. The sisters are ready and willing to let bygones be bygones. In a real sense, it suits them to get on with their work and care for their own family with no more grudges weighing them down. With her death Josefa has given the Chetumal Camíns and the Mexico City Camíns a chance to catch their breaths. It's a death that works for everybody.

I move now to the camp of my paternal grandmother, Juana Escolástica Marrufo.

There's one scene I've already referred to: a night when Héctor knocks on the door at Mexico 15. Luisa and Emma won't let him in. I go to the door and take him home in a taxi. Héctor is crying so hard he can barely speak. Looking back, I suspect the crisis that day had to do with the death of his mother. What follows is based on conjecture.

That night I'd just come in from bowling. I only bowl on days when I work for Condumex, a company that holds tournaments for its employees. It's 1964, and I've only been with the firm for a few months while completing the third term of my college major. Juana Marrufo dies that year on

December 20. Years later Héctor claims to have received news of her death telepathically. He's sitting on a couch in the house of the professional clairvoyant Nelly Mulley, who is his new wife, when he feels a scalding mist grab his chest and wrap itself around him. "This is coming from a bad place," he says to himself. "It's about death." The next day he learns that at the exact moment when the mist enveloped him, Juana Marrufo died in Chetumal. He knows this from a telegram pinpointing the hour of her demise. The minute he gets the telegram he decides to fly to Chetumal. But there's no flight that will get him there until the next day, meaning there's no way he can be on time for the burial. I suspect the news drives him to the bar where he's become a regular, and he stays there drinking until nightfall. Then, I suspect, he takes a taxi to his former house, the one we've called home during the five years of his absence. He needs a shoulder to cry on, someone who's part of the world where his mother died, a world apart from the house on Bucareli where he's lived since remarrying. I suppose he decides to return to the home he deserted because it's only there that the magnitude of his loss will be understood, where the memory of his mother, Juana Marrufo, lives on. Nowhere else in the city is there anyone whose life touched the life of his late mother. He probably came to deliver the news in hopes that it would be met with a torrent of love and tenderness towards the orphan he was becoming and would be for the rest of his life.

Emma and Luisa remember Juana Marrufo as a kindred soul. Their love for Juana goes hand-in-hand with their abhorrence of Don Lupe. In the sisters' memories she comes across as she does in Héctor's: she's the angelic victim of her husband. A ghost, to be exact. Nobody speaks ill of Juana Marrufo, who even speaks kindly of her detractors. There is, for example, the young woman she welcomes into her house in the early years of her marriage. The visitor becomes a long-term guest who ends up sleeping with Don Lupe and bearing his child at the same time Juana is pregnant with Omar, the youngest of her offspring. Juana Marrufo doesn't bear grudges. She's docile by nature, and she believes in self-sacrifice. Though she doesn't complain, there are consequences to be faced. After Omar is born, she starts having convulsions which for years the local doctors attribute to epilepsy. No one in her household questions the diagnosis, and Juana learns to live with her convulsions. She watches her children grow up: Efraín dies; Ángel and Héctor marry; and Juana remains the guardian angel fretting over her family. Like any angel she's invisible. She's the benign spirit protecting her house, but she's nowhere to be seen. Emma remembers a visit when she finds Juana alone in her bedroom while her daughters-in-law chatter amiably, play records, and sing in the sala. They aren't shut up in their bedrooms, Emma observes. Why are you such a recluse? Juana Marrufo smiles: "They never worry about me. I just get in their way." She has frequent medical checkups in Mérida, and always comes home with the same diagnosis. One day the doctors in Mérida decide to operate on her back and do something or other with her spinal fluids. The procedure entails risks that no one but Héctor, who is estranged from Casa Aguilar, pays attention to. Héctor learns that two months earlier Don Lupe sent the wife of a friend to a hospital in New Orleans with all expenses paid by Casa Aguilar. In a letter, Héctor asks his mother why she too can't go to New Orleans instead of going to Mérida where the doctors haven't cured what ails her and never will. The daughters-in-law, who live with their husbands in the same large house as Juana Marrufo, intercept the letter and give it to Don Lupe. After Héctor's letter, Luisa asks one of the daughters-in-law why Don Lupe doesn't seek better treatment for Juana Marrufo somewhere else. The daughter-in-law doesn't mince words: because Don Lupe refuses to be bothered with her. "What Don Lupe wants is for her to die."

That, of course, isn't what happens. Rather than lash out at Héctor, Don Lupe takes his wife to New Orleans where the doctors diagnose chronic anemia and treat her with blood transfusions and vitamin supplements, then send her back to Chetumal with no trace of convulsions. When she gets home, the doctors say, she must eat better and be more active. The ailments that plagued her for so long amount to no more than chronic anemia, Emma and Luisa recall years later: the result of not eating and suffering in silence.

If I'm right, and Héctor comes to our house the day after learning Juana Marrufo is dead, then it's the next day when he gets on the plane to Chetumal. He's traveling with a hangover from alcohol and the scene he made at the door of his former house. He must think his life is a mess, a disgrace, and, what's worse, his mother has died and he hasn't made it to her burial. He's probably wearing his aviator glasses with the green lenses and gold frames. And the feeling of being an orphan that he has yet to get over when I next see him thirty-four years later. He's still navigating his inner darkness with insomniac eyes as large and sad as his mother's. He gets to Chetumal the day after the burial. Don Lupe and Ángel meet him at the airport, and Don Lupe welcomes him with open arms. "I'm so sorry," Héctor tells him. Don Lupe replies, "Not as sorry as I am." He exchanges glances with Ángel but they don't embrace. Ángel just nods as if to say, "What's up?" and Héctor answers in kind. He goes to the cemetery with Ariosto, the family's longtime chauffeur. The Chetumal cemetery is on Efraín Aguilar, the street renamed for his late brother who died in the hurricane that struck Belize. "I'll take you to the cemetery, Don Héctor," Ariosto says. "What's this Don Héctor? Since when have you been so formal with me?" Héctor replies. "All right, Tito," the chauffeur says. The two have worked together for years. In the lumber business, the repair shop, in shared ventures of all sorts. Ariosto takes him straight to the grave and says, "Right here, Tito. This is where they buried her yesterday." The earth appears to have been turned and tamped just hours ago. Héctor gets out his ever-present camera and takes a few pictures. His old friends Pepe and Antonio Musa, Chetumal's legendary policemen, come to the cemetery. "Come to our house," they say. "We asked your friends if they'd like to stop by and have a drink with you." Héctor agrees, and goes with them. Between drinks, they describe what's gone wrong with Casa Aguilar thanks to Ángel's mismanagement. "The place is falling apart," they say. Héctor replies: "There's nothing I can do about it, nothing I can do or could have done." Before Héctor boards the afternoon plane, his brother Ángel catches up with him. Though they barely speak when Héctor arrives, Ángel now says, "Look, I need ten thousand pesos."

"Well, five is all I have," Héctor replies. "I can give you four, but I need the rest for the flight back to Mexico City."

"Four thousand isn't enough. I need ten to meet payroll. Four won't get me off the hook."

"Then don't take it." This is the story Héctor tells me when I see him years later. His version sounds like hindsight, but the details have a ring of truth. Among them is this: at the time of Juana Marrufo's death, Casa Aguilar hasn't met payroll for weeks.

Mexico City, 1969

I've always imagined the city where my father used to live in shades of gray, scratched and blurred like unrestored black-and-white film footage. It's the city of the inn where I went to see him in 1996 after forty years of not seeing him: the city of the old jai alai arena, long-gone trolleys whose paved-over tracks turn corners to nowhere, narrow streets where the sun doesn't shine: Edison and Emparan; Morelos and Bucareli; Ayuntamiento and Abraham González; streets of squat buildings, foul-smelling sewers, twilit stoops, crumbling mansions honeycombed into tiny apartments, and palaces transgendered into government offices. The Ministry of State Security, the place for Mexican politics in their least adulterated form, occupies one such palace on Bucareli Street. It's hunkered down in the shadows of the world where my father lives, a realm of bars and taverns, dance halls, doctors' offices where patients are treated for venereal diseases, antiquarian dentists, seedy lawyers, hotels and funeral parlors, newsstands, businesses with counters overlooking the street, traffic jams, cars climbing sidewalks choked with pedestrians skirting puddles, fruit rinds, cigarette butts, discarded paper: the eternal detritus of an old, dirty, and sleepless city falling apart.

This is the city to which I consign my father like an insect under glass in a natural history museum. In this part of the city time stands still and my father remains forever young. I can picture him there at will. It is, among other things, where this story plunges into a domain about which I can offer few details except my father's odd disappearance. He leaves our house never to return and goes to the seer on Bucareli Street where he ensconces himself. Ironically, perhaps inevitably in the mysterious scheme of things, Héctor was first taken there by his wife Emma and his sister-in-law Luisa, in their shared conviction that his behavior since coming to Mexico City can only be attributed to witchcraft. He's fallen under a spell cast upon him in jungle lumber camps or in the lost city of Chetumal, a curse designed first to confuse him and then to steal from him. As I said before, Héctor's rarely at home. He spends most of his time in a round of meetings and errands that culminate late at night when he assures his wife that it's just a matter of time before things will get better. But they've run out of time to pay the rent or the household bills or the school expenses. The Camín sisters are simple country girls at heart. They're philosophically naive, and they believe in the powers of the unseen. Luisa may be quick to spot signs of trouble but, as will be seen, her gift strengthens rather than weakens her willingness to believe there are those whose predictive powers surpass her own. Except for the chronic melancholy that she battles throughout her life, Emma has no deep affinity for the dark side nor is she constrained or comforted by religion. As a less than liturgical Catholic who believes in generalities, she has no qualms about bargaining with supernatural powers whose existence she doubts will help rescue her household from pending doom and her husband from his delusions of grandeur. The foregoing explains why the sisters take Héctor to the fortuneteller and why he agrees to go. I've already said I don't know who suggests this particular clairvoyant. Perhaps it's just the waves of her notoriety that wash over the city in those years. The history of fortunetelling in Mexico City is not to be taken lightly, and I don't know who is up to writing it. But I can say the following:

In the sixties of the past century, the city is full of witches and seers, ordinary women who spice up their humdrum lives by attributing spiritual powers to themselves. They provide guidance to politicians, console the inconsolable, and advertise in magazines for the lonely-hearted. Their names suggest they're privy to the secrets of the Orient: Ali Jirimichel, Seleiman Jartum, Joselin Caponel, Zulema Moraima, Nelly Mulley.

In his book *The Clairvoyant*, Dr. Jorge Fernández Fonseca tells the story of one such seer, a predecessor of my father's guardian. Her *nom de guerre* is Disle Rally, and her birth name is Luz María Rábago. She was born into a family of wealthy landowners in the state of Guanajuato in 1893, the same year my grandfather Don Lupe came into the world. At fifteen Disle Rally predicts the accidental killing of a sister by a younger brother given to playing with a pistol on their ranch. Disle goes on to run the pharmacy of a mental hospital known as La Castañeda in Mexico City. She marries a philandering husband and salves her wounds in visits to the spiritual ladies whose arts she masters with memorable virtuosity. Dr. Fernández writes about women who preside over ceremonies alleged to invoke the powers of white, red and black magic; who read palms, coffee grounds, and Hindu and Egyptian tarot cards; who gaze into crystal balls; who see signs in the rippling of water, the flickering of flames, and the wax of guttering candles; who can tell why stars align as they do. Also, most prodigiously, they learn the science of purges, how to ward off evil spirits and neutralize hexes in order to induce health, wealth, and lasting love. Times, governments and cities, children's toys, national borders, and life expectancy all change, but the nature of purges and the ancient beliefs from which they spring are immutable. They're practiced with sprigs of tree branches and red flowers, hens' eggs and turkey eggs. They suck the spells from the bodies of the afflicted into branches or flowers that wither or birds whose eggs rot and whose feathers fall off.

In his book Dr. Fernández explains that purges are performed in the patios of the houses where the practitioners live, normally on Tuesday and Friday mornings before supplicants who begin waiting in line at a very early hour. In the center of the patio is a hot stove sprinkled with incense and myrrh. The supplicants come forth with tree branches or flowers or eggs to a chant of: *With two I bind you, with three I unbind you unshackled, unscathed; your enemies are vanquished.* I don't know if Emma and Luisa and the putatively spellbound Héctor are cleansed in this fashion, nor do I know if Nelly Mulley resorts to such coarse remedies because, like her clients Emma and Luisa, she's a princess fallen from on high. Her house once basked in the fickle radiance of presidential favor just as the lumber trade once cast its counterfeit luster on Emma and Luisa.

Dr. Fernández suggests in *The Clairvoyant* that in 1938—the year Emma arrives in Chetumal—Disle Relly is battling for recognition as Mexico's foremost seer, and her main rival is Zulema Moraima, the mentor and older sister of my father's second wife, Nelly Mulley. Zulema Moraima, born Esperanza Reséndiz in a town in the state of Hidalgo, has skirmished with the nation's history for half a century. In 1919, she told poet laureate Ramón López Velarde that a major political figure was about die. The doomed personage turns out to be the revolutionary leader Venustiano Carranza. By virtue of his post as private secretary to Carranza's private secretary Manuel Aguirre Berlanga, López Velarde is one of the executed leader's minor aides. In 1933, Disle Relly accurately predicts that Mexico's next president will be Lázaro Cárdenas. Zuleima regains her exalted status in 1941 when she tells President Manuel Ávila Camacho: "Watch out, there are people plotting to kill you." Three days later Lieutenant Antonio de la Lama, an artillery officer, fires at the president in the halls of the National Palace. His bodyguards, knowing an assassination attempt is likely, intervene in time. Zulema's prediction makes her the foremost seer of the Ávila Camacho years. The analysts from State Security seek her counsel as a matter of routine. Zulema Moraima bequeaths her wisdom to her younger sister, Trinidad Reséndiz, whose nom de guerre will be Nelly Mulley. The Reséndiz sisters will fall on hard times, but for now times are good. The gods of politics are on their side. Top government leaders turn to them for advice about the future, and they're psychic counsellors and advisers to politicians in their home state of Hidalgo. In their halcyon years as readers of star signs, another Hidalgo native, Javier Rojo Gómez, becomes mayor of Mexico City. He goes on to lead the national peasants' organization, falls short in his bid to become president, and settles for appointment as governor if Quintana Roo. Thanks to his influence, politicians from Hidalgo keep a stranglehold on leadership positions in the lower house of the national congress from one legislative session to the next. Nelly Mulley is their reigning oracle, and in two successive sessions the Hidalgo delegation will name Héctor its assistant secretary and its members will simply call him Marrufo. But this will come to pass years later, between 1967 and 1973. In 1964, after his mother dies, Héctor's just a lonely orphan, and nobody knows his sorrows.

Juana Marrufo dies in Chetumal far from where we live. For Héctor life goes on nearby in Mexico City, but so invisibly to us that he might as well have been far away. Emma knows that his trail leads to the home of Nelly Mulley. She knows full well that she and Luisa took him there for an exorcism, and this awareness leaves her feeling guilty and ashamed. Héctor has taken refuge with Nelly Mulley when Emma goes to see him for the last time and exchanges a few words with him: Get a grip, she tells him. Stop chasing rainbows. I don't know if she says this because she hopes Héctor will change his ways or because she wants to disabuse him once and for all of the possibility of reconciliation. Sometimes the guilty concoct their own punishments, and often those who are spurned rub salt in their own wounds. Were Emma to leave the door open for Héctor, she'd have to do so in defiance of Luisa, who dominates the household and considers Héctor a lost cause. Luisa has become the ruler in Emma's house, her partner in raising the children, and her true companion. At a time when Héctor has either lost the battle or just quit fighting, I doubt that Emma is in any position to question Luisa's authority.

Héctor and Emma don't see each other again after this exchange, but Emma doesn't lose track of this man she loved, with whom she set up housekeeping and had children. Emma's not the sort of woman who can easily put these things out of her mind, and she doesn't let go of them in years to come. Héctor's trail grows faint in the urban fog where witches and spirits compete on battlefields of their own.

Josefa's stay with her daughters has opened the way to reconciliation with the Camíns, and there comes a day when Raúl's young sister-in-law shows up at Mexico 15. She's a slender, nervous girl with sturdy legs and a mind steeped in religion. She's named for her late grandmother Josefa, but she's called Chepina. Having seen an ad in a magazine called *Confidencias*, she's come to Mexico City to see a counselor she thinks can help her, and she's asked Emma and Luisa to put her up for a few days. Chepina's been fond of Emma and Luisa since childhood, and her open and loving nature has long since won her a place in the sisters' hearts. At the time, Jesús Rojas, the ex-nanny of Emma's children in Chetumal, lives nearby on Avenida Mexico where she works and lives with her little girl Guadalupe. The story of these two women is a novel in itself. To explain its place in these pages I will say only that Jesús—nicknamed Chuy— is the daughter of the irascible Colonel Rojas, who in 1923 spearheaded the de la Huerta rebellion in Chetumal. The uprising bears the name of its instigator, finance minister Adolfo de la Huerta, an accomplished tenor who, when driven into exile, lives the best years of his life as a voice teacher in Los Angeles.

The de la Huerta rebellion of 1923 gains the support of half the army including Anastasio Rojas, then commander of the Chetumal garrison. The colonel takes over the city, snuffs out the feeble resistance mounted by a second lieutenant named López, and proceeds with the customary reprisals. He lines up twelve local merchants on the main street and publicly demands that they contribute all their savings to the rebel cause. Juan Erales refuses, and the mob of onlookers drives him up the hill towards the cemetery. The mother of Emma Camín's bosom friend Aurora Pérez Schofield will never forget watching Erales being pushed and shoved past the Belisario Domínguez Middle School on his way to the graveyard where he's shot by a ragtag firing squad on orders from Rojas. The remaining merchants all pay a price, including those who avoid doing so in cash. A colleague of Erales named Onofre manages to flee. But first he hides a moneybag in his house, and these gold pesos—as dollars used to be called—are never fully accounted for. When the rebellion is put down, Rojas flees to Honduras where he has a daughter whose mother later dies. This daughter is Jesús Rojas. After the professional turmoil resulting from the uprising has abated, the colonel returns to Chetumal with his motherless child in tow. He leaves her with his godmother while he attends to matters a man must take care of by himself. According to the colonel, he left part of Onofre's stash, some twenty thousand golden pesos, with Don Lupe Aguilar before fleeing Chetumal in 1923. Two decades later he's back, and Don Lupe owns the city. His sons are at a dance with their girlfriends, Ángel with Marion Córdova and Héctor with Emma Camín, when word reaches them that Colonel Rojas is planning an attack on Casa Aguilar that same night. Don Lupe's sons leave the dance, take their girlfriends home, and meet at the family store.

There's no need to defend the place because the attack never materializes. Inexplicably, Colonel Rojas skips town, leaving his twelve-year-old daughter Jesús in the home of his decent but poor godparents where she grows up indigent, consumptive and scrawny. When Juan José, Emma's third child, is born, the colonel's godmother arranges for Chuy to help with the new baby in exchange for meals. This is how Chuy Rojas finds her way into the household of Emma Camín. She's cheerful and keenly attentive to the baby. With Chuy watching over him he sleeps undisturbed by her nagging cough. The child nanny begins to mature and attract attention when she takes Héctor's and Emma's children to the park, and Ángel asks Héctor, "How can you let the daughter of our enemy work in your house?" The girl's cough—which he fears she might give the children— worries Héctor more than her last name, and when he repeats what his brother said to Emma, she replies, "How dare the two of you turn on that girl? What does she have to do with the stupid things her father does? Or that your father does?" Don Lupe will never admit to having kept the colonel's money. He even has receipts to show he gave it to the new authorities after the colonel fled. Don Lupe's greedy, but he's no smalltime thief. That can't be questioned, but Chuy Rojas is destined to be involved with the Aguilar family in other ways. She blossoms into a fine looking girl, stops working for Emma, and takes a job behind the counter in Don Lupe's store until Héctor and Ángel's half brother Galo is smitten by her smile. But Galo's true love is alcohol, and he cleaves to his addiction until, as a very old man, he's overcome with regret.

Galo Aguilar is as good an excuse as any for talking about the women of Don Lupe and his spawn. With his lawfully wedded wife Juana Marrufo he has first Angel and then Jaime, who dies in infancy, then Efraín, who dies at nineteen in the Belize hurricane, then another Jaime who dies as a baby, then

Perfecto and Luz María, who dies in childhood, then Héctor and finally Omar. With Juana Marrufo's friend Julieta Angulo, Don Lupe fathers Narno. With a Mrs. Ávila from Yucatán, he has Jesús. In Belize with Adelfa Pérez he has Gaspar and Jaime, Raúl and and Amira, Bambi and Ricardo. With Ursula Escalante in Chetumal, he has Mario and Bulmaro, Graciela and finally the charming Galo, who becomes an alcoholic at an early age. In the year after the hurricane, Galo abducts Jesús Rojas from behind the counter of his father's store where they both work, and moves in with her. Chuy goes back to working for Emma, who is four months pregnant with Luis Miguel, her last child. Her blissful pregnancy inspires Chuy, and after Luis Miguel is born in 1956, Chuy gets herself pregnant with Galo. Bluntly put, post-hurricane pregnancies are the talk of the town. They give people something to cheer about and remind them that life goes on and you have to make the best of it. Women welcome the advances of their men and use their bodies to show the world they won't be intimidated by the wreckage Hurricane Janet left behind. Chuy has vivid memories of the swarms of midges that precede the storm and the blind cockroaches that bump into everything and crunch underfoot after it passes. When her baby is born, Galo gets her a house and sets about supporting the new mother and the daughter she names Guadalupe. The trouble is that Galo's one person when sober and another when drunk. The sober Galo loves Chuy, and as a token of his affection gives her the title to a lot he bought in Mérida. The drunk Galo stomps in the door one day and demands the title back so he can put it in the name of his daughter. But Chuy knows the ownership papers would only end up in the hands of a saloonkeeper. She walks out on Galo, leaves Chetumal with the papers and her baby, and exchanges letters with female kin of her father's in Torreón who agree to take her in. I have no idea how Chuy gets back in touch with Emma Camín or what brings her to Mexico City. I only know she's holding hands with her daughter Lupita when she comes to our door ready to work. Héctor's gone and is conspicuous only by his absence, which is inexplicable to her since she only knows Emma and Héctor as the indomitable pair they used to be. She may have gotten some explanation from Emma, but it seems unlikely given what follows.

Raúl's sister-in-law Chepina, who is in Mexico City for spiritual counseling, asks Chuy to go with her to the appointment. Together they go to the ground floor of a building in the center of the city. They enter a dark apartment with a hallway that leads from the front door past a parlor, a dining room and two other rooms to a kitchen and laundry room at the back. They're told to wait in the parlor, and while they wait, they see Héctor emerge from the rear of the apartment. He casts a sidelong glance into the parlor but fails to recognize them as he heads out the front door. Chuy and Chepina exchange looks, silently confirming that they've seen the same apparition and that the apparition is real. They don't know if they ought to approach him or speak to him or do as they were told and stay put. Their anxiety grows. They feel guilty of treading on forbidden ground, of entering a realm where they don't belong. What they've seen horrifies them, and the vision gnaws at their souls. They step outside for fresh air and don't go back in. The apartment where they've been is where Nelly Mulley, the woman for whom Héctor deserted Emma, sees her clients. I don't know if Emma Camín realizes at the time where Chuy and Chepina are going for spiritual guidance. I don't know if, in order to get their fresh, involuntary and unskewed impression of what they see, she deliberately keeps them in the dark. I don't know what she thinks or feels when Chepina and Chuy tell her about the apparition. But I at least know what she learns: that her husband has spent the six years since he left her with the witch.

Two thick streaks of oil sprinkled with rock salt appear on the steps of Mexico 15 one morning. Emma makes a point of sweeping and scrubbing away the mess herself. Days later the streaks are back, this time at the foot of the jacaranda that sprouts from the dusty hedge by the sidewalk. On another day they appear in front of the garage. No one knows where they come from or what such defacements can possibly mean. There's something offensive and threatening about them, something for which Emma and Luisa will find a ready explanation. It's part of the war they're waging for Héctor with the witch. As if they didn't have enough to grapple with by day, they now have this to contend with by night. While living with the witch, Héctor must have evinced some spot of weakness or nostalgia that sent her scurrying to her manuals for instructions on how to have her emissaries soil the steps in our entry, the sidewalk, the garage door at Mexico 15. This is the vexed interpretation that passes for fact in our house. Years later I write a story that posits an explanation based on my father's mortifying encounter with my sister Emma. It goes like this:

Emma works as a bank teller. One day she sees Héctor come in and walk toward her cage. But he passes her by and gets in the line two cages beyond hers. Emma is aware that he's staring at her but doesn't recognize her just as he failed to recognize Chepina and Chuy Rojas in the witch's waiting room. Emma goes home that night feeling humiliated and offended. In my story I combine Héctor's hypothetical crisis of conscience with the hypothetical reality of his life with the witch. He returns to her house with the image of the beloved daughter he lacked the courage to acknowledge fresh in his memory. In my story he spends the night drowning his self-loathing in alcohol and rejecting the affections of the seer who has no way of knowing that his foul mood is attributable to matters left unresolved in his prior life. It's possible that some such scene accounts for the petroleum hazards on the steps at Mexico 15 or perhaps it may be what sends Héctor to the door at Mexico 15 in an attempt to assuage his grief after his mother dies. Be that as it may, once Luisa and Emma see Héctor decamp to the seer's house they know they're in for a fight with the powers of darkness and will need an arsenal of their own to fight back. They acquire one where they have in the past and will for years to come, in the consoling presence of a woman named Angelita and her circle of bringers of light.

Angelita is a medium who belongs to the White Brotherhood. Emma and Luisa look to her for advice and inoculation against whatever evil spirits are after them. I remember her as a short, stout woman with a dark complexion and locks of graying hair clinging to her forehead. Her voice is gentle. She nods in impassive yet calculated sympathy as clients bare their souls, then she washes away their understandable ignorance or blindness without condescending. She knows more than they do, and what they're able to articulate or perceive is only a blurred, imperfect and often tearful part of the whole that her knowledge embraces. I never went to one of Angelita's sessions, but my sisters always claim to benefit from them. My sister Pilar tells me about their modus operandi, about this invisible presence my preconceptions can't accept but whose calming effect on our house cannot be ignored. No one else does more to ease my sisters' anguish when things go wrong. Angelita takes her clients' hands in hers and lapses into a trance. Pilar says that when the trance lifts her beyond the walls of the mundane, the change in Angelita's expression and attitude is truly impressive as she summons a being she calls Brother Bernardino. Her voice deepens to an ominous growl, but the comforting touch of her hands makes it possible to understand what Bernardino says through Angelita. His words aren't always clear, and they don't always sound natural.

He can say terrible things and sound as if he's speaking from a great distance, but the trances end in feelings of sweetness and peace. As a medium, Angelita must obey the rules of the White Brotherhood, and rule number one is that she must not be swayed by emotion and must be guided by positive thoughts. Her heart must be untouched by personal feelings of euphoria, depression, displeasure or envy. But the trance itself is electrifying, so much so that it saps the energy that might have helped Angelita get over the cardiac ailment that causes her to die before her time.

Does the search for meaning in some secret clash of hexes and counter-hexes help Emma and Luisa confront the world around them? I've come to believe it absolutely does. They're sure spirits from hidden worlds above and below seep into the nooks and crannies of our lives, but this unshakable certainty speaks more to me of the extreme isolation of the life they share. It's the sole language of a sisterhood that brooks no deviation from a modest, cyclopean way of life. They'll raise children who do well in school and learn to look after themselves; they'll keep their fear of the city at bay and the things they don't understand at arms' length; they'll exorcise loneliness, stick to business, and persevere.

It's a long way to Chetumal in those days, more than a thousand kilometers over bad roads and on flimsy rafts across eight rivers. But time and imagination shrink the distance because the sisters never stop talking about it. To hear Emma and Luisa, Chetumal is a place of loss, futility and graft, but it's also where the sun shines and their family is free from entanglements with its past. I now think of our family as a kind of non-family without grandparents or a father, without the cousins, aunts, uncles and all the relatives whose longstanding friendships sink a family's roots in a particular place. Being so far from Chetumal casts a shadow over our household. My siblings and I haven't been back in eleven years, an eternity as measured in the reckonings of the young.

One afternoon as Luis Miguel waits by the door of Mexico 15 for a friend to come by for a game of soccer in the park, a taxi pulls up, and a small pale man with a receding hairline, baggy pants, a string tie, and his jacket over his shoulder gets out. The taxi driver takes his suitcase to the door, and with a resonant Cuban twang the man asks, "Is this where Emma and Luisa Camín live? I'm Uncle Raúl. You must be Juanelo."

The six-year gap between the ages of my brother Juan José, who's fifteen at the time, and Luis, who's nine, is lost on him. The year must be 1965, and the man's presence is a consequence of the rapprochement that follows the death of Josefa.

"I'm Luis Miguel," says Luis Miguel.

Raúl has come for medical treatment. His nerves are a wreck, and he's suffering from stomach acid and the shakes. It turns out his nerves are fine. His problems are all in his stomach and amount to no more than chronic colitis that won't respond to antacids or diet. The ailment turns the stomach into a torture chamber and must be treated internally. Raúl goes home to Chetumal as miserable as he came. Luisa Camín is convinced the foul potions he was given in Chetumal have left him at death's door.

Raúl Camín has and will always have the soul of a child. Going futilely from doctor to doctor in the city is a bore, and he winds up making friends with his youngest nephew, Luis Miguel. Whenever they can get away, they go to baseball games at Delta Park, the legendary venue that once belonged to the Social Security Institute and is now the site of a huge department store. In his younger days Raúl was a formidable ballplayer in his native Cuba, the star pitcher on the team of a sugar plantation where his father has business dealings. But his father despises baseball. Raúl is obliged to play behind his back, and behind his back Raúl becomes a minor hero in the fevered eyes of local ball fans. He's a natural lefthander with a nasty curveball that ties opposing hitters in knots when they come to Palma Soriano where the Camíns live. Raúl always pitches when his team plays Central Miranda, its perennial rival in Cuba's sugar-mill leagues. Forget about baseball, the elder Camín tells his son; you must become a businessman. But the overgrown kid with the supple left arm never stops dreaming major-league dreams. His may be short, and his skin may be white, but he's just as tough as his acrobatic and combative son Fernando, who in years to come will excel at soccer and be able to do back flips and land gracefully on his feet when his friends toss him in the air.

What Raúl doesn't get from the big-city doctors, he gets from Fernando's godfather Don Salva. As a veteran of General Obregón's peasant army during the Mexican Revolution, Don Salva was given a plot to farm on the Huay Pix Cooperative not far from Chetumal on Lake Milagros. Don Salva tells Raúl he can cure the cats gnawing his entrails if he's willing to spend a few weeks on the old man's farm and follow orders. Raúl agrees. Don Salva makes Raúl drink herbs and vomit for days until he spits up whatever ails him once and for all. Raúl staggers back to Chetumal pale and thin with a look of enlightenment on his face. In the opinion of Luisa Camín, Raúl's body has thrown off the curses of the underworld in Chetumal in a struggle not unlike the one the sisters are waging against Nelly Mulley in Mexico City.

Raúl's visit may have been a medical failure, but it has the effect of continuing to bring the family that talks about Chetumal closer to the one that lives in Chetumal. My sister Emma listens to her aunt and mother go on about this lost world until she feels compelled to see it with her own eyes. She goes to Chetumal on vacation after her classes end for the summer in 1966. She comes back bursting with news of what she's seen but, above all, with news of her blind grandfather. Manuel Camín tries to recognize her by touching her face, but the young woman of twenty-one who says she's his granddaughter Emma doesn't feel like the child he saw for the last time when she was ten. The grandfather who touches her face, Emma says, can go nowhere without someone to guide him though he continues to do household chores his son Raúl does badly or not at all. He feels his way to the bank, signs where the teller puts his hand, shops by touch in stores, and controls his grandchildren by touch as they grow up by touch. Carmen and Raúl have eight children in twelve years, and their house is in an uproar.

The year my sister Emma visits Chetumal, her grandfather Camín is living in a room with a toilet and a broken-down bed on the ground floor of the house, which serves as a storeroom for sacks of grain, buckets of paint, farm tools, and cans. For years it's also where baby chicks are raised. Next to the storeroom is the old store with its counter where staples such as flour, rice, sugar, and salt are sold in bulk and the shelves are laden with canned goods, soft drinks, and sweets. Discarded bags of peanuts and coffee are piled up by the store's iron queen, the German roaster acquired sometime in the 1950s. In December 2011 as I write, it's still intact and in good working order.

The succession of open spaces over the storeroom resembles the quarters where Arab shopkeepers often live with their families, and it's where the eight children of Carmen and Raúl sleep, eat and squabble. Manuel, the oldest, is sixteen. He's followed by: Yolanda, 14; Rodrigo, 13; Fernando, 12; Lourdes, 11; Alfredo, 10; Joaquín, 7; and Verónica, 3. There's no table where the family can eat together and no schedule to keep their daily lives in order. There are no bedtimes, bath times or mealtimes. The young Camíns drop by the store and dip into the till for whatever bills and coins they happen to find. They rip open boxes of English chocolates on the counter and throw them at each other or aim them at a neighbor's bottom with a slingshot as she climbs a ladder to pick mangos in the lush foliage of her backyard.

House, store, storeroom and the town itself are just a playground to the Camín kids whom the good citizens of Chetumal regard with rueful smiles and refer to as The Cubans. The terrible Cubans. They know no restraint at home except a blind grandfather who can hear but not see them tearing in and out of the house. The old man is trapped like a blind minotaur in his grandchildren's labyrinth. They all remember the way he flails at them with a broomstick in his attempts at discipline. Yolanda, the second of the grandchildren, recalls seeing her grandfather asleep on the broken-down bed in a corner of the storeroom. The racket she and her siblings raise makes him angry, and when their footsteps wake him up he thinks they're trying to steal something. He picks up a pitchfork and chases them through the stacks of bags and cartons. "He was blind," Yolanda says years later as she sits with friends overlooking the ocean. "But being blind didn't stop him from going after us with a pitchfork. Why he never caught up with one of us I'll never know, but he wasn't fooling. The more he swung at us the more we made fun of him."

During her trip to Chetumal in 1966, Manuel Camín apologizes to his granddaughter Emma for the way he's mistreated his daughters Emma and Luisa. When they left Chetumal he accused them of prostituting themselves by going off to Mexico City at Héctor's whim. They were doomed to fail, he said, and he wanted them to fail. He'd misjudged his daughters because he was confused and wanted them with him. Admitting he was wrong is all it takes for his daughter Emma to return to Chetumal. She's worried about his blindness and the conditions he's living in. Her ten-year-old son Luis Miguel comes with her. The grandfather calls Luis Miguel to his side as he did with Emma and tries to recognize him by passing his hand across his features. But he can't recognize a thing in the face of someone he's never seen. The local diagnosis of Camín's blindness is that he has cataracts that haven't progressed enough to be operated on. Emma takes him to Mérida and has him seen by the city's highly regarded ophthalmologist, Doctor Vaqueiro. Vaqueiro says Manuel Camín has an advanced case of glaucoma. One eye is beyond repair and is likely to be a source of chronic infection. The bad eye is removed, and the remaining one is treated with drops that burn horribly in such an old man. Emma then decides to take her father to Mexico City where José Garabana, the friend he ran into in Honduras long ago, is now director of the Spanish Hospital. Garabana is the man who first took Camín to Chetumal and for whom he built a waterfront house that has withstood the onslaught of time and tempests. Thus grandfather Camín reappears in the lives of his daughters at Mexico 15 and is taken in by them. Through the good offices of Garabana he's soon admitted to the Spanish Hospital to be treated for his glaucoma, which is incurable but which he refuses to give in to.

My memory of my grandfather Camín in those days is downright harrowing. I'm sent to be with him in the hospital, and the hours I spend there are long and painful. There are no eyes in his face, and his lids come together in lines over the missing eye and the ruined one. His head is filled with refrains he repeats over and over. For example: Who are you? Are you Torucho? Then: Who are you? Are you Torucho? He calls me Torucho because when I was small my grandparents used to embellish my name and call me Hectorucho. Torucho is what remains.

The most vivid memory I have of my grandfather Camín is the welt on my finger. The sash of a window he's trying to open won't stay up unless its side pegs are engaged, and when he loses his grip, the sill comes down on my left thumb leaving an oddly symmetrical lump. Years later, at about the age I was then, my daughter Rosario nearly loses half of the same thumb in another accident. Her mother Tita Ruz saves it in an exemplary show of maternal fortitude. When the window splits my thumb open, my grandfather Camín is at my side. "It's nothing, Torucho. Your thumb will be fine," he says. He lost the tip of his middle finger, and the partial loss of a finger never bothered him very much. It's just something you have to live with. Looking back, I suppose he was only trying to keep me calm and ease the pain of losing a finger by dismissing it as imaginary. I also suspect he's thinking about the scene that's sure to ensue when his daughters see his grandson's mangled thumb. The grandson is his daughters' pampered pet, and no harm must come to him, especially when he's out of their sight. Remembering the time when my grandfather is dying in the hospital, I'm moved to wonder if I ever made peace with him. I tell him I have, but the rheumy discharge that seeps from under the sealed lids of his useless eyes suggests he's not so sure. His inner peace is gone along with his eyes. To him I'm just another grandchild feigning concern for an old man I really couldn't care less about and who doesn't understand a damn thing.

The other harrowing memory I have of my grandfather is of a day when I was eight—I couldn't have been more than eight because it happened in Chetumal before I turned nine. I tell him I'd like to smoke, and he says let's see how you do at smoking. He buys me a pack of unfiltered cigarettes, probably a brand called *Alas Extra*. He puts one in my mouth and lights it with a match whose enticing flame still flickers in my mind's eye. As I take a drag, I see my grandfather snicker at the success of his prank. He tells me to take a deep breath, and the prank quickly blossoms into fits of choking and gagging. My nose and throat feel as if the smoke has set them on fire. Rather than the pleasure I expect from inhaling, I feel as if I'm about to die under the cruel but amused gaze of a grandfather who's taught his grandson a lesson.

These are the unpleasant memories I have of my grandfather, but I do have others that are unforgettably fond. They bind me to him despite all the bad things his daughters say about him in the battle of words that lasts throughout my childhood and into my adolescence. I remember him in his daughter Emma's kitchen in the humid shadows of a tropical dawn. He lifts me up in his rough disfigured hands and sits me on the stove so I can watch him make coffee. The brew's Adamic aroma rises from the small pewter saucepan as Camín spoons two dark rations of grains from the mythic German roaster into the boiling water. He strains the coffee through a woolen cap that makes do for the sleeve Cuban peasants use to strain coffee. He puts a bit of the liquid in a small cup into which he's stirred all the sugar he can into an egg yolk. He mixes the fresh coffee with the yolk, takes a sip, then gives me one; he takes another for himself, then gives me another taste before finishing the dregs himself. He picks me up and puts me in a wheelbarrow. As day breaks, he trundles me to the dock and puts me in a sailboat for a turn around the pungently malodorous bay. It seems to me he's happy, and so am I.

On the way to his death throes in Mexico City, Manuel Camín implores his daughters Emma and Luisa not to give up on their brother Raúl. He worries about Raúl's chaotic household, his utter indifference to practical matters. He doesn't manage the store; he spends his time chatting with whoever drops by. Someone's behind the counter, and his wife Carmen is at the cash register. Raúl talks endlessly with customers who come to shop and be entertained. He's full of his father's old sayings as well as others he made up himself. Some of them have adorned the walls of the Camíns' store for ages: "Work is the people's gold. How else do you expect to get rich?" Like his father and sisters, Raúl is a treasure trove of proverbs and a natural teller of tales. He's never lost his Cuban accent, and he combines the wry expressions and wisecracks of the island with sly local humor. Chetumal is a lighthearted town built on a foundation of jovial cynicism, and Raúl Camín is a mix of peculiarly Spanish and Cuban traits. From the minute the store's doors open in the morning until they shut at closing time, he's a one-man carnival. "Obregón is the only president who didn't steal by the fistful. Why? Because he only had one hand!" "That bastard Fidel Castro is the only one who can get Cubans to work either inside or outside the country." "The only thing Kennedy did right was to get killed, no?" "This is a good country going sour." His soliloquies are both acid and festive, but they're not bitter. He's like the child telling the emperor he has no clothes for the sheer pleasure of saying so, like fans at the ballpark shouting at a hitter who's struck out: "You've been had, asshole!" Raúl's bull sessions with customers may be spellbinding, but the store's a disaster. Lax management lets profits and merchandise alike vanish into thin air. The Camín grandfather may have lost his eyes, but he can see his store is on the verge of bankruptcy, which is why he wants his daughters to go to its rescue. Raúl comes and goes during Manuel Camín's final months. His nephew Luis Miguel is responsible for taking Raúl to the hospital to see his father. They ride the same bus that takes Luis Miguel to Polanco where he goes to *Instituto Patria*, the Jesuit school chosen for him and his brothers by Emma and Luisa. "Off to the bus," Raúl cries out to Luis Miguel. The two take the *Sonora-Penón-Hospitales* bus that stops in front of the house. Its route runs along Avenida Sonora, and nephew and uncle get off at *Ejército Nacional* by the immense *Beneficencia Española* building. They also ride the bus to ballgames at the Social Security Institute's aforementioned Delta Park where Raúl's inner big leaguer is driven to distraction by the quality of play in the Mexican League. If, for example, Poza Rica is playing the Mexico City Tigers, he lashes out with a nervous eloquence that defies imitation. "This is worse than the bush leagues, damn it. It's pure sandlot ball, that's all it is." Luis Miguel pays great homage to the memory of his days at the ballpark with Raúl. He writes a poem set on the ball field of a Cuban sugar mill around 1935. Present at the scene are Raúl, his parents Manuel and Josefa, and Raúl's teammates. It goes like this:

THE BALLPLAYER
Baseball's for Blacks damn it
You're meant to be in business damn it
Damn it Dad it's okay
It's all right Don Manuel let him play damn it
The kid's a natural left-hander
As good a pitcher as we have
And now we're playing Central Maceo
Who gives a damn about Maceo
Come on Raúl give it up damn it
Come on Raúl bear down damn it
That damn pussy Cinco de Mayo can't stop anything
His glove's made of sugar candy for Christ's sake
Do I have to do it all by myself damn it?
Come on Raúl show them your fastball damn it
Damn it here comes Don Manuel damn it all
God damn Dad how the fuck can you do this to me
In front of the team and everybody damn it
Grabbing me by the hair
And ripping my fucking uniform half off
For the love of God you might have waited
Damn it Josefa go burn those pajamas
He's got on right now damn it
He looks like the twerp on the Crackerjack box

For the love of God Raúl you know
Your father doesn't like you playing ball
What the hell's the matter with baseball damn it
Damn it, baseball's for Blacks
Well it's not for Cinco de Mayo damn it
That guy's got a glove like a milk carton, damn it
Baseball's important for Christ's sake
Céspedes go warm up damn it
We lost Raúl for good damn it
Fuck and now we've got to play Central Miranda damn it.

By agreement with their father and Raúl, the sisters go
to Chetumal to help their brother help himself. They open a
clothing store in a small annex next to Raúl's grocery store and
take turns traveling to Chetumal. They dust off their business
skills and name their shop Yolis in honor of Yolanda, Raúl's
oldest daughter. Yolis is wedged between Raúl's grocery and
the wall that marks the edge of the large corner lot that Emma
and Luisa had to give up when Héctor went broke. The lot
compensated Don Goyo Marrufo for his losses to Héctor, and
Don Goyo's widow Carmen Maldonado, who is a dear friend
of the sisters, now lives in the house where Emma once lived.
There follows a period of mutual benefits. Emma and Luisa
help keep Raúl and his family solvent, and the profits from
Yolis are a boon to the sisters and us. By 1968 the Camins'
business and family feuds are over. The sisters will continue
to shuttle back and forth to Chetumal until 1975, and at least
four of Raúl's offspring will spend time at Mexico 15. Manolo,
the oldest, has his nose operated on; Yolanda comes to study
accounting; and Fernando, the middle sibling and godson of
Don Salva, is a soccer standout in a family of talented soccer
players. Fernando's also the protagonist in an incident in *Parque
México* that becomes a family legend. He gets into a fight with
"Mop Head," the reigning tough in the gang that rules the

park. When he breaks his right hand, he battles on with his left. Years later the youngest of the Chetumal Camíns, Veronica, the sweet-tempered, raven-haired beauty we still call Ica, visits Mexico 15.

Manuel Camín never returns to Chetumal. He dies on October 1st, 1969 while his daughter Luisa is with him in the hospital. She calls Mexico 15, and Emma—her niece and my sister—answers the phone and assumes the painful task of relaying the news to her mother at the sisters' store in Chetumal.

I reconstruct all this from the memories of my brothers and sisters. I wonder where I was and who I was in those years. In my memory I find only a foggy sensation of aimlessness. I was about to complete the final year of a communications major at *Universidad Iberoamericana* (1966) with a senior thesis entitled "The Language of Advertising as a Language of Repression" (1967); I served as the ghost writer for a well-known figure in the world of advertising; I worked in the Olympic Village where contestants in the 1968 Olympic Games lived; and I grew disenchanted with the profession of communications for which I'd studied. I decided one more time to become a writer. I wrote book reviews for the newspaper *El día* and began studying for a doctorate in history at *El Colegio de México*.

I made a great point of acting as if my past life were unimportant, as if it had no bearing on anything. I was going to be different from what I was, I would turn my back on the life I'd actually lived.

Mexico City, 1976

Efraín Angulo, known for his boyhood pranks as El Bandido, is one of Chetumal's most successful businessmen. He started out as a helper in the bottling plant owned by my grandfather Don Lupe when Casa Aguilar was in its heyday. In Chetumal the common name for the beverages the plant bottles has always been gaseosas, or soda pop, because they fizz over when you open them or when the caps suddenly blow off in the fierce Caribbean sun. Now, in 2007, Efraín owns the sites where Casa Aguilar once prospered. One after another he bought: the corner lot where the main store used to be; the land once occupied by the Juventino Rosas movie theater; and the elegant wooden house with the pitched roof where my Uncle Angel, Don Lupe's firstborn son, used to live. Efraín lives in the house that belonged to my grandfather, a two-story cement cube where such relics as the pump from the 1940s' gas station and Don Lupe's safe, a steel block the size of a card table, are preserved. Efraín first saw Don Lupe through the eyes of a child, and Don Lupe looms larger than life in his memory. He pictures the formidable Don Lupe as a man who always wears a coat and tie and whose presence looms over Chetumal though he's rarely in town. He comes and goes. He has businesses to attend to elsewhere, other houses to visit, other women, other children, other tastes. He goes to Mexico City or Mérida or the sawmill at Zoh Lake deep in the jungles of Campeche; to Corozal, to Orinchuac (Orange Walk) and Belize in British Honduras, to Guatemala City, the Plancha de

Piedra logging camp—now known as Mechor de Mencos—at the edge of the Petén on the Belize/Guatemala border. He has houses in Havana, Merida, Belize and the French Quarter of New Orleans. He does business in the Panama Canal Zone. In Mexico City he visits government agencies whose Chetumal and Quintana Roo desks are the region's bureaucratic outposts in the nation's capital. There are days when Don Lupe lands in Chetumal for a change of clothes, then is back to the airfield to fly somewhere else. In those days Chetumal doesn't have an airport, just an airfield. Don Lupe's never in Chetumal, but his hand is in everything. No detail ever escapes him. Efraín Angulo tells of the time Lupe comes across an old acquaintance named Rivero in Mérida, a man from Xcalc. Rivero invites him for breakfast at the place he says serves the best breakfasts in all Mérida. The place they walk to turns out to be the city market where peasant food stalls abound. Don Lupe is wearing a Panama hat and is decked out in a suit of finest linen. He stops short at the entrance to the market and says to Rivero: "Let me take you to a different place." "What's wrong with this one?" Rivero asks, and Don Lupe replies: "If my creditors find out I eat in the market, they think I'm broke and foreclose on me."

When Efraín quotes Don Lupe, he speaks in the progressive voice typical of the Spanish of the Yucatán, turning past and present into a jumble of simultaneity: My grandfather at forty is declining to eat in the Mérida city market in a scene being recalled by a man of seventy named Efraín Angulo talking about when he's twelve and looks up to the Don Lupe he's now describing as a force of nature, a shrewd, irresistible giant of mythic proportions.

The things I want to recount next happen in calendar time, but they're timeless in my head. I can only describe them as if they're all happening at once. It's 1975, and Don Lupe is eighty-four years old. He's made a fortune, and now it's gone. He's lost control of Casa Aguilar, and his control of his own fate is slipping. All that remains from his golden past is the general store in Chetumal, which has now passed to his son Ángel. The lumber business has backfired on him and all the lumbermen of the time. He has a bountiful 1955 harvest, but when Hurricane Janet strikes, Governor Margarito Ramírez seizes the timber at his Santa Elena sawmill. Don Lupe spends the rest of his life trying to keep ahead of his debts. Unhinged by his losses, he casts covetous eyes at the concession the Guatemalan government recently granted his son Héctor at Aguas Turbias in the jungles of Petén. Héctor is an inept manager, and for a few thousand dollars Don Lupe wrests the concession from his son in 1957. He logs Aguas Turbias for two years, until 1959. However, Margarito remains a thorn in his side, and rather than market his lumber in Quintana Roo where Margarito rules, he takes it to Cuba where construction is booming. In Havana he sells lumber to builders and starts a furniture business. Timber from Aguas Turbias and real estate fever in Cuba restore the luster of Casa Aguilar. But Don Lupe's luck runs out in 1959, and his businesses are expropriated by the island's revolutionary government. Don Lupe is sixty-nine at the time, and he's burnt out. His son Ángel runs Casa Aguilar, but the only changes he brings are for the worse. Ángel is still logging in Guatemala with mixed results. His concessions are bad, his harvests poor, and his future dim. Omar, the youngest of the brothers, is in charge of the family's sawmill at Plancha de Piedra. One night his wife, a Guatemalan mestiza enslaved by alcohol and jealousy, burns down the sawmill. Omar is relieved of his responsibilities in Casa Aguilar and kicked out the door. He seeks refuge in Mexico City with his brother Héctor. He's always in touch with Héctor, the angel who looks after him and joins forces with him in his clashes with Ángel, the firstborn of the brothers. Ángel is still awaiting the timber harvest that will restore Casa Aguilar to its past glory. He invests more in wood than he earns, and he does it by siphoning off the profits from other businesses, from the store, the movie theater, the gas station, the ice and bottling plants, the local shipping fleet. A time will come when Emma Camín says: "I could get rich on the leftovers from the Aguilars' losses." But that's not how the die is cast.

The account I have of the state of Casa Aguilar in those days comes from a source as neutral as it is unexpected.

It's 1974. Ángel makes contact with a young investor in Mexico City named Silverio Perroni. Perroni is interested in lumber. He's partnered with lumbermen in Mexico City and Chiapas, and he has the optimism and the taste for adventure that the business demands. Ángel invites him to Chetumal and takes him to Casa Aguilar's logging camp and sawmill at Plancha de Piedra, now known as Mechor de Mencos. At the time Ángel's fifty-three, and Perroni's thirty-five. Night is falling as Ángel heads for the airport to greet his young partner as soon as he steps off the plane. He welcomes him with open arms and overwhelms him with hospitality. He puts him up at The Coconut Tree, Chetumal's lone hotel at the time and says:

"I'll be around for you tomorrow at two."

It's eight at night. Perroni thinks his aging host is slowing down. The drive to the logging camp and sawmill near the border between Belize and Guatemala takes eight hours, and Perroni needs to be in Mexico City on other business without delay. He's not about to lose time waiting for a return flight in Chetumal. He asks Ángel if they couldn't leave sooner. Ángel replies:

"We can leave right now if you like."

"But didn't you just tell me tomorrow at two?" Perroni says.

"Right," Ángel replies. "Two in the morning."

The following morning at two Ángel picks up the bleary-eyed Perroni in his Renault, a then-fashionable vehicle meant for city driving. Perroni inquires if a jeep mightn't be a better choice for a trip through the jungle. Ángel tells him jeeps are a bad idea on the rugged road they must travel. He explains:

"Jeeps perform better and last longer, but they ruin your kidneys. It's better to use a good car that doesn't last as long but saves wear and tear on the kidneys."

Perroni tells me this twenty-five years later at The Hayloft, a restaurant in Mexico City:

"Ángel was right," he admits. "On bad roads Renaults fell apart in six months, but you felt as if you were riding on a cloud while they lasted."

Perroni goes on:

"We crossed to the house of Angel's uncle in the city of Belize. The uncle was called Taco, and he was the same age as Ángel. They were born the same year and were nursed by Ángel's mother, Doña Juana. She nursed both son and nephew. Taco lived in a wooden, English-style house and was very orderly, very correct. We ate breakfast in Belize and proceeded to the Guatemalan border at Benque Viejo, a pretty spot on the Mopán River. First, we went to the logging camp on the near shore at a place called Fallabón; then we went to the sawmill on the outskirts of Melchor de Mencos, the former Plancha de Piedra, on the far shore. We spent the whole day there, and it was almost midnight before we started back to Melchor de Mencos for the night. I'd intended to write myself a memo about what we'd seen during the day, but all I felt like doing was sleeping. I was so tired that the rats scurrying about the house where we stayed didn't bother me. I was about to lie down when someone knocked at my door. It was Ángel in a fresh guayabera, combed and perfumed with Yardley's Brilliantine. 'It's time to go sing with the girls,' he said. He liked to sing, and he sang well. The girls were the women working the bars, a whole string of bars that were actually whorehouses in a town made up of bars and a sawmill. Everybody rubbed elbows with the bar owners. They were the richest men around, and everyone else was either a bartender, a lumberman like us, or a cop, a soldier, or one of the girls. In that kind of a place the girls were like beings from Venus. Or from Mars by way of Venus, I should say: the only women in a hotbed of men. They made a whole lot of Ángel Aguilar because he'd been rich and famous in their world, and they were sure he would be again. Ángel felt not just well taken care of but sought after in Plancha de Piedra. I didn't go out to sing with the girls. I stayed in bed, ashamed by my lack of stamina. I don't know how long Ángel stayed out that night, but he wasn't up by the time I was ready to leave. He was a glutton for work. He was twenty years my senior, and I couldn't keep up with him. He wouldn't let me drive. He drove like a madman, but he wouldn't let me drive. He liked old machinery and was good at repairing it. One day we hit a pothole and broke a spring. Ángel stomped into the bush with a machete and came back with the fork of a tree. God knows how he wedged it into where the spring was, but it stayed put until we got to a place where we could make a permanent repair. He was a very good mechanic, and he was very stubborn about replacing parts he thought he could fix. He ended up making the mistake of insisting on a mechanical solution to a problem more easily solved non-mechanically. As I recall, a boiler at the sawmill shut down when it ran out of fuel. We could use the sawdust generated by the mill instead, I said, but he wouldn't listen. 'We'll heat the boiler with a diesel motor,' he insisted. 'But there's no diesel fuel around here,' I said. 'That's right,' he said, 'but we'll smuggle it in.' 'Smuggling's a whole different business,' I told him. 'If we were going to be smugglers, we ought to be moving something more valuable than a few gallons of diesel fuel.' I found out later that he was dismantling some old shrimp boats and wanted to adapt their motors to the boiler. That's what he was up to. He was trying to make old motors serve new purposes. It's what he loved to do, and it's one reason the business didn't work out. The sawmill was getting old, and Ángel had his eye on a derelict boat in Chetumal Bay. It had been abandoned years ago and everyone expected it to sink. Only magic could explain why it hadn't gone down already. It couldn't sink because it had run aground. The bay was too shallow to keep it afloat. It was stuck in the mud."

The boat Perroni speaks of was named *Juanita* for my grandmother Juana Marrufo. Half sunk in the bay, it was a symptom of the declining fortunes of Casa Aguilar. It lay on its side not far from the pier with its keel sticking out of the water, but nobody bothered to tow it away or finish sinking it. I remember the captain who sailed the *Juanita* over the Gulf and the Caribbean in its glory days. His name was Juan Casteleiro. He was white, red actually, but he dressed in white and had glasses with green lenses and gold rims. He had a long chiseled nose, a wide forehead, clear smiling eyes, a cleft chin, and the sinewy arms of a jai alai player. In my memory Justo Casteleiro is a model of well-scrubbed naval propriety.

Concerning his dealings with Ángel and Taco, Perroni concludes: "They were good hardworking people with open minds, but they were a bit old-fashioned in the way they did business." Perroni lost interest in Ángel's and Taco's lumber operations after the Mexican peso was devalued in 1976. Their debts were all in dollars and their earnings in pesos. The devaluation dealt a death blow to Ángel in years to come, a subject I'll bring up later. For now, I'll go back to what Perroni gleaned from Ángel:

"According to Ángel, old age took a toll on Lupe, and he lost his bearings. He'd get engaged to several women at once, then marry but not remember who the bride was. Ángel and Taco didn't know what to do about him. They could manage his businesses, but they couldn't control his engagements."

In 1974, by way of honoring his engagements, the aging

Don Lupe decides to marry Adelfa Pérez in Belize. He's already had six children with her: Gaspar and Jaime, Raúl and Amira, Bambi and Ricardo. He marries under English law with its community property clauses. Before long Adelfa gets a divorce and gains half of Don Lupe's assets in Belize, including the Eden Cinema and the proud family home, a paean to English colonial architecture in the Caribbean. It sits on a picturesque bend in the river that flows through the city of Belize. I remember the two-story wooden house well. It is painted white with a pitched red roof and delicately rhomboid latticework that lets the sea breeze filter in. You can see the water through the latticed windows because the house is on a bluff overlooking the mouth of the river from a height that blocks the teeming, chaotic and malodorous city from view. I remember the breeze in that house and the perfumed neck of a cousin who dances quite close to me during a family gathering in the summer of 1967.

The loss of the movie theater and the house in Belize is devastating to Ángel and Taco. When Don Lupe can't get a court in Belize to find in his favor, he goes to Mérida and looks up another of his women from another time. Her name is Flora Mayo. Born in Holbox in 1909, she's eighteen years Don Lupe's junior. Once upon a time the age difference mustn't have mattered, but when they get back together in late 1975, Don Lupe's eighty-four and Flora's sixty-six. In Ángel's opinion Don Lupe is out of his mind: he thinks he can restore order to a disorderly love life by marrying his old girlfriends. He asks Ángel for money to set up housekeeping with Flora in Mérida, and Ángel says no. As he tells Perroni, he thinks his father's gone mad, and the last thing he wants is a repeat of the episode with Adelfa Pérez in Belize. Don Lupe won`t take no for an answer. When he orders Ángel to do as he's told, Ángel turns him down in no uncertain terms and seizes full control of Casa Aguilar. Don Lupe's fortune passes to the hands of his

favorite son, and he can't get at it. Desperate and penniless, he
looks to Mexico City for help in the person of Héctor, the son
he cheated. In a sense, this is the moment Héctor has always
waited for, the moment when his father prefers him to Ángel.
The irony isn't lost on him. He wins Don Lupe's favor when
the old man has nothing to offer in return, when the losses
of affection and wealth are beyond remedy. Héctor hears Don
Lupe's plea at a time when there's nothing he can win in the
battle with his brother except a spot in their father's heart. He
decides to take Don Lupe into his house in Mexico City and
rekindle the war against Ángel with Don Lupe at his side. It's a
war that can't be won and whose only spoil is the affection of
the dying Don Lupe.

Don Lupe hasn't seen his son Héctor since 1964, the year
his wife, Juana Marrufo, died. What news he gets about Héctor
comes from his other sons, especially Omar, who still touches
base with him on trips to the city. Among their mutual friends
is Gastón Pérez, who represents Quintana Roo in the Chamber
of Deputies where Héctor is an aide. At the time the chamber
is controlled by the delegation from the state of Hidalgo whose
members are friends and clients of the woman Héctor lives
with, Nelly Mulley. She's the widow of a man named Fernández,
and her real name is Trinidad Reséndiz. When Héctor moves
in with her, he's forty-two and she's forty-four. When they
take Don Lupe in, she's sixty and he's fifty-eight. In the years
before I begin to write about her, I always think of Trinidad
as a woman much older than Héctor, a crone who snagged a
younger man. But the fact is that when they first get together
Trini is anything but a hag and Héctor is anything but youthful.
In telling this part of the story, I must describe the place where
Don Lupe takes refuge and admit to my heretofore negative
and twisted opinion of Trini.

Everything my research has uncovered about her tends to

be hostile and unflattering. There is, for example, the absurd story in an Oregon daily in 1957. It says the palm reader Nelly Mulley was stabbed in her office on Bucareli Street by an enraged client after she failed to predict a winning lottery number. Another paper teases Nelly because she seems to have overlooked the disappearance of money mailed to her. "The seer doesn't see she's been robbed," the paper says. Like many of her contemporaries, Nelly Mulley advertises her services as a "spiritual adviser" in the magazines and newspapers of different cities. She occasionally makes personal appearances in the cities where she advertises and gives an address where she can be seen. But her stock in trade is largely written advice requested and paid for by letter. The real focus of the story that questions her powers is a postal worker at the airport who's been extracting money from letters to Nelly. A headline in the September 29, 1949, edition of *El Nacional* says: "Fortuneteller Can't Foretell Her Misfortune." For six months, the story goes on, postal worker Alejandro Ariza has taken "one or two pesos" per letter from correspondence addressed to Nelly Mulley. At the time of his arrest Ariza has on him four dollars he'd yet to exchange (his monthly salary is 226 pesos). Although Ariza is charged with theft and breach of trust, he's released on bond.

Witches are targets of scorn in the newspapers and courts of the time. During her career Trini has prevailed in at least two lawsuits. The press may call her a "spiritual adviser," but in court she styles herself a "social adviser" after the authorities crack down on fortunetellers and put some of them behind bars. In a 1950 pleading, nine years before Héctor moves in with her at Bucareli 59, Trini states that she keeps an office under the *nom de guerre* of Nelly Mulley at that address. At Honduras 48, she gets mail sent to Zulema Osiris Gelo, echoing with scant variation the name of Nelly's late sister, the legendary Mexican seer Zulema Moraima Gelo. Tampering with letters to both addresses, and especially the latter, has nearly bankrupted her,

Trini says. In her petition for a restraining order she asks the judge to enjoin the postal service to cease interfering with mail to the named addresses and addressees, and the judge grants her request.

Nelly Mulley won a more richly nuanced stay in a finding dated June 14, 1948, five days after I turn two in the town called Chetumal where Emma and Héctor live. They have no way of knowing they'll have more children and another life, part of which is already gestating in the world where Nelly Mulley fights her legal battles. The criminal arm of the nation's highest tribunal, the *Suprema Corte de Justicia*, finds in Nelly's favor. The fraud charges for the exercise of her profession are permanently quashed, and thanks to her brains and initiative, Nelly doesn't have to go to jail. One of the justices on her panel, Luis Chico Georna, is absent when her case is heard, but the other four unanimously find that Nelly's accusers "cannot show criminal intent." "A person who believes in the occult arts may be mistaken," the justices explain, "but that does not necessarily mean that the person was duped. A finding of fraud requires a showing that a victim was deliberately misled. Without credible proof of criminal intent on the part of the defendant, it cannot be shown that the defendant acted fraudulently."

This finding appears in its entirety in the *Weekly Record of the Supreme Court of Justice* (fifth session, criminal division, Volume XCVII, page 398). In the years that follow, the treatment of seers in newspapers—or at least in the clippings I greedily assemble and prize—is not so even-handed. Seers are accused of hoodwinking the public, and their practices are frowned upon as "quackery." Calls for a government crackdown—a "social prophylaxis" to get rid of soothsayers—produce a groundswell of prosecutorial zeal against the band of swindlers whose practices are deemed a threat to the nation's health. *"Foreign magicians and sorcerers exploit the gullibility of a certain segment of the public,"* is the headline on the front page of *El*

Nacional on October 11, 1950. *El Nacional* is the government's official house organ. The story goes on to report that Internal Affairs Secretary Adolfo Ruiz Cortines has ordered Chief Inspector José T. Santillanes to look into the *"many complaints about foreigners living in our country who resort to age-old tricks of magic and clairvoyance to prey upon the unwary."* Adolfo Ruiz Cortines is a powerful Secretary of Internal Affairs. Within two years he'll be president of the republic. Upon investigation, the devious foreigners all turn out to be Mexicans and are nearly all female. They're stars in the constellation of spiritual advisers with the guile to give themselves exotic names and lure the desperate and the credulous to their lairs. In dark alleys and modest apartments they speak of times to come and play upon their clients' forebodings. They purge the qualms of the day and keep the shades of night at bay. Necromancers and palmists soothe the city's troubled souls. They satisfy the yearnings of thousands to feel less alone, to be consoled, to be protected against the whims of fate. This hunger for reassurance is insatiable, but it's also tempered by doubt. I cannot help wondering if its fears are real or imagined, and its pangs are eased by the reciprocal fantasies of these spiritual advisers, unchurched apostles, preachers of convenience, and purse snatchers from the occult whose telepathic names I have listed elsewhere and relish listing again: Disle Rally; Seleiman Karim; Ali Joromichel; Joselin Caponel; Zulema Moraima Gelo; Nelly Mulley…

On April 24, 1952, the public threats against fortunetellers erupt in a police action, a dragnet that makes the front page of *El Nacional*. The less worldly among them are caught off guard, proving they can't tell fortunes that affect them personally.

General Cleanup of Tarot Card Readers
and Undesirable Witches of All Sorts

The True Nature of Con Artists Unable to
Divine the Day of Their Own Arrest

The story continues on an inner page that includes a photomontage of the arrestees. The caption says: "Fortunately the authorities are aware of the need to stamp out the swarm of soothsayers and palmists in pockets of ignorance embedded in some social strata." The bylined author describes the figures in the composite photo. First, he identifies a woman with puffy cheeks and a gentle, seemingly forced smile. It's Disle Rally, the leading palm reader of her time who, the writer sneers, "can't even predict the detonation of an atomic bomb (because she doesn't read the papers)." There follows a group of women sunning themselves in the prison courtyard: card readers and fortunetellers who, the writer says, "know their business (gulling others)." The lower-left photo is "the façade of the house where Nelly Mulley, the 'doctor of souls', practiced," on a side street off Bucareli. It's the place where my father will take in Don Lupe and Flora Mayo in 1975, the discordant year of Don Lupe's and Ángel's falling out and of Héctor's reconciliation with his father.

The foregoing is all I've been able to gather about Nelly Mulley from the press. She's a patch of cloud that darkens part of the larger cloud that separates my life from Héctor's. As I say, the clippings paint a bleak picture of Héctor's world: a rickety stage for misadventures that sound like folktales and border on the picaresque. The scraps of history I get straight from Héctor don't do much to brighten the picture. There is, for example, the assortment of credentials Héctor has been careful to preserve as if to keep alive events that would otherwise disappear from his fading memory.

There's something strange about all Héctor's credentials and the stuttering way he tries to explain them. The oldest has a photo that shows how he looked at twenty-six. He's a handsome, swarthy animal with a full head of tightly curled hair and perfectly formed ears; he has a wide forehead, the neck of an athlete, sensual lips, a cleft chin, and precisely drawn eyebrows; his eyes look into the camera with a romantic stare. The photo is attached to a credential dating from May 27, 1944, that identifies him as a member of the First Volunteer Battalion of the Territory of Quintana Roo. Typed above it with a black and red ribbon is the following: PERMANENT MEDICAL RELEASE. The card states he belongs to a military unit in which he's not required to serve: now you see him, now you don't. Body and soul, he's a chip off the old block. Given the card's date of issue, I suppose it speaks to Mexico's rhetorical commitment to fight in World War Two on the side of the United States and its willingness to allow the United States to build an airport on the island of Cozumel. Cozumel, it seems, is crucial to the defense of the Caribbean. The streak of asphalt laid down for this purpose underlies the runway where planes land and take off today. From the date of issue, I also deduce the arrangements Héctor must make in order to marry Emma Camín less than a month and a half later. The urgencies of a later time have also left their mark on this document. Héctor wants its date of issue to read 1964 instead of 1944 and in the elegant hand he either imitated or inherited from his father, he's turned one of the fours into a six. Then he puts 1964 in the upper right corner. He does likewise in the lower right corner as if to settle a dispute over dates and stress that the changed date is the right one. I don't know what the altered numbers are all about although 1964 happens to be the year his mother, Juana Marrufo, died.

The next credential Héctor preserved is a thirty-day

provisional driver's permit issued by the government of the state of Tabasco on March 28, 1958. It's a trivial document except as it bears on this story: it's the only photo of Héctor at a key moment in his life. It was taken a year and a half before he vanished from my house and my life, and though he was riding high at the time, he knows he's headed for a fall. He has a streak of gray at the temples, he's put on weight, and he's wearing a foolish smile. His features have coarsened, his brow is no longer elegant, and the sultry stare of times past is gone from his eyes. He's become a bloated adult.

The next vestige to survive is a card dated July 4, 1962. It confers upon Héctor the rank of honorary captain in the police force of Laredo, Texas. The document seems as improbable as it is enigmatic. It bears the signature of David O. Gallagher, Chief of Police, and is good for four years. I suppose Chief Gallagher is something of a legend. News stories that come up in a Google search show he first took office in 1942, and by the time he signed the credential he'd held the job for twenty years. Google has nothing similar to say about Héctor Aguilar Marrufo. There's nothing to show why he obtained or needed the post of honorary captain in the Laredo, Texas, police. I have a few snippets that suggest he may have had his reasons but nothing definite.

What is there to say about his passport? It dates from July 10, 1983, when Héctor was sixty-six, two years older than I am as I write. The passport says he's five feet nine inches tall with brown skin, brown eyes and graying hair. But his eyes were always black, and black dye disguises the gray in his hair. His features have thickened, and he looks into the camera with the conventionally cheerful but frozen expression of a man unable to hide a dawning awareness or pained recognition of a misspent life. The passport says he's married, but there's nothing in the blanks for the bearer's name, surnames, and marital status to support this claim, and the spaces for information about the bearer's spouse are left blank. In this respect the passport is as virgin as it is in all other respects. The thirty-two additional pages show no departures from or returns to the country. Nor are there any entries regarding persons to be notified in case of accident; no name, no place of residence. He's a man with no references or proof of identity. My father in body and soul.

In the years he lives with Trini, Héctor does jobs of many kinds. He's an aide on the administrative staff of the Chamber of Deputies and secretary to two deputies from Trini's home state of Hidalgo in successive terms. He seeks import permits on behalf of singers, politicians, judges, and other bureaucratic fauna with similar needs. These tasks must have something to do with his unlikely possession of a credential making him an honorary police officer in Laredo, Texas. Though he mustn't be doing badly, he's not doing well enough to make up for the fortune he'd counted on. One evening as the dinner hour gets under way, Héctor notices a group of acquaintances from Chetumal sitting at a table near the back of a bar on Bucareli. He goes up to them and says: "Don't act as if you know me. Around here, I'm not the person you knew." He exudes an air of prosperity. At this table of well-fed diners he assumes the role of a generous and good-natured host.

The scene, as described to me long afterwards by an elderly Chetumal politician, conforms to my telepathic image of my father in those years. It reproduces with stunning similarity a scene I concoct for my friends and myself of a supposed encounter with Héctor. I picture him as my imagination wants him to be: a self-assured and relatively wealthy man who invites me to a luxurious meal at a popular bar on Bucareli. In flawless diction of my own creation, he explains what forced him to flee and why he remained silent for so long: "Unless it hurts to break away and hurts even more to stay away, there can be no coming back."

This scene that I concoct captures at least something of the life Héctor and Trini must have led from 1959 to 1975, the year Don Lupe moved in with them. Héctor himself will later offer me a disorganized account of his aspirations at the time. For a while he was in the good graces of the ultraconservatives who dominated the legislature, and he thought he could fashion a political career for himself. He even lets slip that at one point he dreamed of becoming governor of Quintana Roo. It was, I suppose, an illusion based on his links to the politician Javier Rojo Gómez, a client of Nelly Mulley/Trinidad Reséndiz and, like her, a native of Hidalgo. Rojo Gómez had been mayor of Mexico City. He once made the short list of possible presidential candidates, but he ended up as a popular governor of Quintana Roo in the days when the post was filled by presidential appointment rather than election.

In Héctor's later reminiscences about bit players in the political dramas of the time, the figure of Ferrer McGregor stands out. Ferrer McGregor was a minor celebrity in Mexico's political underworld. For years he was the federal district judge in Chetumal where he met and became friends with Héctor. Later he joins in the effort to cloak the violent events of 1968 in judicial respectability. He never questions the trumped up charges against student protesters jailed in the aftermath of the bloody uprising which preceded that year's Olympic Games in Mexico City. Ferrer McGregor committed every abuse a lower court judge could commit, and Héctor will recall watching him do it with no complaint. The friendship comes apart when the judge's carousing in the finest saloons and whorehouses of the time culminates in a two-day bender. Still drunk out of his mind and without a shred of prudence, he staggers into Héctor's office to show off a briefcase he received from the president's office. It has a red velvet lining and is stuffed with cash.

Héctor also recalls his dealings with a wildly popular

crooner whom I will call Antonio B. Together they tried and failed to finagle a permit to import prohibited merchandise into Mexico's closed economy. Getting foreign products into the country entails either smuggling or the pulling of strings, and the profits from marketing such items as cigars, Scotch whiskey, pork bellies, German cars, and Christmas trees could be huge. Among Héctor's assets there is no record of these efforts and no whiff of enrichment. Instead, the facts suggest that his dream of being his own boss and beholden to no one hobbles his efforts at entrepreneurship. Anyone can see that his fierce, arrogant and self-defeating quest for absolute independence is simply the obstinance of his father Don Lupe writ small.

I do know that his quest for independence leads Héctor to open an office that provides bookkeeping services to small businesses in the streets around Bucareli where he lives. It's a district of restaurants, hardware stores, dress shops, law offices, newsstands, and XEW, Mexico's largest radio station. One of the celebrities who come and go every day is the station's star announcer, and Héctor convinces him of the need to normalize his tangled accounts with the fiscal authorities. This attracts lesser taxpayers in financial trouble. He goes on to set up shop as a preparer of computerized payrolls for other businesses.

No sooner does Héctor receive his father's call for help, around Christmas 1975, than he travels to the city of Mérida where he finds Don Lupe living in what he describes as a state of "decadence and ruin." He has an acquaintance who works for *Mexicana de Aviación*, the national airline, arrange two tickets to fly his father and Flora Mayo to Mexico City. He moves the couple into the one extra bedroom in the apartment where he lives with Trini. In my mind's eye, the added occupants make for cramped quarters in a place consisting only of Héctor's room, the extra bedroom, a kitchen, a dining room, and the front sala where Nelly's clients tell her their woes. It's possible that Trini suspends her consultations with Nelly's followers in order to accommodate the formidable presence of her father-in-law in her tiny home. She's eager to help the man she lives with disengage from the shadow of his father. However, by February 1976, Don Lupe and Flora Mayo aren't just lodgers in their son's house; they have plans for the future.

It's a period, Héctor recalls, when he works from early morning until very late at night. The bathroom in his office has a shower, and at times he bathes there before work. At other times he doesn't get home until dawn the following day. This austere account of a period when he does nothing but sweat and slave omits details that others with him at the time are glad to fill in. Missing, for example, are the many attacks of depression and dissipation that cause him to repair in virtuous abstinence to restaurants, bars and saloons in the company of such dissolute friends as Ferrer McGregor or his brother Omar. In the aftermath of the fire that burnt down the Piedra de Plancha sawmill, Omar has broken with Ángel and, according to Héctor, has been welcomed in the latter's business of the time. The fact is that in the days when Don Lupe and Flora live with Héctor and Trini, Héctor always rises early enough to take up the Phillips electric razor with which he chisels the accreted stubble from his father's stony countenance. He's awed by the toughness of his father's beard. His solid rock of a father.

One day Omar comes to visit, and Don Lupe greets him with a smile while holding hands with Flora Mayo:

"I want you to know I'm going to marry this strapping girl."

Omar knows all about mad romances. He pretends to accept Don Lupe's announcement at face value, but he doubts it's more than a whim to be forgotten from one day to the next. When he exits the bedroom and repeats what he just heard to Héctor, he's told it's not a whim. It's a firm intention, a scheme which Héctor may have engineered and is willing to help make happen. Years later Héctor reconstructs the dispute that follows. Omar is outraged and indignant, Hèctor says; he can't abide a situation he's powerless to change.

"How can this be, *papá*?" Omar says to Don Lupe, stuttering as he always does when his emotions get the better of him. "Wha.. what makes you th.. think you can do such a th.. thing at your age?"

"So now you're going to scold me?" Don Lupe replies. "You're going to scold me because I'm getting married? Do I have to remind you of how many times you got married?"

"This is sh.. shameful," Omar says and slams the door as he stomps out of the apartment.

"Daddy Lupito was right," Héctor will say years later. His use of the double diminutive reflects the double bind that forever ties him to his father. "Omar was a libertine. He married four times. His first wife was a school teacher named Julia who ran him out of the house when he had friends in for drinks and made her wait on them. He used to hide his bottles of Old Parr in a chest of drawers, but Julia found them and smashed them on the floor of the patio. When Omar found they were missing, he demanded to know what happened and beat her up. That ended his first marriage, so he took up with a physical education teacher who'd been with every man in Chetumal. One day, when he got too drunk to know what he was doing and didn't bother to shut the window, he was seen naked and dancing the mambo with her in broad daylight. Then he came to Mexico City. I gave him a job in my office and tried to get a little work out of him, but one Monday he took the whole staff out drinking at La Mundial. La Mundial was a bar run by a Spaniard who was a good friend of mine. I went there myself because Judge Ferrer McGregor was a regular customer. I asked the judge if he'd happened to see my brother anywhere, and he said, 'Isn't that the bum in the back?' I check the back, and there's Omar with my staff. He's strumming a guitar and singing Jealousy. 'Back off, Tito,' he says, calling me Tito because it's short for Héctor. (His nickname is *"Cuino"* because that's what we used to call fat kids who ate a lot.) 'You can't tell anyone not to have a good time,' he says. 'I can tell you,' I say, 'Who the hell do you think you are anyway? You think you can rub the asses of the women who work for me and not worry about anyone but yourself and your next drink? You're like an animal in heat. Get out of my sight.' I told my employees to pick up their severance checks, and I signed a 4,000-peso check to Omar. 'Here's some money for you,' I told him, 'and don't let me see you around anymore.' And despite that he says, 'Could you let me have a 100-peso bill for a taxi?'"

After Omar's mad scene Don Lupe is more determined than ever, and he says to Héctor:

"What do you think about my wanting to marry this strapping girl?"

"Well," Héctor replies, "there's nothing to stop you. The death of my mom Juanita made you a widower, and you're divorced from Adelfa Pérez. How do you want to marry? In a civil ceremony of in the Church?"

"Either way," Don Lupe replies.

At this juncture Héctor´s fluctuating memory goes off on two different tangents. On one tangent Héctor sees a judge named Elvia, whom he describes as a friend with a sharp tongue.

"I'll do the ceremony for your dad. But you're the one who ought to be marrying me."

"No, my dear, I'm through getting married," Héctor tells her.

The judge is well prepared for such contingencies. She's performed lots of marriages. On request she can provide witnesses to sign the marriage documents and a trio to grace the occasion with music. At the appointed time, she gathers the required seals, stamps and paperwork, proceeds to the home of Trini and Héctor, and marries Don Lupe. In this version of events there's no mention of Trini or what she thinks of the way the judge practices law. Nor is there any mention of the judge's opinion of Trini or her lawyer's assessment of Héctor's marital status.

In the other version—offered by Héctor a few weeks later—he goes to a male friend who's a justice of the peace and says his aged father is desperate to marry.

"Fine," says the judge. "I won't even charge you."

"But I'll make it up to you," Héctor vows.

He gets three acquaintances from the branch bank where he does business to serve as witnesses. He buys food and drink for a suitable dinner and arranges for his father's third wedding. Instead of the signature of a judge named Elvia, the marriage documents are signed by an attorney in the registry of civil records named Benigno Jiménez. Among those signing the documents are three witnesses who really are identified as bank employees. The wedding takes place on Friday, February 6, 1975, under the laws that define the state of marriage. The law will soon turn out to have practical implications that matter far more than the unparalleled extravagance of newlyweds who marry so late in life.

The wedding marks an unexpectedly major turning point. According to Héctor, who never ceases to regard his father as one of a kind, Don Lupe's amatory prowess is unflagging. Florita Mayo seems both coquettish and exhausted when she says, "Héctor, honey, your dad's too much for me. He's insatiable. He won't let me sleep."

Héctor responds with a sly smile:

"Come on, Flora, you know how to handle him."

"Handle him?" Flora exclaims. "Honey, you don't know your father!"

In the days of his last honeymoon Don Lupe's gonads may be plenty active, but when the February chill sets in, it spawns a cough that makes him take to his bed. When the cough spreads to his lungs, it triggers a major bronchial crisis. On April 21, a wide-eyed Flora Mayo bursts from the bedroom where she cares for Don Lupe. In a faltering voice she says to Héctor:

"Get in there, honey. Your dad wants to speak to you."

Héctor goes to the bedroom and sees his father lying on his right side fighting for breath. Héctor tries to listen to the old man's chest. He seems to be asleep, but he isn't asleep. He raises a calloused hand and pats his son on the cheek. He draws him closer and kisses him. Héctor pulls back with a start.

It's the second time in his life that his father kisses him. The first time was years ago. Héctor's twelve, and he's just had his tonsils out. He's lying in a room next to the operating room with his throat on fire and his mouth full of blood. Don Lupe comes in to see him. Héctor pretends to sleep. Don Lupe thinks he really is asleep and kisses him. Héctor pretends to wake up. Don Lupe asks him how he feels. "Fine," Héctor replies. Don Lupe nods and leaves the room. He doesn't kiss him again until now, in the wee hours of April 22, 1976. when Don Lupe also looks as if he's sleeping though he's really awake. He draws Héctor close. He kisses him and after kissing him, says in a rasping voice:

"Forgive me, son."

Héctor will cleave to this scene and those words for the rest of his life. He'll replay them to me several times. The shades of meaning and significance change, but there's always a lump in his throat when he speaks of that time. It's a moment that mystifies Héctor, and he always ends by saying:

"I don't know why I'm supposed to forgive my father. I don't know what he thought I should forgive him for."

The following morning after a restless night, Don Lupe's condition stabilizes. He's unconscious, but the rattle of his breath is steady and rhythmic. By afternoon his fever gives way to a cold sweat. At nine in the evening he stops breathing, and Héctor holds his hand until the undertaker arrives. Héctor and Flora keep watch over the body at the Gayosso funeral parlor on Rosas Moreno.

Don Lupe dies intestate, and after his death a legal battle ensues. Flora Mayo invokes her recently acquired conjugal rights. Héctor, Omar and Perfecto invoke their rights of inheritance and file suit against Ángel. The brothers join Flora in claiming equal shares of Don Lupe's estate, but Ángel is able to drag the case out for six years during which the disputed assets slip through his fingers. First he uses the income and then the properties of Casa Aguilar to underwrite lumber ventures that go bad. The devaluation of the peso in 1976 leaves him buried in debts he's incurred in dollars while provisioning the lumber camps. He reimburses his creditors by selling one of the blocks the family owns in the center of town and begins borrowing from Efraín Angulo, who has become one of the city's more prosperous businessmen. Ángel makes a habit of using real estate to cover the costs of lumbering operations that don't pay off. First, he sells the building that houses the Juventino Rosas movie theater, then the block occupied by Casa Aguilar, and, finally, Don Lupe's own house on the lot next to the store. The devaluations of 1981 and 1982 take the last of the family's properties: the beautiful wooden house where Ángel and his family live. From its veranda on the second floor Héctor watches Emma Camín go by in 1938 and tells his cousin Licha: "If I jump from here, I'll land face down right there." By "there" he means the supple young haunches of Emma Camín as she traverses the sidewalk on her way to Hidalgo Park.

Ángel's wife has a special place in my memory for being the mother of César, a cousin my own age. César has the good sense to go to Efraín Angulo and ask him not to let Ángel have all the proceeds from mortgaging their house. Whatever Efraín gives Àngel, Marion says, will disappear into the bottomless pit of the lumber racket. Efraín agrees and deducts from the deal enough money to pay for the modest house in one of Chetumal's new subdivisions where Marion and Ángel spend the rest of their days. Héctor and his brothers will fight for years over their share of the assets Ángel has sold off to Efraín Angulo, the onetime helper in Casa Aguilar's bottling plant. When next I see Héctor, it's 1995, and he's still going on about the shady real estate deals which a fair trial would overturn. Justice would demand that the lost properties be returned to their legitimate owners and would indemnify the third-party purchasers who bought the properties in good faith. But by 1980 the case has fallen into judicial limbo, and the devaluation of 1982 speeds the handover of Casa Aguilar's assets to its creditors.

All this time the *Juanita* remains stuck in the mud of Chetumal Bay, and the parts of the craft that are still above water can be seen from the shore. There's no dearth of members or friends of Casa Aguilar who speak of its enduring presence as a miracle.

"Isn't it strange," they say, "that the *Juanita* has never sunk?"

Mexico City, 1991

It's four in the morning and I'm half naked with my back sticking to the tub in the bathroom of my house at Mexico 15. I'm hiding to avoid detection by my Aunt Luisa Camín. The bathroom's on the upper floor of the house. A few moments ago I heard Luisa open the door to the sewing room on the ground floor where she works nights with her sister Emma, my mother. Luisa's heard something upstairs and is determined to find out what. The noise she's heard is part of my skirmish with Micaela Haas, then our guest from Germany. Together we've been having a clandestine party. In the boarding house that's my home alcoholic beverages are forbidden as are parties in the guests' bedrooms, exactly what Micaela, I and other boarders have been having. Following the festivities, I ask Micaela to climb the stairs to the room on the top floor, wait until the coast is clear below, then come down to the second-floor vestibule where there's a sofa that will serve our purposes. For several minutes I lie back on the sofa, waiting for her in the dark. She descends in a blue cotton shift with the rubicund flesh of her long, shapely arms and legs on full display. She has a lovely mane of ginger hair and freckles from head to toe. I take off my shirt and fumble with her shift. She does and doesn't let me unbutton it, playfully taunting me for being more eager than deft. Her rebuffs lead to a gentle struggle that ends when I knock over the metal side table next to the sofa. A crash of biblical proportions rends the night and shatters the concentration of Luisa Camín. She flies from the sewing room, flips the light switch at the foot of the stairs, and demands to know what's going on.

Micaela rises from the sofa and flees to her room, as quiet as only a barefoot woman can be. I too am barefoot, and I'm wearing just a pair of briefs. I sleep in the garage on the ground floor, and with Luisa Camín standing in my way there's no way I can get there unseen. I remain on the couch hoping Luisa will forget about the noise and go back to her sewing. But Luisa doesn't forget about the noise and doesn't go back to her sewing. She doesn't give in to the fear that might freeze her in place waiting for the noise to be repeated. Fear is a stranger to Luisa Camín. She turns on the light on the ground floor and heads up the stairs while I slip into the large bathroom on the second floor with its tiled niche for the tub. I enter the bathroom on tiptoes, leave the door partly open, get in the tub, and close the plastic shower curtain while Luisa Camín is mounting the stairs. She doesn't turn on the upstairs ceiling light. The one on the wall suffices for her to see there's no one in the vestibule. I hear her footsteps as she rounds the sofa. I assume she's heard my footsteps since she goes straight to the bathroom where I'm hiding. She pushes the door fully open and takes two steps in with the light still off. Something tells her her inspection of the bathroom won't be complete unless she draws back the shower curtain. Her small hand smoothly slides it open, and there I am with my heart in my mouth, gasping for breath. She smothers her surprise upon seeing me and says: "You're quite a sight. Get out of there." I get out and face her, shivering in my underwear. She nods accusingly and whispers: "With the German chippie, right?" I nod helplessly and suppress a smile upon hearing Luisa Camín use such language. "They're all whores," she goes on; her words snuff out both my pride of conquest and the uninhibited radiance of German femininity as embodied in the brazenly pink person of Micaela. "They're no different from the Swedes and the French," Luisa adds. "And Gringas," she hisses, "and all that trash." She steps out of the bathroom and points to the clothes I left on the sofa. "Put your clothes on," she says. "If the guests see you like that, they'll be making fun of you for the rest of your life." She descends the stairs head down, saddened or, perhaps, exhausted because by then she's spent half the night working. I follow her down thinking about the corrective scourge that awaits me in the morning. But there's no correction, no scourge. Luisa doesn't say a word about Micaela nor does she ever again speak to me about the incident. I don't know if she says anything to her sister Emma. I'd bet she doesn't.

Luisa Camín's the father. She speaks in a voice that leaves no doubt as to who's boss. In my mind's eye I see her foreground smile against a backdrop of unsolved riddles, one more sign of her authority. In the imaginary biography I create for her she has depths she keeps to herself. She has the power to see through time and people. Luisa *knows*, and sooner or later you're absorbed into what she knows. Luisa also *chooses*; there's a wall around her; its gates open only from the inside and cannot be forced from without. People who remember her in Chetumal say she falls in love with the dresses she sells. She either makes them herself or culls them from catalogues, and she's reluctant to part with them. She acts as if she's giving customers a piece of her flesh. "Let them take what they like," her sister Emma scolds from behind the counter. But Luisa can't stop making comments that are a drag on sales. "This color doesn't suit you... That's not your size." It's a quirk to which her sister Emma is never fully resigned. "Luisa refuses to sell!" Her aversion to selling is a daily source of friction in their store at the corner of Avenida Héroes, the town's sweltering main street where Lebanese shopkeepers ply their wares. They're not like Luisa Camín who has a way of wrapping things in a mantle of belonging the minute she touches them.

She feeds her own chickens and thinks letting them eat out of her hand makes them happy. Once they enter the temple of her possessions, they're immune to being cooked and eaten. I especially remember her small but aristocratic hands as she shows a seamstress how to backstitch with fingers that once shuffled tarot cards. As a girl in Palma Soriano, she dismisses her way with the cards as entertainment until the day she sees death in the hand she dealt a neighbor. Two men are vying for her affections, the neighbor says, and they're both her relatives. She bursts into tears as she reveals her tragic plight: for the past two days her brother's been gripped by a fit of jealousy because her boyfriend wants to marry her. He's been stalking the boyfriend for a day and a half, pistol in hand. The fear-stricken boyfriend is holed up in his house while her brother is standing outside on the corner. Which means Luisa's cards have told, or are about to tell, the truth. "So death is in the air," Luisa intones and puts her thumb on the fatal card, possibly the king of spades. She takes all her predictions with a large grain of salt, but for the girl who hears this one it's no joke. "He's going to die, my brother's going to kill him," she sobs. Her brother is an enraged gunman, and the boyfriend is just a bookkeeper with bottle-thick glasses. The poor girl can't stop crying. Through the open window she hears her friends in the street shouting, "Santiesteban killed Perico!" It seems the myopic bookkeeper stepped out of his house with an old revolver, and her brother shot him in the eye. For Luisa Camín, the bookkeeper's death bespeaks the power of the cards, and she never touches them again. She goes to her teacher for help in solving the riddle she's become to herself. The teacher casts the cards and right away tells Luisa she cheated on her husband in a past life and will never know happiness with a man in this one. Her head fills with childhood memories she thought were long gone. As a child, for example, she was taken to live on her grandparents' farm in Llanes. Upon arrival at the family's ancestral home, she sees the ash tree that used to grow in the patio is gone. Nobody pays her any heed, but Luisa won't stop talking about the ash tree. Finally, her grandfather starts to wonder if there ever was an ash tree in the patio. An old man who lives nearby thinks he remembers one, but he can't recall what happened to it. The grandfather has a hose drawn to the spot where the tree supposedly grew and orders that the water be left on overnight. The next day the dead trunk of the ash tree can be seen deep in the mud. A short time later, in a game of hide and seek, Luisa and a cousin enter a barn where fruits from the orchards are stored. The floor of the barn is carpeted with a thick layer of onionskins, and at the back is a cupboard. As if knowing what she'll find, Luisa approaches the cupboard. She opens it, rummages through the dust and dead leaves, and brings out a small box. It's encased in a metal sheath but has lost its top. Inside, wrapped in graying canvas, is a porcelain Lady of the Pilar, Patroness of Spain, with a black smudge on her face as if in observance of Ash Wednesday. She has arms that move, one eye is missing, and she's wearing a black chasuble. The apparition knocks the cousin back on her heels, but Luisa stands her ground. Her child's fingers prod the fabric's darkest fold to expose the delicate purple of the vestment underneath the grime. Years later the yellowed fingers of an old woman tell me the tales of a lifetime. I watch them rub together as they once did over the chasuble, as a reader's might upon finding a dried flower hidden between the pages of a book. When she's a bit older Luisa learns that a woman, a countess, who once lived on her grandparents' farm died at the hands of a jealous husband. It all comes back to her when her teacher's cards say she'll never be happy with a man because in another life she made a man unhappy.

It's worth noting that on October, 21, 1939, the year after the Cuban sisters land in Othón P. Blanco, the 26-year-old Luisa

Camín, daughter of Manuel Camín, a construction worker, and Josefa Camín, a housewife, marries the Cuban-born José Gene, age 25. The groom is a Santiago de Cuba merchant whose father, Genaro Gehne, is a native of Gashar, Lebanon. The ceremony is a crowning achievement for José Gene who, though he regards Mexico as the end of the earth, nonetheless travels there in his quest to return to Cuba with Luisa by his side. As soon as the wedding is over, the couple sets out for the island. José has won the hand of his beloved, but not for long. Less than a year later Luisa escapes from her husband's house and is back in Payo Obispo, or Chetumal as the town is renamed in her absence. She gives three reasons, or at least she remembers three reasons, for her flight. First, Gene loses more at poker than he earns as a jeweler, and two, gem smugglers looking for Gene have been to their house. Luisa isn't about to wait for the police to come. The third reason is anatomical: "I'm not having a child with a nose like that." Luisa's excuse for leaving Gene's house in Havana is that she wants to visit her parents in Quintana Roo. She travels to Chetumal and does in fact move in with her parents. She never turns back. She files for divorce in Chetumal, and the divorce decree appears in the press of both Yucatán and Cuba. Gene awaits her return for months before flying to Chetumal on the assumption that his appearance will prove his concern for her, if not his love, and will make her change her mind. There comes a morning when Gene goes to the house on Othón P. Blanco where the recently wed Héctor and Emma live, and knocks on the door. It's opened by Héctor, who finds the Cuban jeweler standing before him in a white linen suit. Héctor's never met the man, but he knows who he is because Gene has announced his pending arrival in a letter. The word is out that he got off the morning flight from Mérida and checked in at the town's one hotel, The Coconut Tree. Luisa has the whole town on alert to keep Gene away from her in a state of induced limbo.

"Luisa's not here," Héctor tells Gene. "You better go back where you came from."

Gene refuses to go away. He'll only leave if Luisa herself tells him to, and he promises to be back to see her later on. Héctor steps out of the house and walks to police headquarters where he meets with Comandante José Muza, a Chetumal native of Lebanese descent whose broad shoulders and deliberate step leave no doubt that he's a man to be reckoned with. The foreigner they've all been waiting for has come to town, Héctor reports, and he needs to be sent back to where he came from. This is not news to José Muza because he disclosed it himself and is just waiting to be told what to do. He takes half a turn around town before finding the foreigner, his Lebanese compatriot from Santiago de Cuba, drinking a soda at The Coconut Tree. He doesn't put him in jail because he's a fellow Lebanese, but he does put him under guard in his hotel room. The next day he escorts him to the airfield and buckles him into one of the six seats on the twin-engine puddle jumper to Mérida. Gene licks the wounds of his Mexican humiliation before flying on to Cuba where he finds solace in other arms or maybe shoots himself. Nobody in these parts knows what happened to him. He never again sets foot in Chetumal, and Luisa never says another word about him.

I know in my heart that the very thought of marriage is repugnant to Luisa though I don't know if her horror of the conjugal state is inborn or acquired. Maybe José Gene is to blame, maybe it rose from the muck and mire of another life. In any case, it's of a piece with the views of Tolstoy and Lear who speak of life as nothing but "slavery, gluttony, and filth," proof that the rule of the gods ends at the waist. "From there down is the dark realm of the devil, the inferno, the burning sulphur pit that scalds, stinks and consumes."

All her life Luisa will be plagued by the premonitions of her childhood and adolescence. She compiles a list of her forebodings that really do come true, of secret visions and prophecies both trivial and terrifying. She remembers a light she's seen at the foot of her bed. A voice from the flame calls out to her, and she sees the gentle face of Jesus who tells her not to be afraid. Then, when two gunshots pierce the chirping of crickets in the Chetumal night, Luisa says to herself, "Pedro Pérez has been killed," and it so happens that two gunshots really did claim the life of Pedro Pérez. "If you give in to your father, he'll destroy you," she warns her brother-in-law Héctor, and Don Lupe really is Héctor's downfall. She foresees the death of Don Lupe as it really happens: "He'll die a broken man in the house of a stranger." He's buried and remains to this day in the family crypt of Trini, his son's second love. The night her nephew Juan José goes missing Luisa silently reneges on her vow to kill Ángel provided young Juan is found alive. When he's found, she deeply regrets a promise made in haste.

I repeat these things because they say something about Luisa Camín as she emerges from the depths of my memory. She was very much a presence in our lives, and though she didn't talk much about them, she was always on the lookout for invisible forces that might do our family harm. She was modest to a fault and hated to be touched. The barrier she built around her person was beyond penetration by passion, physical love, marriage, or even motherhood. Her experience of childbirth was strictly vicarious and came solely through conversation with her sister Emma. Luisa knew about the things she was determined not to learn, and she was intimately aware that what she shunned left her at the mercy of forces she might have been able to neutralize. If you refuse to wield the powers you have, you'll be hobbled by the powers you eschew. It's a saying familiar to historians and politicians, but I apply it to my musings about Luisa Camín. Relinquishing her powers made her vulnerable, and she was resigned to her fate. But she was no martyr; she had a purpose in life, and that was her saving grace.

On the morning of April 16, 1991, in the breakfast nook
of the house at Mexico 15, I sit Luisa and Emma Camín down
with a tape recorder and ask them to talk about their lives. Luisa
is 79 at the time, Emma's 71, and I'm 45. My daughter Rosario,
19, also asks to be present. I turn on the tape recorder and
explain my idea: to have them retell the stories they've told so
often in recent years over meals and as they go about their daily
lives. They hesitate at first, but soon they're off on a freeform
reminiscence. They butt in on each other constantly, adding
details, insisting on corrections, or debating conflicting versions
of the same or similar events. Some two hours later, they've
laid the groundwork for the family history which takes up half
this book. They've told how my grandfather Lupe appropriates
the business and the life of his son Héctor and how Héctor
vanishes in a fog from which he emerges thirty-six years later
as wounded and dazed as a shell-shocked soldier. In the weeks
that follow, during more sessions in the breakfast nook with
Rosario and me, the sisters indulge the endless questions with
which I interrupt the eloquent, meandering flow of their
narratives. Emma and Luisa tell the stories of their parents
and grandparents, of my paternal grandmother Juana Marrufo
and their mother Josefa as well as stories about themselves:
Luisa's childhood in Asturias; Emma's in Cuba; their respective
girlhoods in Camagüey. They describe their arrival in Chetumal,
a coastal town of eight sandy streets deep in Mexico's southeast
jungle. Chetumal and Cuba are the stages on which their stories
play out, the axes on which their memories turn. Passages
derived from their recollections fill the pages of this book
which in many ways is just a prolongation of the stories they
tell, an attempt on my part to make their words last since I lack
the means to extend their lives.

My own memory of Emma and Luisa is more sharply
drawn. It gathers up their jumbled recollections of Asturias,

Cuba and Chetumal, then brings them into focus at Mexico 15 where the two will live from 1959 on. When the man of the house disappears, they form an ironclad bond. Together they'll raise five children and mourn the deaths of their parents. In my mind's eye they're always together; I can't picture them any other way. They preside over Mexico 15 as a team. Luisa's hand is firm, and Emma's is gentle. Luisa lays down the law, and Emma grants the dispensations; one scolds, the other smiles; the father's stern, the mother's a pushover. Or so it seems. You may do battle with the father, but it's hard to disobey the mother. They're unsurpassed at the game of good cop/bad cop. Meanwhile, they sew to earn a living. They usually work at night, often with my younger brother Luis Miguel beside them. They put him down in the security of the sewing-room sofa and work until dawn. While working, they chat and drink Cuban coffee which, they insist, doesn't make it hard to sleep, it just keeps you more alert while awake. Their business leaves them no choice but to burn the midnight oil. There's always a wedding in the offing, and the bridal gown must be ready on time.

Luisa and Emma have sewn since the 1920s when they were girls in Camagüey. They copy designs from the fashion magazines that reach the city from Spain and Paris, and though the Camagüey of the time is rigidly Catholic and conservative, it's also snobbish and very pretentious. There's a ready market for the styles Luisa copies from magazines and turns into garments that can be worn and shown off. Soon she creates designs of her own. Emma proves as deft with a needle and thread as Luisa, and a day will come when my sister Emma inherits this dexterity. Years later, when Luisa and Emma open their store in Chetumal, the styles they sell are largely of their own design. The shop is supported by a bevy of seamstresses—"seam-sewers" as they're called in Chetumal—girls whose mothers want them to learn a skill and make some money. The sisters will do the same in the Polanco District of Mexico City, cutting out and assembling the elements of Luisa's creations. They've been sewing as long as they can remember but never under the kind of pressure they must endure in their early years at Mexico 15. In Héctor's absence it's up to them to pay tuition for private schools and bills from Chetumal while also fighting off delinquent debts that stem from the burglary of their store in Polanco. They fill the house with student boarders and the nights with sewing. They sew from need and hate doing it on a deadline. They can't stand the thought of having their daughters stuck in the same trade, and a time will come when they refuse to pass it on to their granddaughters. Still, they must derive some satisfaction from the way fabric is transformed in their hands. The intense concentration they focus on the intricacies of backstitching and shoulder pads, on pleating to enhance busts and streamline hips by draping innocent rags over vain bodies must afford them some solace. The clothes they make pass for designer fashions. Some clients show them the tags of famous couturiers and tell how they impress their friends by affixing them to bridal and baptismal gowns sewn by Luisa and Emma. Others confide the secret of their stylish wardrobes to friends who in turn come to the sisters for outfits of their own. To keep up with orders from new clients, they work more and stay up later.

The youthfulness of Emma and Luisa during those cloistered years amazes me. Their lives consist solely of sewing, raising a family, and running a boarding house. For some arcane reason, Luisa put an end to her love life years ago while she was still young and beautiful. The closest Luisa Camín comes to romance in all her years at Mexico 15 is a boarder from Yucatán nicknamed Slim. One day, when he'd had too much to drink, Slim makes a pass at Luisa. He gets his face slapped in return and is chased to his room. The next day he's thrown out of the house.

Emma's thirty-nine at the time. Just about any woman that age would now catch my eye, and I wonder about the passions that can still smolder for so long. I'm incapable of thinking of Emma in those terms, but I understand how many eyes would see in her the delights of an older woman. She never fell for anyone. I was wary of the favoritism she showed an engineer whom she treated with childlike deference. She was all smiles when he was around, and she was never so attentive to any other boarder. It's likely that the flames he kindled had more to do with my jealousy than embers burning in the heart of an older woman because, once Héctor was gone, there were no more men hanging around my mother, just my aunt who was the real man of the house.

Many men figure in my memories of Luisa and Emma in their kingdom at Mexico 15: students from the provinces, office workers, sales reps for pharmaceutical companies, interns in hospitals, travel agents, an ex-army officer from Guatemala, an Ecuadoran revolutionary, a judicial policeman, the engineer who made me jealous, relatives from Chetumal, three homosexuals, my friends from high school and college, fellow history majors, copy editors, literary journalists, and others in public life. Thoughts of so many different men always bring me back to the pair of matriarchs who hover over them all. Frictions of one kind or another were bound to be a fact of daily life in the house, but even the most demanding boarders left with warm memories of Emma, and of Luisa too, though she ran the place with military precision.

My sisters' closeness to each other is part of the greater picture my memory paints of the world of women overall, a world populated by women of all states and conditions. My sisters orbit slowly and happily around Emma and Luisa, not as dependents but as part of a planetary system of grandmothers and mothers-in-law, aunts, cousins, and sisters-in-law. The system extends in concentric circles to friends and acquaintances who remain close no matter how far away, to unforgettable guests who go on to become allies or rivals, and to the array of clients and daughters of clients whom Emma and Luisa have dressed since time immemorial. Last but not least are the nannies, servants, maids and cooks who over time become part of the family as godmothers, goddaughters, and bosom companions.

Some of these women have already played a part in this book. Others mustn't be left out.

The sisters' friendship with the beautiful, mild-mannered Aurora Pérez Schofield dates from their girlhoods in the primitive streets of Payo Obispo. Aurora appears at Mexico 15 with the regularity of a comet on her way to El Paso, Texas, where her daughter Mansky lives. She's bright-eyed and soft-spoken; for the sisters she's a breath of fresh air.

Señora Velasco is the ideal client, a mother whose sons are doctors and whose daughters are all married to politicians. Though her children reach adulthood, they succumb too soon to cancers that medicine and the law are powerless to cure.

In the course of her life, Doña Lala, the cook, has been blessed by the love of two men but no children. She's tall, plainspoken, and hardheaded as only women from the north can be. She's the exact opposite of the gentle Carmela, who cooks and does the dishes. Carmela is pencil-thin and doesn't like to say "no," which accounts for her five children with four different partners. Francisca, our other cook who over the years becomes family, has four children with four fathers. She's plump and cheerful and wouldn't hurt a fly.

Another regular visitor to Mexico 15 is Mercedes Alavés, the widow of the aforementioned Pedro Pérez, whose murder on a night when Chetumal was young stands out in the memories of Emma and Luisa. Mercedes shares the sisters' gift of gab, and the three of them can rummage through memories of times gone by from early afternoon to late evening. Of lesser duration but greater intensity are their colloquies with Guadalupe Rosas, mother of Tita, my first great heartthrob.

Angela, our cook in Chetumal, is foremost in the memories of my sisters, and in the same breath they often speak of her daughter, Valentina Mena, our nanny. Her skin is black, her eyes oriental, and because of the flare of her nose, we always call her *La Chata*. She frightens easily, and—as happens whenever I visit Chetumal—she bursts into tears at nearly anything. The minute I walk into her store she starts sobbing. Wiping her tears away, she invariably says: "You didn't tell me you were coming, darling." She looks much the same from year to year, and I always picture her behind the display cases that gave her two small stores in Chetumal the feel of museums as diminutive and modest as she is herself. After the hurricane she opens her first store on a stretch of sidewalk along Othón P. Blanco where the storm leveled all the houses. There La Chata dispenses candy, soft drinks, and such party items as sequins and costume jewelry. Years later she sets up shop in the front part of her old house in the Cerro district, whose gentle hills have now become a residential neighborhood near city hall. There she keeps a parrot, and as soon as anyone enters, it croaks "customer" in its inimitable shriek, then tells the customer, "Out of Cokes." Each time I visit Chetumal I stop to see La Chata if only for a minute. When she sees me, she always says, "You didn't tell me you were coming, darling," and starts to cry. In later years she looks after her husband, José Sosa, who is dying of diabetes as she is herself although her case is less advanced. Ever since we left Chetumal in 1955, my four siblings and I always get a telegram from La Chata on our birthdays. To me she's the platonic ideal of faith and love, its incarnation here on earth: the palpable, unconditional and unquestioning expression of pure love.

There's a witch called Angelita, a sister of the light whom Emma and Luisa call on to combat the malign influence of Nelly Mulley.

Among the guests who sometimes stay at Mexico 15 are Isela and Emma Valencia. In days long past, their father and mother, Inés and Amparo, were our godparents. They lived in Xkalac and used to bring strings of lobsters from the reef protecting the town's white sand shore to our house in Chetumal. I can still picture Amparo's head of brilliant white hair and hear her voice in the voices of her daughters repeating: "When things go wrong, the best remedy is a good conversation."

Last comes Ceci, the daughter of Francisca. I might well have put her first since she's the one who stays longest at Mexico 15. She grows up attending to Emma, and, as the lone occupant of the room where Emma once lived and where nothing ever changes, she looks after her to this day. Ceci's the sole custodian of the sacred cardboard boxes of Emma's letters and papers which I'll one day revisit as a historian in pursuit of the truth once I finish writing this book as a historian of my own emotions.

The quintessential public space at Mexico 15 is the front room on the ground-floor. It's dominated by a black and white Motorola television that's turned on and watched according to the differing tastes of boarders draped over the sofas by the stairwell and over the steps of the stairs. On Saturday nights I watch boxing. Sundays attract quorums for the midday soccer matches and the late-afternoon bullfights. During the week someone's sure to tune in a soap opera or the news. People may go in and out of the house or go up or down the stairs en route to the dining room or the door, but they all stop to check what's on television. Luisa is leery of idleness and technology, and she thinks watching tv is a waste of time, an alibi for sloth. "Having that trash on all the time makes people lazy," she says. Walking clients to or from the door, she glances at the black and white screen out the corner of one eye then the other. "My lord," she says incredulously. "Don't you get tired of watching that garbage?" She never has a good word for the medium, and her disgust comes to a head on a night in July 1969 when the whole house is transfixed. Boarders hang over the bannister on the stairs, squeeze onto the sofas on the ground floor, squat on their haunches, or sit on the bare granite floor watching astronauts land on the moon. It's Emma's month to be in Chetumal, and Luisa's at Mexico 15. From time to time she looks in on the unusually large gathering in front of the television and wonders what's going on.

"Can't anyone tell me what you're all looking at?" she demands. Her voice crashes over the rapt audience like a wave on the shore, and the voice of an announcer trembling with feigned emotion fills the room. "We're watching a man land on the moon," someone says.

"Someone's landing on the moon?" Luisa snickers. "Who says? You people will believe anything!"

"It's the moon landing, Doña Luisa. The astronauts have landed on the moon."

"The moon? The moon? For God's sake!" Luisa exclaims. "The Gringos are filming it in the desert of Sonora."

"On the moon, Doña Luisa."

"The moon the Gringos built to cast their spell over the rest of humanity," Doña Luisa asserts with an epic sneer. "The moon they stuck in your mouth with their fingers and you swallowed whole. Get out! You're as gullible as a bunch of old women."

She's immune to television to her dying day. In Luisa's opinion, no man ever set foot on the virgin moon.

Luisa and Emma spend the sixties of the past century within the confines of Mexico 15 raising their children, dealing with boarders, licking the wounds inflicted by their family. Near the end of the decade the country stumbles into the crisis that boils over in 1968 when the government and dissident university students reach a violent impasse. Meanwhile, Luisa and Emma begin to assume commitments that draw them apart from each other for the first time in fifteen years. What first separates them is the death of their father, Manuel Camín, whose dying wish obliges them to come to the aid of their brother Raúl in Chetumal. As his family grows, so do the debts he runs up mismanaging his store. Emma and Luisa spend the ten years after the demise of their father commuting between Mexico City and Chetumal. This new division of labor sends Emma on shopping trips to Miami, New Orleans and Panama to buy clothes and fabrics while Luisa cuts and sews garments for sale at Yolis, the shop next door to Raúl's grocery store. This arrangement works to the sisters' advantage since profits from the shop add to the income from Mexico 15 at a time when their children are finishing college, getting jobs, or going to graduate school; they're also getting married and moving on. Which is what I do in 1970. Juan José follows suit in 1974, Pilar in 1975, Emma in 1976, and Luis Miguel in 1982. By then we're all self-supporting and no longer a burden on the sisters whose mission is now accomplished.

Here I should point out that in the sixties, while they combine raising us with paying work, they also apply things they learned at home to the house where we live. They demand more from nieces than from nephews, they're stricter with the two sisters than with their three brothers. As I look back, I'm amazed at the tolerance and freedom granted me by Luisa and Emma. I can do just about as I please. I have no need to explain my comings and goings, to work or not work. I can party to my heart's content, disappear for days on end, and ignore their hope that I'd find a job as soon as I'm old enough to help keep the strapped household solvent. They only put their foot down when I get bored with college and threaten to drop out. Although I chose my major in a rush of idealism and against their advice, quitting is the one whim they're not about to put up with. They'd looked into the heart of Héctor, and I suppose they see in mine the same willingness to give up in the face of adversity and equate evasion with freedom rather than fear. They know that quitting is sure to lead to despondence, indolence, disillusion.

In the seventies, when work pulls them apart instead of together, the sisters watch a parade of grandchildren come into the world. Emma has a baby, my wife has three, Pilar has two, and Juan and Luis Miguel are each the fathers of three. At the end of the decade, when they feel they've met their commitments in Chetumal, the sisters withdraw to Mexico 15. They stop accepting male boarders and live at peace with their female guests. They're home again with few worries except the aches and pains that remind them they're growing old and the lukewarm affections of the children they raised and who are now too busy to be very sensitive to the feelings of elders who love them.

Here I reach a point of narrative breakdown. My memory is becalmed in a narrow space where the sisters are neither old nor young, and that's how I picture them for a very long time. The years seem to pass them by. They're always wearing the same simple clothes; they wear their hair the same way, and they wear the same bifocals. They have no illnesses that separate before from after. You don't see them grow shortsighted by looking at them, and you can´t see the cataracts that cloud their vision and eventually become inoperable. Tests show their bones are brittle with age, and there comes a time when their osteoporosis reaches a critical stage. They must watch their step when walking or climbing stairs, and the combination of failing eyesight and fragile bones makes these two sedentary women more sedentary than ever. It's all they can do to contend with the tree roots sticking out of the sidewalks around their house. Mexico City makes a specialty of crumbling, uneven sidewalks like the ones that confine Emma and Luisa to the few blocks they know well, but most people in this vibrant, neglected and perilous capital worry about other things.

I've said that after Héctor leaves in 1959, there are no men in their lives. That makes one less metric by which to establish dates. A friend of mine could pinpoint key dates in his life by remembering who his mother's lover was at a given time. By simply counting her marriages, he could estimate the dates of his adolescence, his first wedding, the birth of his third child, his mother's fiftieth birthday, and her appearance at the baptism of his first grandson on the arm of her latest surrogate husband. Like wines, lovers have their seasons. But this doesn't work with Emma and Luisa because their lives have no such markers. All of a sudden the fortyish sisters who endure my teenage years are the seventy-year-olds who spoil my children. Age sweeps over their bodies like the pale sun of an arctic summer. They live in the mist of evenings that never end and invisible nights that turn suddenly into days. To my eyes the sisters are embodied in the glow of a twilight that lasts for fifteen years, and I'm shocked when it's over. Their advanced age catches me by surprise. The two of them were always the same static age for me. Then one one day I looked at them and saw they were old.

I saw them a lot in those days, once a week, sometimes several days a week. To me it seemed as if age crept up on them in a slow, natural process that was never cause for alarm. New wrinkles were barely perceptible extensions of old ones. The changes from one week to the next were no more noticeable than the gradual thickening of their bodies or their occasional lapses of memory. They paused more often when speaking, but their speech was as colorful as ever. To me, the faces and bodies of the two elderly ladies—their skin, their features, their sprightly step around the house, their way with words— remained the same while the rest of us changed in ways that couldn't be ignored. We had children of our own and got new jobs while the sisters looked on from Mexico 15. They sewed less now, and their children and grandchildren visited more often. They presided over meals and celebrations without complaint, and though many things had fallen out of their lives, the pleasure they took upon opening their door to friends and family did not.

One day, with time at a standstill, Luisa makes Emma stop working on a dress after an epic battle with a client who comes to complain that that her dress isn't ready. Emma has been laid up with a bad cold aggravated by chronic allergies. When the congestion in her lungs doesn't abate, she falls behind on the dress she's agreed to make rather than say no to a first-time client. The woman, who came recommended by the friend of a friend, tries to sweet-talk her into doing a rush job on the dress which she just has to have for some unforgettable occasion. "She can go to hell," Luisa tells Emma. "She thinks she can get her way by flattering you." But Emma gives in, and a few hours later the cold lodges in her lungs. The next morning when the client calls to request a change in the outfit, Emma says she's come down with a cold. A few hours later the woman calls to see if Emma's too sick to finish the dress. The next day she wants to know: Is the dress going to be ready? The third day brings more of the same: Is Emma any better? Can she finish the dress? On the fourth day she comes to the house in person to see about Emma's health for herself and to see firsthand how the dress is progressing. Luisa meets her in the sewing room and explains that Emma is sick. The client goes into a song and dance about how urgent it is for Emma to finish the dress as promised. Luisa hears her out, then takes a deep breath.

She repeats that her sister is sick and unable to work. But how can that be, the client whines; how can she do this to *me*? "She can, and she will," Luisa snaps. "My sister's not doing any more sewing." "Your sister Emma's going to have to tell me that to my face," says the client. "You're hearing it from me, and that's that!" Luisa fumes. "I'm also telling you to get out, and don't come back unless you want to hear what I really think of you. What don't you understand about get the hell out of here?"

Luisa raises her arm and points furiously towards the front door. The client storms out in a burst of clattering heels. She doesn't come back. Her departure from Mexico 15 marks the day Emma and Luisa stop sewing for pay. Their D-Day.

More than to children and grandchildren, they commit themselves to what they like to do best: keeping each other company and reminiscing. They're prodigious tellers of stories about their world. Every Saturday when the family gathers for dinner, the table talk turns to stories the sisters tell after the meal. There are tales about Cuba or Chetumal, the shady doings of Don Lupe, anecdotes to illustrate the sayings of Manuel Camín, a choice bit of Cuban chicanery that leaves the whole table convulsed with laughter. They have stories and opinions about everything. In the days when my friends and I are enamored of the Cuban revolution, Emma says: "You're right, it's a country that needs a dictatorship, and a dictatorship of the proletariat will do." One afternoon when someone frets about who will and won't go to heaven, Luisa replies: "There's a heaven for everyone, for people and for dogs. There must even be a heaven for lions." Which leads her to compare her former husband to a Charlie Chaplin skit about a man who adores his wife when sober but beats her up whenever he comes home drunk. "Hit the creep with a stick the minute he comes through the door," Luisa tells the wife of an abusive spouse. "Don't let him hit you first." The husband is subsequently hospitalized with a blow from a log in the couple's fireplace. It's the last time he comes home drunk, and the two live happily ever after.

Her grandchildren harbor memories that tell a lot about the Luisa Camín of those years. She has secret rituals to be performed in very specific places after the family meal. For some these rites bring forth candy or a favorite dessert such as chocolate or toast she delicately sprinkles with sugar. Others get storybooks, puzzles or a surprise. For my daughter Rosario the memory of her Aunt Luisa evokes feelings of warmth and wellbeing. For my niece Ana Lucía, daughter of my sister Pilar, she's a human version of the jacaranda whose roots force their way above ground and which only blooms for a few splendorous days in March. My son Mateo sees her as the woman who lets him root through the sacred contents of drawers and closets his cousins are forbidden to open. When he's thirsty she lets him drink from the glass that sits by a candle in the small shrine of the sacred heart in her bedroom.

Luisa's bifocals enlarge her beautiful old woman's eyes as her small fingers flick a hem inside out to show me how it's made. It reminds me of how she once found the robe of a virgin under a patina of dust and how her fingers brushed aside the grime to reveal the fabric's original purple. She knew beforehand what her fingers were about to uncover, and the memory brings a smile to her face.

Many who know the sisters in those years see in them the profound serenity that comes with a sense of mission accomplished. Their struggles have ended, and they know deep down that they played the hand they were dealt, and, against all odds, they won. That's certainly the tone of the six recording sessions we began in April 1991. We do six sessions of two to three hours each, and the last one takes place on June 18, 1991.

Nothing seems to change as the sisters hold forth from the pinnacle of their years, but time doesn't stand still. Each dawn draws them a day closer to changes that are sure to come, a fact brought painfully to my attention just months after we finish recording. In September 1991, I'm invited to teach a one-semester course at Colombia University. October has barely begun when Ángeles returns from a week with me in New York and pays a visit to Mexico 15. Luisa Camín is bedridden with a backache thought to be sciatica. For several days she's also been bothered by stomach pains which she alleviates by eating beans and chili. She refuses to see a doctor, she knows what ails her and knows what to do about it. But the pain doesn't subside, it increases. Enrique Peña, the doctor of family friends, comes to see her, but Luisa won't let him near her. She's offended by the idea of lifting her clothes to be examined. Years before she suffered the worst humiliation of her life when we insisted on having her checked for cardiac arrhythmia and the doctor made her undress and put on an indecent green hospital gown. Unable to examine further, Peña confirms the sciatica as best he can by sight. The next day Luisa is groaning with pain. By the time she gets to the hospital she's in serious condition due to a possible mesenteric infarction that requires an operation. Exploratory surgery reveals a ruptured ulcer, a perforated intestine, and septicemia. In short order the operation becomes an emergency procedure to rid her digestive tract and intestinal lining of a raging infection. Luisa chokes. The doctor suggests a tracheotomy. My brothers and sisters ask the advice of the surgeon treating the abdominal infection, and he says: "If she were my mother, I'd do it." The siblings agree to the tracheotomy, and Luisa starts to breathe again. There follows a month in intensive care. Luisa is unable to eat or breathe on her own, but she's awake. I remember her expression of revulsion and horror as she struggles to understand her condition in choked silence. What's going on? What are they doing to me? In my head I translate the look on her face to: Get me out of here.

We fall into the hospital trap: you can't be cured, but you're not allowed to die. I arrange for Luisa's transfer to the intensive care unit of a public hospital when the bill from the private one becomes unpayable. She's taken to Hospital de la Raza on the north side of the city. The care is as good as at Hospital Inglés, but there, too, though she can't be cured, she's not let die. Hospital de la Raza is a world apart from the city we live in. At Hospital Inglés we can visit Luisa whenever we want; at Hospital de la Raza visiting hours are strictly limited. The only people she sees are the nurses and doctors who change her tubes and drips. In this hospital her family must come and go at visiting hours. No one can stay with her for long and talk to her the way Emma had at the old hospital. In November the family suffers another blow. Eduardo, the infant son of María Pía and Luis Miguel, was born with a shortened esophagus that must be surgically connected to his stomach. After many months' care Eduardo is able to begin the gluttonous life of a normal infant. Then one morning when he takes a sip of *atole*, the corn-based porridge sticks in his throat, and he stops breathing. The blood flow to his brain ceases in the few minutes it takes to get him to the hospital. He too is prevented from dying. His life is saved, and he's given back to his parents in a vegetative state that lasts until he dies.

We know Luisa isn't leaving the hospital. Her life is over though the devices measuring her vital signs say she's still alive. We decide to get her out of the hospital so she can die at home. We get the rooms on the ground floor of Mexico 15 ready for her. But on December 29, the day we set aside for the transfer, a nurse calls my brother Luis Miguel and says our aunt's life is over. When we get to the hospital, her room is empty, and the sheets have been stripped off the now bare mattress. An orderly says: The patient died early this morning. My nephew Eduardo also dies. He passes away on August 12, nine days after my mother's birthday.

Death takes a heavy toll in those months, pruning the

oldest and youngest branches from our family tree.

I've barely touched on an incident that stands out like no other in my memories of Luisa Camín. It's winter 1955, and we're staying at a country house with a blue swimming pool in the city of Cuautla. The place smells of a herbicide called Lindana which is used to get rid of the vermin that hide in its nooks and crannies. Lindana has a pungent dry odor, and though it's now outlawed worldwide, its glorious aroma has stayed with me since boyhood. It brings back the chill of the red tiles of the house in Cuautla when our feet first touch the floor in the morning. The sensation marks the start of days of idleness and freedom unlike any others in my life. The house in Cuautla is in a bucolic neighborhood of cobblestone streets and luxuriant jacarandas that I'm sure the city swallowed up long ago. A viaduct flanks the neighborhood on one side, and under its arches is a spring that feeds a quiet pond that spills over into a beautiful crystalline brook.

We spend our days in Cuautla outdoors the way we used to in Chetumal. We eat breakfast very early and stroll through empty streets lined with houses that only come to life on weekends when their owners are around. We have the run of the neighborhood, and Luisa shares the pleasures of our walkabouts. We soon develop a routine of picking the watercress by the spring and taking dips in the pond. We go back to the house for lunch, then dive into the swimming pool from which we only emerge in late afternoon with chattering teeth, purple lips and wrinkled fingers. Indoors we're greeted by the smell of Lindano followed by hot baths with soap and scrub brushes to rinse off the chlorine from the pool. Luisa makes sure we all have our pajamas on with the buttons buttoned and our hair dry. We sit down at the table by the radio and listen to the nightly soap operas. I especially remember the staccato lines of the one with Detective Lacroix and his secretary Margot: "Watch out, Carlos! Watch out!" "Fire, Margot, fire!" The soap operas make us drowsy, and we lapse into a silence broken only by the crickets of Cuautla, just like the ones in Chetumal. These are the times when we grow homesick and most feel the need to be cared for. Luisa brings us mugs of dense hot chocolate and oven-warmed rolls or bread with thick layers of butter and a generous sprinkling of sugar. We gorge ourselves on rolls that come out of the oven with crisp golden crusts and bread flavored with a sublime mix of sugar and salt. We use the bread to soak up every drop of liquid from our mugs, and our melancholy lifts without a trace. The feelings of sadness are gone, I only remember the fullness of evenings by the radio with Luisa's sugared bread and hot chocolate.

Mexico City, 1995

On August 3, 1995, Emma Camín turns seventy-five, and her children celebrate the occasion with the traditional family dinner. They also conspire to organize a surprise party that brings together people who, one by one, crossed Emma's path in the course of her life. Everyone except the guest of honor is apprised of the event which takes place in December. The invitees who keep the elaborate secret belong to what could be called Emma's extended family, some three hundred people of all ages beginning with her children, grandchildren, and multiple degrees of in-laws. In addition, there are longtime clients her own age, boarders, godchildren and parents of godchildren, hired help, friends and relatives from Chetumal, and several generations of her children's friends who at one time or another enjoyed Emma's hospitality.

A video registers Emma's surprise upon entering the ballroom where the party is held and preserves her spontaneous joy at what she sees. She goes from table to table with the ease of a veteran politician, smiling, speaking, kissing and hugging people she's surprised to see. Although she's elated now, she's been anything but pleased by an event in the immediate past. A few days ago she received disturbing news: after a thirty-year absence her husband Héctor has reappeared. This news was not unexpected, in a way she'd always known it was inevitable. In mealtime conversations she told her children: If your father comes to the door one day and asks for a glass of water, don't give it to him. That's exactly what happened a few days before her grand party: Héctor came and asked for a glass of water. But the door he knocked on wasn't Emma's; it was mine.

Héctor reappears on Friday, November 24, 1995, two weeks before the party. That Friday I arrive at the magazine *Nexos* and my assistant Martha Elba regards me with the look of a paramedic.

"Héctor Aguilar Marrufo called," she says.

"Who?"

"Your father. He told me he was your father."

"What else did he say?"

"That he was calling from a law office."

"What else?"

"That he's staying at a boarding house with no phone."

"If he calls again, put him through to me."

Martha puts calls through to me all day long. The last one comes at three in the afternoon when I'm about to leave. On the intercom she sounds like a paramedic:

"Héctor Aguilar Marrufo."

Instinctively I pick up the phone, letting the moment carry me in directions I can't anticipate. Foolishly, on the spur of the moment, I say:

"How are you?"

Those are the first words I speak to Héctor since the night I found him sobbing head in hand at the door of my house at *Avenida México, 15.* Thirty-one years after that scene Héctor has reappeared at the other end of a phone line. His first words are as awkward as my own:

"I haven't called you because four years ago I fell down."

He gasps, and after a pause, he continues:

"I had a fall, and I was an invalid. Then they burned the soles of my feet, and I'm just getting over it. That's why I hadn't called you."

His voice is weak and halting. He speaks, as I will later

learn, of an accident he suffered ten years ago while moving furniture out of his office after it was shaken to bits by the earthquake of 1985. I tell him I'm pleased to hear from him and would like to see him, if possible the following Monday after I return from the Guadalajara Book Fair which I'm attending the next day. He asks if I could see him right away. He lives in a rooming house called the *Posada Alcázar* at 24 Ramón Alcázar, room 104, in back of the ancient jai alai venue, *Frontón México*. His speech is hurried, giving me no time to remind myself it's an address I've been seeking for years. It surprises me to learn that reality comes with a whiff of telepathy. I'd always imagined him living in exactly that part of the city, in the streets surrounding the fronton and the Monument to the Revolution, a district of cheap hotels and unpainted buildings where drunks and pimps hang out.

I grant his wish. At eight that night I park by the Posada Alcázar under the only lighted entry on the street. I give my father's name to the woman who keeps watch on the door from behind the front desk, where a single lamp sheds just enough light to reveal her presence. The woman disappears wordlessly into the dark patio, and like a character in a bad Mexican movie from the fifties, I pace back and forth until, finally, I hear voices in the patio. A light flicks on, casting shadows that dance about in the gloom. It shines on the woman returning to her post at the front desk followed by a man with a limp and a flashlight that bounces up and down in his hand as he lurches across the patio. The hunchbacked man who at last steps into the light of the reception area has dyed black hair; his head sticks up from between his shoulders like the head of a turtle sticking out from its shell. His small eyes home in on me with a crazed stare. His face is covered with freckles, and time has reduced his eyebrows to irregular patches. His legs are bent, and his speech is halting. The decrepit person before me is no one I recognize. He in no way resembles the sturdy, affable and often ebullient man I remember. For a second I think he must be my father's chauffeur or an aide come to take me to him. But he's my father, the father who fits the surroundings of the city I've imagined him living in for so long, the city of ghosts to which I condemned him for leaving me. He's standing right in front of me after so many years, but the people who confront each other aren't really us. We're our images of each other, the father who went away and the son who once was, trying to reconnect in the shadows.

The ghost of my father has difficulty looking up at me from beneath his hump, and his wild little eyes can't keep still.

"I'm so glad to see you here. So glad."

He clutches my elbow and presses his head against my arm. His slurred words are spoken in the voice of a delirious old man.

"Just look at you. What a big, big boy you are."

His flashlight pushes back the darkness as he walks me towards the patio. The lodgers aren't supposed to waste energy, he explains. I let myself be led by the wobbling beam of the flashlight, still doubting that the man I'm with is really my father. This may all be a gigantic misunderstanding I think, but that doesn't keep me from following my doddering guide into the back of the rooming house. He stutters with indignation while he points out obstacles I might stumble over, and he complains that his pleas to turn on the lights fall on deaf ears. The flashlight dances to the fractured rhythms of his speech as we feel our way ahead, and I'm suddenly reminded of how my grandfather Camín grew frail and lost his eyesight in his final years. All at once the air is filled with an acute sense of loss, of a family ground down by the onslaught of age.

As we walk, he says, "I watched *'La China'* interview you on television."

I'm slow to grasp what he's talking about. He's referring to the writer María Luisa Mendoza—nicknamed *La China*—who interviewed me on Channel 11 ten years ago. Héctor speaks as if the interview happened yesterday, as if the years without seeing each other don't matter. I begin to understand that for him time is relative; it's not measured by the clock anymore.

The patio is a rectangle defined by paths of broken bricks and planters gone dry. Héctor's room is at the far side of the rectangle. He's left the door open, and even before I step inside I smell the dampness, the stale odor of its interior. The lime-based plaster on the walls is wrinkled and cracked. There's a large bed in the middle of the room, and in the middle of the bed is a hairless doll with a disconcerting stare. On a chest of drawers between the bed and the window two televisions perch one on top of the other. The larger one is on the bottom and appears to be out of order; a jumble of wires taped to the smaller one serves as an antenna. Empty cracker boxes, empty cans of powdered milk, and two boxes of straw-colored paper are stacked against the wall under the window. A manic sense of order prevails over these piles of trash: milk cans on milk cans, cracker boxes on cracker boxes. I take note of this hierarchy of empty containers. Héctor says:

"Everything's ready to go. It's all here."

He opens the armoire in front of the bed. I hadn't noticed it before because it was in back of me as I walked in. He takes out a bundle of file folders, puts them on the bed, and opens one. In it is a motion asking a court to find him the rightful owner of a building he claims is legally his.

"The building on Callao," he says.

By Callao he doesn't mean the Peruvian seaport, he means a street I never heard of in the Lindavista district of Mexico City.

"The case is settled," he says. "It's not the biggest one, but it's the one that's going to pay off first. Look..."

He hands me a document dated 1990, five years ago, with the address of a judge he's named as his agent. The address belongs to the law firm he called me from this morning. He spreads the contents of another file folder over the bed.

"This is the good one. Look."

He fumbles through the file with his arthritic fingers and fungus-infected nails.

"It's on the toll-free road to Cuernavaca, kilometer 16.5. It's a property I saw in 1970 when I was driving an Impala. I told the owner, Doña Chonita, 'I like your property. How much is it?' She told me, and I said, 'Fine. I'll pay in installments. Let's agree to a payment plan, and when we're through, you can give me the deed.' I made the payments, and she gave me the deed, but I didn't go back to see her or the property. Then, in 1981, on October 21, 1981, I happened to go by, and I saw houses being built, one-story condominiums. I found out that the engineer doing the construction also built houses without permits in the state of Guerrero. I had a lawyer notify him he was building on my land. When he ignored me I said, 'I'll file a lawsuit, and that'll cost you more in the long run.' That lawsuit has dragged on since 1981, but it's now moving ahead and is going to be settled. What happened is my desk fell on me, then my feet got burnt, and I've been stuck here for three years, since June 14, 1991, when I went to the Tepeyac hospital. What a bunch of bandits. I was doing fine. I had my business on Bucareli, and we were getting IBMs so we could do all our clients' accounts—inventories as well as payrolls—by computer. But then, on September 19, 1985, I lost everything in the earthquake."

"Didn't you have insurance?"

I know it's a foolish question before the words are out of my mouth. He isn't listening, and he isn't going to answer. I'm spellbound watching myself watch him from a distance so I can write it all down. Although I look him in the eye and listen carefully, I don't believe him, and I can't imagine anyone else will.

In 1985, he tells me, while going down the stairs, the

mahogany desk, which is one of the few items he can save from his office, lands on top of him. It fractures his spine and leaves him permanently bent over. He makes me run my hand down his spine.

"Go ahead, do it."

There's an inverted Y in his lower back. The twisted bones form an unnatural arch, but they don't hurt. Then he tells me how he wound up in Tepeyac hospital in 1991 with just a liter and a half of blood left in his body.

"A liter and a half. The doctors said my blood volume was two thirds below normal, that I was on the verge of coma. They gave me transfusions and I left. My stomach was like a sieve. I ate and ate, but I kept losing blood. I had just a liter and a half left when I got to the hospital."

He goes on to recount the saga of his feet. He burnt them while undergoing treatment by the quacks he calls "nutriologists." From a box under the window he pulls out a sheaf of drawings of the soles of the feet marked with the pressure points purportedly connected to different parts of the body.

"There's a pressure point leading from the feet to each part of the body," he says while showing me the drawings. "There's nothing you can't cure through your feet, which is where the nutriologists come in. They started squeezing my feet, then they applied heat to the sore parts. Everything was fine until they treated me with the embers from lit cigars and callused my feet. You can see my calluses."

He takes his shoes off to show me his feet. They're exceptionally long, narrow and well formed with toes that descend like organ pipes from long to short. They've never been mistreated or exposed to the elements. But the soles are grotesque. There are calluses around their backs and sides and all over the heels and arches.

"I've been taking care of my feet. I went to a chiropractor

named Camilo Gómez. He checked me over and said, 'You'll be better in a year if you do as I say.' He gave me the reflexor I'm using to get rid of the calluses. Camilo Gómez has an office in the Guerrero district. Twenty-five Violeta Street, Suite B.'"

I ask about the reflexor. He extracts a wooden dowel with rings on it from a box at the head of the bed. He's supposed to roll his foot over the reflexor to dissolve the calluses.

"An hour on one foot, then an hour on the other," he says. "So here I am getting over the calluses. That's what comes first right now. It's all I can do to walk until they get better. Just look what's happened to my big toes."

He points to the big toe of his right foot and lifts it with his hand. Its flexibility seems normal. He pushes it down and pulls it up.

"Now look at the other one," he says, meaning his left big toe. "See? The calluses underneath won't let it come back up. When I started using the Reflexor six months ago, my feet had no arches. They looked like tamales made out of calluses. They were just like duck feet, and I couldn't walk. Before I was laid up in bed in 1991, I was fine. I did forty-five pushups and an hour of calisthenics every day. So I'm going to get better again. I'll settle the lawsuits I'm telling you about and get back what I'm owed so I can pass it on to you, your brothers and sisters. Because I'm doing this for the five of you. That's what's kept me going all these years. But first I have to get over the calluses and get back on my feet. It's written that before I die everything must be ready for my children to inherit. Otherwise I'd already be dead. If I lived through brushes with death in the past, it's because it's written that there are things to be settled before they're passed on. The Callao building is good for 2.5 million old pesos. The land on the road to Cuernavaca is also ripe for settlement and will bring in plenty more. Then there are the matters left hanging in Chetumal and Belize that are worth even more. I need to go back and get what we're due from them."

He puts his socks on, sits down on the bed and asks:
"Is Doña Emma alive?"
"She is," I reply, "but Doña Luisa is dead."
"She died?"
"She did."

He receives this news with no word or sign of sorrow. He says Luisa didn't want me to be named Héctor after my father; she wanted me named Cirilo for the saint whose day I was born on. But he said no, and he won.

"I was right," he adds. "Imagine being on television and having the announcer say, 'Cirilo Aguilar'." Your grandpa Lupito would love to have seen you. He'd have said, 'He's not like the others, he's a real Aguilar.' Your grandpa Lupito would have seen it in your face."

I repeat the question I asked the last time I saw him: Does he have a wife and children?

"No wife, no children after I left the five of you. That was it."

He keeps talking while he puts his shoes on his wounded feet with the tenderness of a nurse.

"I have to go back to Chetumal," he says. "As soon as my calluses and my eyesight are better, I'm going to Chetumal. I'll tell you about my eyesight later, but I'm going to Chetumal to retrieve what's ours. My brother Ángel broke the law when he sold the corner where Casa Aguilar used to be. That lot was the community property of my dad Lupe and my mom Juanita, but her name's not on the bill of sale. In the eyes of the law the transaction was defective. I filed a complaint about it too, but I have to get better before I can follow up. The same thing happened in Belize. Doña Adelfa Pérez took over the Eden Cinema on the basis of her illegal marriage to your grandpa Lupito. The wedding was in a church only, but that's all she needed to get hold of your grandpa Lupe's assets in Belize. I'm getting them back, too. Do you remember your grandpa

Lupito? I have a picture of him right here."

He goes back to the armoire and gets out another collection of folders wrapped in multiple layers of crepe paper. The adhesive tape they're sealed with makes them resemble medical sutures. He spreads them over the bed and opens them just as carefully as he must have wrapped them untold years ago. In them are photos of the Aguilar family in its glory days. Photos of a close-knit family when the children were little. A photo of my grandmother Juana Marrufo when she was very young and looked at the camera with an engaging smile.

"Just look at my mom. She's so beautiful. And here's your Uncle Ángel who declared war on me. I always loved him, but he was jealous because Dad pampered me so much. And here's your Uncle Omar when he wore a necktie and was such a ladies' man. I need to go see him, I promised his little boy Eugenio a gift."

"My Uncle Omar is dead," I tell him.

He turns pale. The terrible news twists his face into a grimace of pain or chagrin. Later, I'll see that same look in his eyes when he remembers other things he lost or that made him happy. For the moment he's speechless with grief, with indignance and outrage at his inability to turn the clock back with a scowl. He isn't despondent for long, he can't let it take up too much of his time. Letting grief linger upsets the balance of his shrunken universe. It interrupts his stream of consciousness and takes his mind off his ailments; it undoes the rigorous logic of the world where he lives in memory, the world of his father and brothers in Chetumal, the lumber ventures, the lost kingdom he preserves in reams of paper, in photos and carefully kept stacks of empty boxes and cans.

The bald doll he has in the middle of his bed is a boy.

"His name is Hectorcito," he says. He picks it up and shows it to me in a tender rapture that brings tears to his eyes. "Look at this." He lifts a chain on the doll's chest with his fingers and holds it before my eyes. It's a tiny golden heart. "Look at the inscription."

Looking closely, I can read, "For my beloved son Héctor from his mom Juanita." But the date is illegible.

"Your grandma Juanita died in the afternoon," Héctor goes on. "I was sitting on a sofa, and I felt this blast of heat, an ill wind that swept through my chest and took my breath away. I sat on the sofa and said to myself: This is bad, it means death is on the way. And it came over me just when your grandma Juanita was dying in Chetumal. The next day I got a telegram. I have it right here."

He takes the telegram from one of the boxes where he keeps it together with other papers charting the days of his life. He puts it away and puts the doll back on his lap. He says:

"At bedtime I put my mom Juanita's medal around Hectorcito and put him on the shelf at the head of my bed. I wish him goodnight, and we fall asleep together."

I go into a bathroom that smells of old drains. On the floor by the door is an electric hot plate. Héctor explains that he uses it at night to cook rice and beans. He cuts ears of garlic into millimetrically precise slices with his jackknife and adds them to his clandestine meals as a nutritional supplement. The owners of the rooming house forbid hot plates and space heaters because they draw too much electricity. He can't afford to eat in nearby restaurants because they're too expensive. He knows the exact price of each brand of powdered milk and which box of rice is forty centavos cheaper than the others and tastes better. He's equally savvy about beans, sardines, and the different kinds of Maruchan instant soups. He ends his dissertation on the cost of rice, beans and restaurants by asking for money. That, he admits, is why he looked me up. He's behind on his rent and owes 350 pesos to the family that cleans the building and staffs the front desk.

"The room is 1,050 pesos, and I live on 1,500."

"So, you need 2,500 pesos a month?"

"No, 1,500. If you bring it to me by the morning of the sixteenth each month, I'll get by. And we'll keep an account. Because I`m just a bit short at the moment. It'll be a loan to tide me over until the things I told you about are settled and I can get by on my own."

With mixed emotions I set out to find an ATM machine. I`m puzzled and elated as I make my withdrawal. While I pocket the money I recapitulate the events of the night in my head:

My father—or what remains of the man who turns out to be my father—lives a dog's life, alone in a precariously obsessive world of daft routines and lawsuits. He's granted the law office that handles his affairs full powers of attorney. He's filed complaints and proofs of evidence against the engineer who usurped his land in Cuernavaca. The case he's pursuing in Chetumal is about the flawed sale of community property. In his world there's no real cause for concern, just fleeting reverses that come and go like dust in the wind. I tell myself this with a condescending smile, then it hits me: I'm crushed by how frail he is. I'd wanted to find him in control of his faculties and up to settling scores with me. As things now stand, there are no scores to settle.

I return from the imperfectly lighted streets to the perfect shadows of the rooming house. I leave him the 350 pesos I'd had on me plus the 1,500 I got from the ATM machine. It's November 1995, and the peso's at seven to the dollar. I put the bills in his hand, give him a hug, and assure him he doesn't have to see me out. Embracing him, I feel his need to get on with counting the money I gave him and that he's clutching in his hand. I make a strangely hurried departure as if I were fleeing the scene of a crime. After I leave, I'm overcome by a sense of unreality and begin to laugh aloud as if recalling a hilarious scene from a movie. I picture my father spreading the money I gave him on his bed to count it. He memorializes our transaction by entering the sum on one of his slips of paper, then he adds the date and how much he'll owe me when the loan comes due. When I get home, it strikes me that he never asked about my brothers and sisters or about his grandchildren.

There's something indecent about my father's reappearance. His weakness enervates me as much as it saddens me. It combines in a single picture all the things I fear about growing old. It makes me see myself in the worst possible light. I can pretend to be Aeneas carrying my father around on my shoulders, but there's nothing mythical or romantic about the void left by the years he was gone or the knowledge that I'm the one who will have to prop up what's left of him. I'd rather have come upon a cynical old man who could argue with me with his senses intact. But all that's left is the mad reappearance of someone I went to see more out of curiosity than love, the man I can't abandon now that I've seen him. His fate is now my fate.

I spend the weekend at the Guadalajara Book Fair nagged by the knowledge that I must face trial in the court of Emma Camín upon my return. I have to go see her and tell her I gave him the glass of water she told me not to. I broke the law she laid down: "He walked out on us, my son, and it will cost him dearly." I didn't make him pay.

On Monday I go to see her. She listens impatiently while I tell her about the unexpected phone call, the rooming house on Alcázar Street, the peeling walls, the piles of paper. She's more curious than annoyed, but her displeasure mounts as I go on with my story. She shakes her head in disapproval. My description of Héctor and the room where he lives saddens her. She finds the phantasmagoric folders and the tale of his burnt feet rather touching, but she has no sympathy with his plea for a loan. I can't tell if, on the whole, my story pains her more than it pleases her. The facts of Héctor's life tend to vindicate her own life, and after so many years she can see that he's ended up just as she thought he would. It's now clear that when Héctor chose the witch, he didn't just walk out on his wife and children, he also walked out on himself. I fall silent, and Emma asks what I'm going to do. I tell her that once I've seen him, I can't just abandon my father to his fate. He's nearly indigent, and he's incapable of facing up to himself or his indigence.

"I'm going to help him out," I say.

Emma looks down at the floor and takes a breath as deep as her chronic asthma will allow.

"I understand what you're doing," she says. "You're acting out of Christian charity and as a son. It speaks well of you. Your father knew where to turn. But I don't want him around here. Don't bring him to me."

Her harsh words come as a relief. They repeal the prohibition against denying him water provided I don't abuse this dispensation by begging my mother to forgive him. The lifting of the decree comes with a condition. I can help Héctor so long as he stays away from Emma. Bringing him to see her is out of the question.

Emma Camín's grand party is the following weekend. I know how much the party will boost her spirits, but she doesn't know it's about to happen. I pick her up Saturday on the pretext of joining my sisters at a new restaurant she's sure to like. She enters the ballroom and finds herself at a fiesta in her honor. I don't care for ballrooms or the family parties normally held in such places, and the idea of a party in a rented space doesn't come naturally to Emma Camín either. The image that best preserves her spirit for me is not an impersonal party space but a house with open doors, good food, and good friends, the proper place for the ritual of a tribe sharing its tent.

The ballroom we chose is a monument to bad taste:

artificial waterfalls, bright lights, garish flower arrangements, laminate floors, blue murals, gold lamps. An elegant nightmare of the sort dreamed up in the Navarte district of Mexico City. I have no idea how we came across it, but it's clear none of this matters. The décor in no way reduces the warmth of a celebration that is simply the extension of a family feast that happened long ago. No one understands this better than the guest of honor. Her surprise upon arriving is quickly replaced by the pleasure of hugs and kisses, exclamations of recognition, and tears of joy.

She enters the ballroom accompanied by her daughters Emma and Pilar, my brothers Luis Miguel and Juan José, and Ángeles and me. Ángeles is wearing red, and her beautiful hair bounces up and down when she speaks as if to sweep away the sadness of a day that began at the graveside of another Emma, her best friend and soulmate Emma Rizzo.

There's a video of the occasion, the work of my two brothers-in-law: Emma's husband, Miguel Marín, and Victor Guerrero, who's married to Pilar. The facial expressions captured on the video add up to a time capsule of surprising vitality. Emma is alert and full of energy at seventy-five, and when she appears, the orchestra greets her with a resounding fanfare. The electric piano is less musical than strident and the drummer more obstreperous than rhythmic, but the applause that fills the ballroom is absolutely genuine. After the fanfare a ragged succession of boleros serves as background music while an elated Doña Emma makes her way through the throng of admirers.

A table at the middle of the ballroom is decked out with flaming orange tablecloths. Around it are chairs with crisp white slipcovers. Emma sits framed by flower arrangements that pale by comparison to her radiance. Her children are seated on either side of her, and they, too, pale in her radiance.

The orchestra starts to play, the guests applaud, and, one

by one, Emma's sons invite her to dance. More partners wait in line as if they were her beaux and this was her fifteenth birthday.

When the dancing ends, the meal begins. Waiters serve the first course with the flare of gauchos on parade, and the musicians urge the diners to wave their napkins over their heads in the manner of spectators calling for the award of an ear to a bullfighter. To the tune of *When the Saints Go Marching In*, the waiters scurry among the tables with tureens of soup in one hand and ladles brandished like shoeshine cloths in the other.

At the end of the meal, Emma is prevailed upon to stand by a cake that looks like a pier. Colored icing at its center proclaims *Doña Emma 75 años*. The numbers are repeated in the form of two lit candles. Emma blows them out in one breath and in doing so drags the hem of her tailored jacket across the cake. The call goes up for her to say a few words before she cuts it.

"You're very kind," she says. "You're in my heart."

A fanfare brings forth a fresh round of cheers and applause. Emma is about to cut the cake when Ángeles, who's just come from the burial of her best friend, asks her to recite an epitaph cherished by the family, a stanza from the headstone of Dolores Rendón, a woman long remembered in Camagüey for her kindness and good works. Emma agrees as she always does when called upon for a story. She tells how a schoolmate died young and the whole class joined the procession that carried him to the cemetery. The teacher wanted to turn the tragedy into a teachable moment, so she led the children to the mausoleum where Dolores Rendón lay. Doña Emma takes a deep breath and repeats the verse on the headstone. Her index finger rises and falls like a metronome marking time for her words:

Here ended the journey / of Dolores Rendón. / Come, mortal, consider / what matters most. / Pride and pretense, / wealth and pleasure

/ are soon gone. / All that's left / are wrongs set right / and deeds done well.

Her speech ends with bravos and another fanfare. But she's not done yet. When the ovation subsides, she adds:

"Our teacher told us to memorize that, and I did. Now it's your turn to learn it."

The fiesta lasted for hours, and Emma lay awake all night savoring the occasion.

Many years later I replay the video of Emma Camín's party. I watch her go from one group to the next, sharing her joy. She sways as she walks like a ship plowing a high sea. I measure her years against those of her husband. If spouses are rivals, or end up as rivals in the Darwinian drift of their years, Emma has come out ahead, not in a race she chose but in one that chose her. The daughter of the dour Manuel Camín joined forces with the son of the imposing Don Lupe, and in the years that follow, she builds herself a world while Héctor lets his fall apart. Other people—Emma among them—are Héctor's undoing. He sees his life in the mirror held up to it by other people. All Héctor sees in the mirror is himself, a fantasy version of what he was or could have been. Emma is surrounded by friends and loved ones in her old age while Héctor has no one in his. Though he's taken a beating, he still has his health, and he's in no hurry to die. He's due to live for quite a while.

Mexico City, 1998

On September 19, 1985, a devastating earthquake strikes the heart of Mexico City, the old part where my father lives. Among the damaged buildings is the one on Bucareli Street where Héctor's office lies in ruins two blocks from the dead-end street where he still lives, where he's lived for years with his second wife Trini, and where he brought his father to die. That morning the blocks around Héctor's home and office are a wasteland of fire and devastation. At the time I work for *La Jornada,* a newspaper with offices in an old building on Balderas, a street parallel to Bucareli two blocks from where—as I now know—Héctor's office and the domicile he shares with Trini are located. I've always known he lives in this part of the city without knowing exactly where, and I've been coming to work at the paper every afternoon for a whole year. His imagined presence darkens the shadows in this shabby landscape of streets choked with sidewalk kiosks, saloons, old movie theaters, newspapers, and newsstands. I'm sure Héctor walks these cheerless streets. He's as remote and as nearby here as anywhere. I'm as likely to cross paths with him here as on a trip to the moon.

The quake shakes Ángeles and me out of bed at seven in the morning in a very different city. We live in one of twenty houses in a horizontal condominium on the edge of the San Jerónimo Lídice neighborhood at the foot of Mount Ajusco. All the houses in the condominium are two stories with an interior patio and parking for two cars. The tremor jolts us awake. Longtime residents of the city can date the events of their lives by remembering what they did in the periods between one quake and another. We live in a city of earthquakes and the threat of earthquakes. The one on September 19, 1985, reminds me of the one on July 28, 1957, the night when I learn Héctor is incapable of protecting me. It hits with the rude, lacerating snap of a quake that, instead of swaying, jerks you up and down. These are the ones that do the most damage in the old city, which is built over dry lake beds, depleted water tables, and vast subterranean grottos that collapse under the weight of the buildings above them and the immense force thrusting up from beneath them. Only part of the city is built over these empty grottos. Only part is damaged. The first damage reports we get come from the early morning news on the radio. We descend from the unscathed city where we live into the old city where hospitals and offices, schools and apartment blocks have all crumbled. We're dazed by the devastation we see on our way to the old city. We drive past one mountain of rubble after another. Pedestrians on street corners gape up at the fractured Roble Cinema, the gashes in the Hilton Hotel, the columns of smoke announcing the smoldering ruins to be seen in the city's main historic district. It's nine thirty in the morning. We're headed towards the offices of *La Jornada* where we hope to find a base of operations from which to gauge the damage. Wherever you look from the offices of the newspaper, fire and destruction evoke the oppressive certainty of people trapped in these ruins. Two blocks to the north on Avenida Juárez the quake has toppled the legendary Regis Hotel famed for its ornate baths, its bar, its political intrigues and venereal hijinks. A blaze fueled by ruptured gas lines consumes the hotel's remains from the inside out, and a plume of smoke and flame curls upwards from its bowels into the sky as the building caves in on itself. Avenida Juárez is closed to traffic. There's a dreamlike quality to the absence of cars on the enormous thoroughfare which is now the domain of pedestrians who walk among the ruins like tourists at an archaeological site. Ángeles and I are among the somnambulant browsers staggering about in the rubble. We sit down on a curb beside the avenue, exhausted by what we see but unable to take our eyes off the column of flames and smoke rising from the ruins of the Regis Hotel.

While Ángeles and I wander about and get lost in the smoke, the offices of Héctor's most recent business crumble in the building next to the daily *El Universal* on Bucareli. I suppose he assesses the damage to his office that same morning and realizes it's beyond repair. He curses his luck and goes back to brooding about how unfair life has been to him. He's sixty-eight years old and needs to start over. I don't know if he's overwhelmed or encouraged by the thought that his father was seventy when he, too, had to start over after his business was seized by the Cuban Revolution.

Up until the '85 earthquake, Héctor's situation isn't all that bad. He has a small but thriving business managing payrolls on his computer. He has some savings and a car. I think he has a girlfriend twenty years his junior (more about the girlfriend later). But the harm done by the earthquake is irreparable. The building where he rents an office is unusable, and the tenants must move out. In the days that follow Héctor sets himself to the task, and his zeal is his undoing. He's keeping an eye on the movers from his vantage point on a stairway landing when a desk falls on top of him and breaks his back. Though the benign fracture causes no pain, it puts an end to his working life. Bent over and unable to stand up straight, he becomes a solitary tenant in his own body. He lives on his savings for ten years, until the November morning in 1995 when he calls me to ask for help. The source of his savings is a mystery to me until, years later, I come across the small folder where Héctor's kept his most important papers. Among them are documents concerning the death of his partner Trini, known in my house as "The Witch."

Trinidad is born on May 6, 1915, in Huichapan, Hidalgo, and dies on March 3, 1980, in the apartment on Bucareli Street that she's shared with Héctor since 1959. According to the death certificate, she succumbs to liver failure after falling into a coma two weeks prior to her demise. She'd waged a six-month struggle with cirrhosis, and she dies in the same apartment where my grandfather Don Lupe died in 1959. He's buried in Trini's family crypt in the old French Cemetery. Trini gives Don Lupe her spot next to her mother, her father, and a sister who died in 1973.

A paper in the folder documents Trini's purchase of a two-year certificate of deposit from the National Bank of Mexico on May 30, 1978. The interest rate is twelve per cent, and it's signed by Trini and nobody else. She's still holding it at the time of her death. Héctor petitions to become the executor of her estate, and a court finds in his favor on April 13, 1982, two years after she's gone. On April 28 of the same year he signs a Bank of Mexico withdrawal slip for the balance of Trini's account which totals 1,428,667.67, about sixty thousand dollars at the then-current exchange rate. I don't know what Héctor does with the money. He may or may not shield it from the devaluation of September 1982 when the exchange rate soars from 26 pesos to 150 pesos to the dollar. This is the devaluation that ruins his brother Ángel in Chetumal by forcing him to sell off the remaining assets of Casa Aguilar.

To protect his savings, Héctor has to have done more than just cut his expenses as a now solitary consumer. These must be the years when he begins his descent into the state of urban hermit in which I find him. He survives an entire decade alone in a world of his own making while spending the remainder of Trini's assets on litigation. The only papers I have from his lawsuits are those concerning the building on Callao Street in the Lindavista district, the one he tells me is about to settle when I find him thirty-six years after he left Mexico 15. He's 78 at the time.

"He's like a character out of Beckett," Ángeles says when I describe my meeting with Héctor.

Somewhat inaccurately, I begin referring to him as Godot. I've spent my life waiting for him, and that's good enough for me to call him Godot. But he has the flaw of his reappearance, and that makes "Godot" a less than perfect fit. Calling him "dad" doesn't sound right, and "father" doesn't ring true either. He's not the young man who lives in my memory, nor is he the elderly parent I might have watched grow old as I grew up. He's a stranger whose reappearance I've waited for all my life: Godot but a flawed Godot for having reappeared. Who can he possibly be?

Our first outing is the Wednesday after our encounter of November 29. I invite him for a meal and arrive at his lodging at five minutes past three. The concierge, a Guatemalan woman named Irma, says he's been waiting for me in the reception area since noon. He takes my arm, limping as he walks. We reach the corner of the so-called Plaza of the Republic in the middle of which is the column where the Angel of the Revolution is perched. On the plaza a restaurant opportunistically named in homage to the women who fought alongside the men in the revolution has opened: La Soldadera. It's the only place Godot is able to suggest when I ask where he'd like to eat.

"I don't go out," he says. "I don't go to restaurants."

He remembers this one because it just opened. We stop by the door and peer inside. It looks elegant and empty. Godot prefers a prix fixe place minus the angel on the next block. He walks with his eyes on the sidewalk. He comes to an abrupt halt and picks up a nail. He inspects it closely, then shows it to me with childish glee.

"I pick up all sorts of things," he explains. "Screws, brackets, whatever I come across. I save them for the mechanics who took care of my Impala. I had a '74 Impala, then a '75. Then I got a '76. They took care of it for me."

He puts the screw in his coat pocket and clings to my arm as his eyes fill with tears.

During the meal he describes the wedding of Don Lupe—whom he calls Lupito—to Flora Mayo. In time I'll get used to these unexpected outbursts of memory and the tortured logic that goes with them.

He explains:

"Your grandmother Juanita was dead. In Belize he married Adelfa Pérez in a church and lived with her as man and wife, but that was no obstacle to a civil ceremony here in Mexico. On Saturday, February 6, 1976, Lupito and Flora got married. February went by, then March but not April. Daddy passed away in the night between April 20 and the morning of April 21st."

"How old was he?"

"Eighty-six."

"And Flora?"

"About seventy-five."

He goes on describe the crucial scene I spoke of earlier:

"The night of April 20, Florita called for me and said, 'Come in here, darling. Your daddy wants to speak to you.' I went into the bedroom and saw him lying on his side. He could hardly breathe. When I put my cheek on his face to listen to him breathe, he reached out his hand. He drew me closer and said, 'Forgive me.' Then he gave me a kiss. For the second time in my life."

"When did he give you the first one?"

"When I was little, when they took my tonsils out. They were infected, and he came to tell me they had to come out. 'There are two doctors in Mérida who can do it,' he said. 'One is crazy, but when it comes to tonsils he's the best, better than the one who's an all-around good man.' I asked him to take me to the crazy one, and he did. Afterwards, when I was lying in bed with a very sore throat, Lupito came to see me. I pretended to be asleep, and thinking I was asleep, he kissed me on the forehead. I turned over as if I were waking up. If he'd thought I was awake, he wouldn't have kissed me. He asked how I felt, and I moved my lips as if to say 'fine' because I couldn't talk. That was the other time my father kissed me."

He follows up with a non-sequitur:

"All these years my only thoughts have been for my children. I did it all for you. Once everything's straightened out, I want you to have it all."

The following week, when I take him out to eat again, I ask where he wants to go.

"Wherever you like."

I insist that he think of a place. He thinks of *Victor*, an eatery on Bucareli Street. It's across from his old office near the venerable Mexican radio station XEW. He hasn't been near there in twenty years.

On the way he shows me the building where his office used to be on Bucareli next to the El Colmenar grocery store. It's a gray building pockmarked by the corrosive brew of automobile and truck exhaust that permeates the street. He makes me stop to see if the newsstand on the corner still carries the same array of periodicals. The Victor's parking lot attendants embrace him like an old friend. They're not so young anymore, but, as he explains, "I left a lot of love in these streets."

Inside the restaurant he and a waiter named Gerardo recognize each other. He gazes nostalgically—I might almost say lustfully—at a waitress who is now an older woman.

"She was really good-looking when I used to come in here," Godot says. "You have no idea what a fine figure of a woman she was."

She hasn't lost the come-hither look that bespeaks a turbulent past.

Godot declines the glass of water served with the meal.

"There's cholera all over the place."

He tells me about his friendship with the singer I've called Antonio B. He went everywhere with Antonio except the parties the singer arranged to let the cabinet secretary whom I'll call Miguelito P. meet girls. Miguelito P. arranged the permits that let Antonio B. and Godot import such extravagant goods as pork bellies and Christmas trees.

Another friend, he says, was a judge named Ferrer McGregor who conducted mass sentencings of protesters in the 1968 student uprising and is known on the street as the Meat Grinder. The Meat Grinder's in the habit of starting fifteen-day, fifteen-thousand-peso benders in Godot's offices on Bucareli; he ends them in a whorehouse run by a madam named Teresa on Pachuca Street. One day the Meat Grinder invites Godot for a fling with a girl he highly recommends, a former favorite of the legendary singer Javier Solís. Godot declines.

"Spare me, dear friend," he tells the Meat Grinder. "I'll do whatever you want, but I'm not getting involved with any of those girls."

He takes a deep breath and swears, "I didn't have a woman. I had no children after I left you and your brothers and sisters. No other involvements."

On our third outing I take him to the *Rio Bravo* restaurant at the corner of Álvaro Obregón and Orizaba Streets. I've been going there since my student days at *Colegio de México*, when it was located two blocks away on Guanajuato Street. We receive a festive welcome from the owner. She's delighted to meet Godot and says it's kind of me to bring him in for a meal. Beto the piano player sings Mexican and Cuban boleros from the forties, old favorites such as *Nunca, Lágrimas negras,* and *Temor.*

"Doña Emma was such a wonderful dancer," Godot unexpectedly asserts, carried away by the music. "She danced beautifully."

We finish eating and leave the *Rio Bravo* to the strains of a Cuban love song. Godot can't walk upright, but his hips can still sway to the beat of the music. He lifts his arm and spins like an accomplished dancer. He draws a round of applause from a table of good-natured kids.

Upon returning to his room, he shows me a credential issued in 1962 by the Chief of Police in Laredo, Texas. It identifies him as an officer on that city's police force.

He speaks to me of his children—meaning us:

"You've been in my thoughts all this time. I've cried for you when I was alone. I don't know why I keep starting things. Something always gets in the way and won't let me finish."

"We worry about him," says the Guatemalan lady who's the concierge at Posada Alcázar. "Do keep coming to see him."

I visit him twice a week loaded down with food from the supermarket: cereal, juices, crackers, and the dry Maruchan soups he likes to rehydrate with boiling water. The day I bring him the first of the biweekly checks we've agreed upon his mood darkens, and he says to himself, "I've always worked. I don't deserve this."

He twirls a rubber band between his fingers as he speaks. The rubber band holds a packet of slips of paper together, and he twists it until it snaps. The slips of paper annotate whatever he does, his expenses, the dates when he takes his pills. He compares the number of pills he takes with the number left in the bottle. He takes notes on bags of chamomile tea. He flattens them out and uses them for his log of dates and doses.

He repeats himself:

"I don't know why I don't finish anything. When I start something, it goes well for a while, then, all of a sudden, it's gone."

Sitting down on the bed, I accidentally dislodge Hectorcito—the doll with the disturbing blue-eyed stare—from its spot in the middle of the headboard.

"Be careful with my son," he says. "He's been with me so long he's my grandson now."

He tells me the best room in the inn is vacant. It looks out on the street and has a small sitting room and kitchenette. I ask about having him moved, and Irma, the concierge, tells me that would be hard because the owner wouldn't be likely to agree. Godot is a difficult tenant who refuses to let anyone clean his room. I tell this to Godot and, without meaning to, unleash his formidable ability to feel offended. From that moment on, Irma ceases to be his ally and becomes his enemy. Godot withdraws deeper into himself, and his dealings with Irma turn hostile. The very idea of changing rooms becomes anathema to him. It stirs his wrath and puts him on a war footing. "I have a silver pistol that was made in Brazil. It fires hollow-tip bullets. Just let them try to get me out of here." He's certain beyond a doubt that they want to be rid of him.

Mention of the non-existent pistol brings to my mind the Laredo police credential, a document which I suspect has a dark and outlandish history: Officer Godot, trigger-happy cop.

He ends the year walled in from the outside world. In early January I have a talk with the woman who owns the place. She agrees that Irma's fears are not unfounded; Godot's presence has become a problem. Not only is the owner unwilling to rent him the better room, she'd rather I move him out of the one he has. Her wish is a self-fulfilling prophecy.

I tell Godot he has to move. I can feel the rage and humiliation welling silently up in him. He's not interested in another hotel or rooming house. He wants to live alone with no visitors, he wants nothing to do with anyone, he just wants to be by himself.

I take it for granted that he's able to live on his own, that his mind and body are equal to the demands of self-sufficiency. I set out to find him an apartment. For two days I walk the streets and scan classified ads in the newspaper. I focus my search on the parts of the city that would feel familiar to Godot, barrios like the one he's lived in for so many years, places where he might settle in with his memories and not too many changes of habit. I see close up the ruthless stratification that the laws of supply and demand impose on an ugly, unglamorous city. The available quarters range from pigsties to over-priced garçonnières. Beyond the façades and prices lies an odd world of patronizing doormen, peculiar neighbors, shifty tenants, and deceitful landlords. Though I'm looking for a place to rent, a for-sale sign on Bucareli catches my eye. The sign hangs on the imposing wrought-iron grillwork of a three-story apartment house dating from the late nineteenth century, the sort of dwelling coveted by the francophile elites of the Porfirio Díaz era a century ago. It's one of the many decaying structures that once exuded an air of Parisian elegance along the verdant edge of the old city. Four bachelors—all members of the Fernández family—live in the apartment that's for sale: the grandfather, the father, and two sons in their forties. To me they look like Godot's spiritual twins shut up in a sumptuous ruin with a rusting cage elevator, worn rugs with the pads showing, black baseboards yellowing with age, hallways with broken windows and burnt-out light bulbs that no one's bothered to change.

When I knock on their door at one in the afternoon, the Fernández men are watching television in their bathrobes and pajamas. They come and go from the kitchen with dirty plates and boxes of crackers which they eat standing up or sitting on the crumbs. The apartment has four large bedrooms, a big dining room, and a living room where myriad styles of furniture have piled up according to the caprices of old age and neglect. It must have taken generations for the Fernández family to acquire so much junk. Its bachelor remnants live on in the forlorn hope of selling this cavernous apartment, the last jewel in the family crown. Leaving this once handsome neighborhood, I think of Godot, and a line from Marco Antonio Montes de Oca comes back to me: "Strictly speaking, we might all be ghosts sooner or later."

On the third day of my search I come across a ground-floor apartment in a three-story building on Tehuantepec Street in the Roma district. It has a bedroom, a bath, a small sala, and a half kitchen plus rooftop quarters for a maid. Its windows look out on an interior patio at the bottom of an airshaft that supplies a modicum of light to all the apartments in the building. The district meets with Godot's approval as well as mine. It's not far from Medellín Street where I grew up. Tehuantepec is a quiet street that preserves a bit of soul from days past when single-story houses with low walls and a tinge of art deco were in fashion. Houses from a time when people were less frightened.

I take Godot to see the place, sweetening the pill of his having to move by telling him that, like Bajío Street, Tehuantepec comes to an end at the gates of the French Cemetery where his father Lupe is buried. "Can I walk there from here?" You can. "How many blocks?" Seven. He thinks he'll walk the seven blocks to Lupito's grave every day. I think so, too. When he lived on Bucareli, he tells me, he could run all the way to the French Cemetery on Cuauhtémoc Avenue, the continuation of Bucareli. Cuauhtémoc separates Roma's quiet streets from the squatters' settlement in the illegal district of Buenos Aires. He ran both ways, he says: fourteen blocks to the cemetery and fourteen back. He could do fifty sit-ups. His memories brighten the prospect of moving. "I know my way around here," Godot says. "I used to come here in one of the four cars I had. I'd turn on Viaducto and come down Monterrey." The apartment on Tehuantepec is also near the office of Mr. Guerrero, the lawyer who handles his multiple lawsuits. I drive him through the rundown streets of the district in my car, and though the area is shabbier than it used to be, it's still familiar to him.

"Here on Manzanillo Street is where the lawyer Pérez Wachimar used to live," he says. "I wonder how he's getting on. He drank a lot."

The lawyer in question is Federico Pérez Gomez, the husband of my mother's friend and namesake Emma Wadgymar (Her name sounds like Wachimar.). They lived at Manzanillo 67, and when we arrived from Chetumal, we spent several weeks in their house prior to renting an apartment for ourselves on Medellín. Neither address is far from where we are now, and it's just a few blocks more to the house my mother took us to see and once dreamed of buying on Tlacotalpan. While driving Godot through these streets, it occurs to me that for us Roma is more than a neighborhood. It's a hotbed of family secrets, the locus of our identity and our first big-city dreams, a place we can't help coming back to.

The house where Federico Pérez Gómez lived is gone. It was torn down and replaced by a building that takes up the entire lot and looks like a bunker. Behind its faceless exterior and barred windows are laboratories of some sort. Federico Pérez Gómez died more than ten years ago. His older son Federico and his younger son Fernando are also dead. Emma Wadgymar, whom I recently saw at Doña Emma's surprise party, suffers from Alzheimer's disease.

I take advantage of Godot's situational euphoria to win his approval of the apartment and the area. Then I exploit the modest perk of having an office by getting someone else to prepare the rental agreement for Godot's new home. The move creates a symmetry that's both obvious and comforting to Godot: I'm coming to his rescue just as he came to Lupito's. Rescuing Godot appeals to my vanity; in a way it's liberating. Finding the real Godot dispels the myth of the imaginary

Godot whose absence has been my lifelong torment. Héctor is no longer lost in fog and steeped in melancholy. He exists within the parameters of his reappearance: the rented apartment; meals; money; the simple fact of his presence; his soliloquies; his hangups; the hoary countenance I find so compelling; the battles he fights with his ghosts. And, at bottom, beneath his mad obsessions, the leftover charm of a once charming man.

I don't keep a diary now, but I did when Godot reappeared. I thought my recollections were quite accurate, but the diary entries expose the encyclopedic scope of what I forgot. I proceed from here according to events recorded on the days they happened. This explains the abundance of detail and precision in the dialogues that follow.

It's Godot's second Sunday in his new home, the apartment on Tehuantepec. Ángeles and I set out on a blitzkrieg shopping spree for furniture: a bed, a living-room suite, a refrigerator, a television, bed sheets, pots and pans. We get the electricity turned on and order a telephone. My office takes care of the rent and utilities. Every two weeks I give Godot cash in the amount agreed upon. Every third day I take him groceries or have them sent from the supermarket. Every third day Tonya, our cook for life, goes by to prepare meals and clean. Though she's stopped working, she agrees to help look after Godot.

I phone Godot almost every day to check on how he's doing. I visit whenever I can and on Sundays without fail. On Sunday, February 9, we watch a soccer match. At least I do. He spends the first half showing me diagrams of pressure points on the feet where aches and pains elsewhere in the body may be alleviated through acupuncture. He leafs through a manual that tells where to apply pressure to different parts of the body with the thumb and forefinger in order to relieve insomnia (earlobe), sexual impotence (the deep muscle of the calf), colds (cheek), and menstrual irregularity (the middle of the forehead).

I've brought him clothes: underwear, which he hasn't used for ages; long-sleeve undershirts he can wear under his regular shirt to ward off the cold. It's winter, and the apartment doesn't get much sun. I take the clothes to his twilit bedroom with its closed windows and drawn blinds that keep out what little sun might otherwise shine in. A damp odor affronts my nostrils, something I'd mentioned to him a day earlier; he's left the vent partially open in deference to me and points out that the air quality is better now. He's also hung the bathroom air freshener on the bedroom wall. But the damp smell hasn't abated. It emanates from his old clothes. His confinement. I see he's reproduced the moat around his bed with chairs and shelves of cereal, medicines, cookie tins. Ritual objects that protect his cloister, that form a magic circle around him, the Maginot Line of his solitude.

He's happy, he says. He's sleeping better by night and eating better by day. He needs to eat less every day.

"I'm not so anxious. I've settled down. I'm becoming more open."

He's getting back on his feet. He shows me that the abductor muscle in his left foot doesn't work, which is why he can't raise his big toe, which is why he shuffles when he walks. He doesn't have the strength to pick up his foot.

During the second half of the soccer match, he asks:

"You didn't chase skirts the way Lupito did, did you? Women were your grandpa Lupito's downfall. He never got over them. When he was dying, Flora Mayo called me 'Darling.' That's how she talked, she was from Corozal. 'Darling, your dad's too much for me, darling. He wants to screw and screw all night. I'm not up to it anymore. What can I do?' Dad loved the women. At twenty-eight my mother, Juana Escolástica Marrufo Coral, gave up on sex of any kind. She said sex gave her epilepsy. You never met your grandma Juanita, did you?"

"Yes, I did."

"In Chetumal I kept my mom company every night from six to ten. She liked to watch the people leaving the movie theater. She'd pinch my pant leg, and it was as if she were pinching my skin. And she'd scold me, 'Just you behave yourself!' I adored my mom."

"And did you behave yourself?"

"I certainly did."

"Like Lupito?"

"Lupito was a ladies' man. The girls in Belize used to fight over him. He was very strong and very handsome, and, on top of that, he was very rich. He could have any girl he wanted. And he idolized his mom, Natalia. You can't imagine how that affected me. Your grandma Juanita was pregnant with me when Doña Natalia announced she was sick. She went from bad to worse while I was on the way. My grandmother died on October fifth at four in the morning, and I was born at two-thirty that very same morning. My father spent the day of my birth mourning the death of his mother, and that coincidence cast a shadow over my whole life. In our family, October 5 was a day of mourning, and I never got any presents. On my birthday your grandma Juanita set up an altar in memory of her mother-in-law. Shortly after I turned thirteen my dad Lupito gave me a bicycle. 'Go to the store,' he told me. 'There's something there for you.' It was a beautiful bicycle, and I was in awe at the sight of it. I asked Antonino Sangri to take care of my bike. Then, one day, Antonino came to me and said, 'Even if it makes you mad, I have to tell you your brother Ángel came and took your bicycle. Just look at how he brought it back.' It was covered with mud. 'Tell Ángel he can keep it,' I said. A few days later, when my father saw Ángel riding it, he said, 'I saw Ángel on your bicycle. What happened?' I told him, but he never did anything about it. Lupito loved me a lot, but he had a soft spot for Ángel. I tried hard to please my dad, but Ángel was the oldest, and he always got his way. At least that's how it seemed to me. When he was in Chetumal, Lupe used to go to the dock in the morning for fish. I'd wake up very early and stand by the door. 'What are you doing here?' he'd ask, and I'd say, 'Waiting for you.' I could never say 'dad' to my father, and I always said usted, never *tu*."

"What did Ángel call him?"

"I don't know, but I always said *usted*. Then he'd say, 'Come on, let's go.' He'd take my hand, and we'd set out for the dock. We'd walk by the barracks, and the soldiers would all come to attention. It frightened me to see the soldiers with their rifles, and your grandpa would pick me up and carry me. At the dock your godfather Inés Valencia would hold out a string of red snapper. 'The best of the catch, Don Lupe.' And we'd take home the best of the catch. That's the way it was with your grandpa Lupito."

Sundays I visit Godot. Usually our conversations are carried on while we watch a soccer match. Which is to say, we talk without looking at each other. Speaking in asides lets us bare our souls with no outward sign of intimacy. In true masculine fashion.

One Sunday the conversation begins with a question:

"Why would my dad Lupito ask me to forgive him just before he died?"

"I don't know. Did he want you to forgive him for something in particular?"

"I don't know. It puzzles me."

"That's a puzzle for you and me to solve," I say.

On another day he says:

"When he got sick and I went to get him in Mérida, he was in very bad shape, he seemed all worn out."

"What wore him out?"

"Sex. Sex is what got him. I put him and Flora Mayo in a bedroom of my apartment on Bucareli. Every morning at six I gave Lupito a shave before going to my office and getting down to work. I worked very hard."

"You shaved him everyday?"

"With a Phillips electric razor. It broke because Lupito's beard was so tough. I looked in on him every day until the morning Flora Mayo called me. I went to the bedroom and saw him lying there. He lifted his hand and gestured for me to come closer. Not once but twice. I said, 'What is it you want?' I said, using *usted* as usual. I could never break the habit. When I got close to him, he kissed me on one cheek and then the other. And he said; 'Forgive me, Héctor.'"

"I'll ask you again, what did he want you to forgive him for?"

"I don't know. Nothing. He didn't need my forgiveness for a single thing."

Another day:

"The day after Hurricane Janet I flew to Chetumal from Belize in the plane of company X. I'd been working for Richardson, its competitor, but Mister X said: 'Come on. You're a friend, and I'll take you.' From the air I saw how the jungle had been flattened. In Santa Elena drums of gasoline had broken open and were strewn all over the place. 'My God. What is it like at home?' I wondered. 'What happened in Chetumal?' In the distance I saw a mountain of splintered power poles, downed trees and mud. We had to walk from the airport because there was no way cars could get through so much rubble. I got home at last, and right away I put on my khaki pants and work boots. I started shoveling and washing away the mud with the high-pressure hose we used to wash cars with in the shop. Do you remember the shop? There was mud all over the place. The rushing water didn't take all the buildings with it because I'd put up a cement wall around the property. It was just high enough to keep the water from doing more damage. It protected the shop and the house, too. I found my dad Lupito, and told him, 'I need lumber.' He said, 'Go get whatever you need. Go to Santa Elena and sign for whatever you need.' Casa Aguilar's sawmill was in Santa Elena. And my dad just let me have it."

His voice cracks.

"And I let him have it back. I don't know what he wanted me to forgive him for."

Another day:

"I brought him to Mexico City. I got him settled in, and when everything was taken care of, he died."

He asks once again:

"Why did my father beg my pardon when he was about to die? I just don't understand. But whatever is supposed to happen does happen. How can I not believe there's such a thing as destiny when my father only kissed me twice, and the second time he begged me to forgive him was the day he died. I wonder what he thought I should forgive him for. He didn't have to beg my pardon for anything."

On another day:

"I had 1900 trees marked for cutting in the Petén. The taxes and logging fees came to six thousand quetzals that were supposed to be paid in advance. I went to my father and told him, 'I'm leaving Guatemala. You can take over. All you need to do is pay up and wait for a full moon before you cut and haul the logs.'"

"Why wait for a full moon?"

"If you don't the wood rots as soon as you cut it. When the moon is full, the tree gets waterlogged, it gets swollen and hard. Cutting it down under a full moon keeps it fresh. So you pay up and wait until the moon is right, then you get all the trees you cut down out of the jungle before the rainy season. It was a done deal. I had everything ready to go."

"How were you going to chop down the trees?"

"With axes."

"And why did you want to pull out of Guatemala with everything ready to go?"

"Because I'd had enough. I was on the verge of losing my wife and children. I rarely saw any of you. And the communists had the place in an uproar. They shot at me with a .22 caliber rifle. Encalada, one of my most loyal hands, was with me when it happened. Two shots rang out, and a bullet whistled over our heads. Encalada said, 'They're shooting at us, Don Héctor.' A bastard named Ceferino Domínguez was to blame. Guerrilla warfare had broken out in Guatemala, and he had the whole Petén on edge. That's when the fighting began, and it didn't end until just now when a peace agreement was signed. I mounted my animal and went to look for Ceferino."

"Your animal. A horse?"

"My animal. A burro with a saddle. I rode it on the side trails. The only way I'd go down those trails—the road-cuts to haul the lumber out—was on my burro. I had to go a hundred, three hundred, five hundred meters into the jungle. 'Come look, Don Héctor.' I was going to go look, but the others were way ahead of me. I brought up the rear, riding my burro down the path."

Another day:

"What happened to Ceferino?"

"I went looking for him, and I found him. I said, 'Your people wanted to kill me, but they couldn't, so now I'm here so you can kill me yourself. What's your problem?' 'There's no problem,' he said. 'I've given your people work,' I said. 'I put real beds in the barracks for them to sleep on. I built a bridge so they wouldn't have to swim across the river. There's a dining hall and a clinic in every one of my encampments. But they want to kill me, so here I am. Go ahead and let them kill me.' I drew the .38 pistol I kept under my hat and fired it at a pile of cans. The cans flew all over the place. 'Is that what you want?' I said. 'No, you've got it all wrong,' he said. 'I'm not wrong,' I said. 'If you want me dead, then kill me, but do it right. Otherwise, I'm going to get you.'"

"Who was Ceferino?"

"He was a hunter in the Arab encampments of Don Enrique Sagua. He hired hunters with guns to supply the meat for his encampments. Ceferino was a hunter who liked to make trouble. Someone else was after me, too. I got out of my car in Egar on the English side, and this Guatemalan shrimp comes up to me and says, 'Héctor Aguilar Marrufo?' I told him yes. 'You're the man I'm looking for,' he said. 'I am?' I say. 'What you want? What can I do for you?' 'This,' he says, and takes a punch at me. I go into a crouch, and with my left hand." He holds up his arm and clenched left fist; it's contorted with arthritis and covered with freckles. "My counterpunch knocks him down. A black cop on the English side came to see what was going on. 'Hey, man,' he says to me, 'you a boxer, man?' 'No,' I told him. 'It was an emergency, and I was frightened.' So many problems. So much effort, so much toil and struggle."

His eyes fill with tears.

Another day I ask:

"Why in the world did you pull out of Guatemala? You took so many risks, and all it was going to cost you to move that timber was six-thousand quetzals. How much were the 1900 trees you cut down worth?"

"A bundle. I went to see Jalil Sagua, the Arab, and in broken Spanish he said, 'You take me Guatemala, I get wood, and you and me go fifty-fifty.' 'No,' I say, 'you have a very bad reputation in Guatemala. There'd be hell to pay.'"

"So you went to Lupito for help?"

"I went to see him in Mérida and, in the presence of Frank Vadillo, I proposed that he pay the tax on the wood and get it out of the country. Vadillo said, 'Don Lupe, do it. Pay attention to your son. Just this one time, trust him. You always bad-mouth him, but he's the best of your sons, and he's making you a good offer.'"

"But you didn't offer to make him a partner in your business."

"No."

"You just handed it to him on a silver platter. Why not offer him the same deal the Arab offered you, fifty-fifty?"

"That's not what I proposed."

"Not what you proposed or a promise he vowed to keep and then broke?"

"He gave in to your Uncle Ángel. Lupito let your Uncle Ángel take over, and he ruined everything."

"But why did you let it happen? It was your business. Why didn't you look for a loan somewhere else?"

"I went to the Arab."

"But not to anyone else?"

"It never occurred to me."

"So Lupito got his foot in the door, and you let him cut you out of your own business?"

"He wanted Ángel to be the boss. I didn't want to fight with my brother."

"And now I know what Lupito wanted you to forgive him for."

"For what?"

"He stole your business."

"It didn't do him any good. He lost everything. Moving the sawmill from Santa Helena to the Petén was the stupidest thing Ángel ever did. It was Oscar's fault it burned down."

"But why did Lupito give the whole business to Ángel if it belonged to you, and you started it?"

"Lupito told Vadillo that Ángel was his oldest son. It's customary for the oldest son to come first. Vadillo replied, 'Don Lupe, listen to Héctor.' He paid no attention to Vadillo or me either."

Another day:

"Lupito paid the taxes and headed for the Petén?"

"Yes."

"And he got the timber out of Guatemala?"

"Yes."

"And for all the things you did you got nothing?"

"Ángel ruined everything."

"Ángel ruined everything, but Lupito ended up with your business."

He extricates himself from the corner I put him in with a smile and a memory. He says:

"I should have wound up owning a sugar mill. I left Guatemala with Romandía Vidal, an old school friend. He told me he needed some trucks like mine to haul sugar cane from the fields to the gin. He was really down in the dumps. I asked him what was the trouble, and he said, 'My uncle's a real son of a bitch.' 'How could he be worse than my dad, Lupito?' I asked and answered my own question. 'I don't believe it. Nobody could be a worse s.o.b. than my dad Lupito.'"

He laughs until tears run down his cheeks. When he gets over the tears and the laughter, his mirth becomes a lament:

"So much loss, so goddamn much!"

He chokes on his own breath and sobs uncontrollably.

This foregoing dates from the months between November 1995 and November 1998 when Godot drives Toña out of his life. Little by little, he's developed a grab bag of grudges against her. According to Godot, Toña cooks meals to her liking, not his. Toña's too fastidious. She talks too much. She's a snoop and a spy, not a housekeeper. The truth is she spies on him; she keeps me abreast of the ups and downs of Godot's whimsical daily life. Every day he walks to the nearby market where lottery tickets are sold and to his lawyer's office. A taxi driver has started hanging around, and Godot comes and goes in his cab. One day he comes home without the money I'd given him that same morning. On another occasion Toña spends the day waiting for the missing Godot. He's not in when she arrives early in the morning, and he's still not back at four in the afternoon. He's finally comes in with some characters Godot describes as the mechanics who helped him with his '74, '75, and '76 Impalas. Toña says they look like a bunch of really a bad kids who are up to no good with Godot. Robbing him is the least they're likely to do. I talk to Godot, I tell him to watch out, to use the driver in my office when he has errands to do, to have someone with him when he goes out, to keep his eyes and ears open when he takes a walk. He's not about to be a shut-in. Some days he spends the whole morning in the parish church talking, he says, with his mama Juanita. Other days he visits Lupito's grave in the French cemetery. It annoys Godot to have Toña keeping me informed of his doings. He thinks it diminishes his stature in my eyes. There comes a day when he won't let her in the apartment, he flatly refuses to open the door. The woman who minds the building's entrance knocks on his door. On the strength of occasional gratuities, Godot maintains cordial relations with her. She's his new confidant in a world full of enemies. But he won't let her in either. Thinking that something may have happened to him, I get my keyring and enter the apartment fearing the worst. I find him inside sleeping like a log. In the conversation that follows he demands that I fire Toña. He'll spare me the expense of her severance pay by compensating her out of his own pocket. He knows how to do these things without causing any problems with the law. I've already discussed how to meet his needs with the woman who minds the entrance, and she agrees to pick up where Toña left off and do better than Toña. "Let me take care of this. I'll straighten things out," she promises. She's as good as her word, and Toña steps aside. In a matter of weeks she becomes the target of Godot's complaints. She watches him through the windows, he says. She's ruined some of the shirts I gave him in the wash; he'd grown fond of those shirts and kept them looking like new. What's worse, she'd lost a sweater of his and couldn't explain its disappearance.

One day I call to ask how he is.

"I'm all right now," he says with an undertone of reproach.

"Were you sick?"

"I had a fever. A woman named Carolina came for me with another woman. 'What are you two doing here?' I said. 'We came for you,' they said. In English. 'No,' I told them. 'Go away. It's not my time yet. I can't go out a failure. In a time of loss, in this city. I have to leave on my own time.' 'I'm here to get you,' she said. 'No,' I said. 'It's not my time.' I stood up to those women and scared them off. I know what they're up to. They did quite a job on me, but I know about these things. I know exactly how she got me off track. I remember very clearly. It was when Valentina Mena came. When she left, the secretary said, 'Don Héctor, who was that woman? Look what she left here.' She showed me a string of garlic. That was when my troubles began."

"You mean to say La Chata, our nanny Valentina Mena, cast a spell on you?"

"Well, who else? Why has my luck been so bad for so long? In 1985 my desk fell down on me. The building where my office was fell down, and not a thing went right from then on. I know all about curses. I saw how they did it in Belize lots of times. They find your weakness; a quick look is all it takes. First they stun you, then they drain you like an empty wineskin. I know all about it. I was doing fine. I was back on my feet, and my office was off to a great start. It occupied a whole floor, and the seventy employees I had under me were human spark plugs. When my dad Lupito saw my office he said, 'You did this all by yourself?' I think he realized I could have cut our losses in Chetumal if he'd let me. And now Catalina's after me."

"Catalina?"

"This is where she used to live, and the other woman, her sister, heckles me and says in English, 'We're coming to get you.'"

I don't know what to do about these leaps into the abyss inside Godot's head. I had assumed he could live alone, but he can't. I'm not dealing with an old man able to fend for himself, an elderly person who matters to me, who's stable and can fill the gaps in his half-told story. I'm dealing with an old man who is a danger to himself. At this critical moment in the life of Godot, Rita Tenorio descends straight from heaven or, to be exact, from the rooftop where she lives. She's Godot's latter-day guardian angel.

Mexico City, 2005

I don't think I've described the power of my mother's physical presence. Naturally, it changes over time, but throughout the years her face is lit up by eyes that put a smile over deep sadness. She has small, well-formed lips that lend themselves to speech; soft, even cheeks; a forehead lined by life's metaphysical setbacks. Her usual expression suggests that she finds herself in a world that's hard to understand but which she must confront daily without ever admitting defeat. I've already spoken of the scene that typifies her spirit in my memory. Hurricane-force winds batter the planks that comprise the front wall of our house in Chetumal. Emma rushes at the endangered wall and holds the boards in place with her bare hands. She's imprinted on my memory in just that position, keeping the catastrophe that threatens her house at bay despite the mindless fury of the storm. She's driven by an iron will that forges relentlessly ahead despite all obstacles. She's as lucid as she is determined, and the possibility of failure buzzes ceaselessly in her brain. It jars her awake at night, and she's shaken by its persistence, by the way it haunts her rest like water that won't stop dripping from a faucet. At certain times in her life I picture her as a good-natured woman molded by misgivings that pose no real threat to her unbending determination and which she brushes impatiently aside like tropical mosquitoes. I see her standing on a patch of spiritual high ground, swatting away signs, both real and imagined, of adversity, weakness, and the suspicion that her strength has limits. She blindly resists anything she thinks might harm her or her family. There's never a time when she isn't ready to pit her bare hands against the storm trying to knock her house down.

My mother is always Doña Emma in my thoughts, but, as I've said, in the depths of her soul she's a girl from Cuba who loves to sing. I remember her singing day and night. When she cooks, when she's lost in thought, when she goes from one room to another. It's a source of pleasure, a cure for the doldrums that bubbles up from deep within her. There's no explaining her need to sing; it's an abstract pleasure with a life of its own. Her memory works in much the same way and is as natural to her as breathing. In a sense my memory of my mother is simply an extension of her memory, of a long life more remembered than lived. Her most vivid recollections date from her Cuban girlhood and her early years in Chetumal. She tells tales from these places over and over like the old-time bards who traveled the countryside polishing their narratives by repeating them in one town after another, preserving old storylines while adding fresh details to hold the attention of their listeners. She remembers without nostalgia or melancholy. She begins in the flower of youth and ends with a smile at things no life can escape. The passion for storytelling gains strength as the years go by as does her love of a good meal. Her tales, like her cooking, become simpler and sweeter. There is, for example, the story she tells her family after dinner on April 19, 2004.

As told by Doña Emma:
"Julio Antonio Mella was mad about Communism. In Cuba he married Oliví, a girl we knew in Camagüey and who eventually became the mother of the eight-year-old daughter they called Natacha because it sounded Russian. Her real name was Natalia, but they preferred Natacha because in those days

communists ruled Russia. Oliví left the little girl in the care of her younger sister Hilda. Natacha was just our age, and Hilda and Natacha used to come and play with us. While awaiting her husband's return, Oliví complained about the communist dream that so enthralled her mate. The day Mella arrived in Moscow in the twenties, Oliví said, he jumped off the train, embraced the first Russian who crossed his path, and loudly proclaimed the man his communist brother. He was later murdered here in Mexico by fellow communists. Cubans have always been mildly nuts."

In her telling:

"Every year Father read the list of petty crimes and punishments published in the Cuban law journal. Once a defendant was convicted, judges heard the arguments of the opposing sides and pronounced sentence without delay. In a case that drew father's attention, a judge was called on to find a black man who had lost an arm guilty or not guilty. The man had a stump just below his elbow. A Spanish storekeeper accused him of stealing a carton of cider. The police caught him as he was running home with the box of cider on his shoulder. The one-armed black man claimed the box of cider was a gift. The Spanish merchant said he'd left it on the sidewalk until he had a moment to put it in his storeroom. In answer to a question from the judge, the black man said, 'Your Honor, how do you think I could get that box on my back and carry it with only half an arm? It was a gift that was put on my shoulder so I could take it home. How could I get it onto my back all alone?' The judge agreed. He added that all too often courts found against blacks due to racial discrimination and ruled that the defendant could keep the box of cider. The black man was delighted with the verdict. He lifted one side of the box with his good arm, put his stump under it, and lifted it onto his shoulder in a single motion. He was on his way out of the courtroom when the judge ordered his arrest because, 'He confessed to what he did.'"

In her telling:

"Regarding the death penalty, I remember a man named Adolfo Pérez who lived in Chetumal. He was the father of my friend Aurora, and this is what happened. Don Adolfo Pérez was a hardhearted man. In the blistering heat of Chetumal he owned a café called *La nevada*, The Snowcap, where all his children had to work. My father said, 'You're a slavedriver to your own family.' They were always arguing. Once when I went to Belize to visit the Pérez-Schofields, they took us to a dance at the Pickwick Club. While he was dancing with me, Aurora's brother Manuel said, 'You and I ought to get married.' 'But, Manuel,' I said. 'How can we marry when our fathers get along like oil and water?' 'When we marry they'll stop feuding,' he told me. But I didn't marry him. He married a girl from Corozal, and a year later she came to Chetumal for Christmas with a baby daughter. Even then, the father wouldn't give his son a moment's rest. He sent Manuel to close *La nevada* for the night and bring him the earnings right away. Manuel did as he was told. The family had a two-story house with offices on the ground floor and living quarters for the Pérez-Schofields above. In the back patio there was a small house where the servants lived: a cook called La Cacariza because of the pockmarks on her face and a colored maid who used to tell me, 'When you marry and have a family, I'm going to come and work for you.' And I'd tell her, 'No way. I couldn't let you work for me and leave Doña Flora all alone.' Flora was Don Adolfo's wife, the mother of Aurora and Manuel. Well, Manuel's on his way home with the money, and the brother of the colored maid was following him. In his hand, he had a club made of machiche, a hardwood tree used to make fenceposts in Chetumal. He hit Manuel over the head and left him for dead on the ground. Doña Flora was upstairs chatting with her daughter-in-law, and they heard the commotion. The daughter-in-law said, 'Something's going on outside.' 'No,' said Doña Flora. 'It's just drunks making a racket in the street. There are lots of drunks this time of year.' But it was the sound of her son being beaten to death. He was barely alive when they got to him, and with his dying breath they heard him say, 'Toilette, toilette'. Everyone thought he was saying *'tolete,'* or club, that he'd been killed with a club. In the investigation that followed, the colored servant—the one who wanted to work for me when I married—was asked if she heard anything, and she said no, 'I went to my room at seven and didn't come out.' Then La Cacariza told the police inspector, 'That's not so. I saw her on the balcony at nine. She seemed to be waiting for someone.' So they re-interrogated the colored maid who admitted her surname was Toilette and that her brother had murdered Manuel to get the money. Toilette was arrested, and the town was outraged. General Guevara came, then the territorial governor came and told Adolfo Pérez and his wife Flora, 'We're going to start the investigation all over again. If you want, while the new inquiry is in under way, we can have the man who murdered your son killed.' Which meant they could make it appear that he attempted to flee and was killed while trying to run away. Doña Flora said, 'Killing him won't bring my son back.' She turned down General Guevara's offer. She mourned her son's death the rest of her life, knowing she'd heard him being killed and paid no attention."

One night in Mexico City, Doña Emma takes the bite of bread and sip of coffee that costs her life. I'm in the city of Oaxaca where I've gone for a wedding. In the hotel where we are there's a painting described by Italo Calvino in his story about how the palette and kitchen are related to each other ("Under the Jaguar Sun"). Food is Emma Camín's only remaining source of sensual pleasure, and at eighty-four she looks forward to her evening dose of bread and coffee with milk. She lives in the two large rooms that overlook the park from the second floor of the house at Mexico 15. One of the rooms opens onto the balcony on where wilted flowers land each year from one of the 163 jacarandas around *Parque México*. Here she spends long years mourning the death of her sister Luisa, mired in a loss she cannot share, a sorrow she doesn't let come between her and the people she loves. Her mourning is intimate and unrelenting, its depths barely hinted at when her look becomes a stare. Her eyes glaze over, then slowly blink as if she's recovering from a fainting spell. So much of what added a ration of joy to her daily life is gone: her partner, her older sister, her surrogate mother. There's no one left who shares her memories, no ready listener, no complicit voice. Luisa's passing deprives her of what matters most to her: the unfettered intimacy of their conversations. Nothing ever fills the enormous silence of the long years without Luisa. It follows her around the house. She misses the table talk at mealtimes and over evening coffee and takes Luisa's silence with her into the silence of the night.

It's April 30, 2005. The jacarandas in the park are still in full bloom. The season when their lilac hues are on display begins in the dry month of February and lasts until the rainy season in May. For several days rain showers have been carpeting the city's parks and medians with purple flowers. In the air there's a whiff of more rain to come that afternoon. Trees in the park sway in the breeze, and if you listen closely, you can hear the rustling of leaves above the rumble of traffic in the street. Hundreds of kilometers to the south in Oaxaca, the wind doesn't just blow, it unleashes a tempest: a classic Mexican cloudburst that comes on strong and quickly dissipates. The rain scours the outdoor air and ushers in the kind of sunset a biblical prophet might have called down. From the window of our hotel room we see the heavens turn bright red and battleship gray over the city.

The storm bears down on Oaxaca with a fury that blackens the sky and streaks it with silver as thunder and lightning make the ground tremble. The conflagration goes on for half an hour after which the corridors of the hotel are ankle-deep in rainwater. A golden light breaks through the clouds, and the city's sky is restored to its customary blue. We leave the hotel to attend a party on the outskirts of Oaxaca. We drive past the stand of Montezuma cypresses that clusters about the enormous *Árbol del Tule*, the tallest and largest tree of its kind. By comparison, the giant's lesser neighbors, though imposing, are dwarfs hidden among the houses and buildings that have gone up among them. A bolt of lightning has struck the heart of a smaller tree, severing a limb and setting it ablaze. Plumes of smoke rise from the stricken tree, and a stump of charcoal and ashes sticks out from where the missing bough used to be. I remember thinking the damage resembled a wound before reminding myself that the notion of wounds or injuries doesn't jibe with a tree or any other form of vegetation. Life that grows up from the ground is indifferent to scars or losses. When we return from the party, the remains of the tree are still smoldering with a few pink flames flickering up from inside it.

We ride past the charred tree around the time Doña Emma has her supper in Mexico City. Something has delayed her partaking of the small pleasure she derives from her nightly repast. She falls asleep a bit late for a person who's been an early riser all her life. An aftertaste of coffee lingers in her throat while a familiar voice on the radio keeps her company. It makes her drowsy, and for the last time she lays her head on her pillow. Then comes sleep and then comes the bile that rises from her stomach, floods her throat, pours out her nose, and surges into her lungs. I know full well how Emma Camín feels on this night when an acid torrent erupts through her esophagus and sets her throat on fire. I've choked at least twice from overeating at dinners I went to before being told I had a hiatal hernia. I know the kind of terror that comes when acid gushes into sleeping lungs, the bitter asphyxia of bronchial distress, the coughing and cold sweats, the convulsions you wake up to when you're on the verge of dying. As she begins to suffocate, I know Emma's body tells her to sit up in bed and staunch the flow of liquid burning her trachea. But she isn't strong enough to answer her body's demand to jolt herself upright, stop the downward flow of fluids into her chest, and cough them up. These are the moments when I think Emma Camín actually dies, the moments when she knows she's dying and is about to die. Ceci sleeps in the adjacent room and comes to her aid as she starts to gag. Ceci sits her up and tries to make her clear her throat, but Emma can barely breathe through her congested windpipe. The fluids collecting in her lungs are drowning her. By the time she reaches the English Hospital Emma is semiconscious. The doctors' first report is conclusive. The fluids Doña Emma choked on have scalded her lungs. She's suffered for years from a mysterious type of emphysema that strikes non-smokers. Her lung capacity was a third of normal before last night's crisis, and now it's close to zero. Her chances of recovery are poor. Though a tracheotomy might help keep her alive, it wouldn't cure her. My brother Juan José tells me what the doctors say when he phones me in Oaxaca at nine. Doña Emma's condition is serious but under control. She's in intensive care but stable. Her condition, though critical, is not life-threatening at the moment. He suggests I come home. I take the first flight I can get on at four that afternoon. My first talk with the doctor makes it clear that the emergency has passed, that the one remaining question is what to do next. We'll try everything, the doctor says. His sincerity and good intentions are palpable, but the only message I hear is: We'll delay her death.

I know right away how this will end. More time in the

hospital won't change very much. The only question is when to end this ordeal of lookalike days. In the emergency room Doña Emma was immersed in the limbo of sedation. She feels no pain, and she'll remain as she is now until she's unplugged from the machines keeping her artificially alive. She shares the vegetative grandeur of the tree struck by lightning in Oaxaca.

Eighteen days go by with Doña Emma in intensive care.

"Is there anything you need?" the doctor asks as he steps onto the elevator.

"A miracle," I reply.

When I get off the elevator, I continue the conversation with the doctor in my mind. I think, "I've already had my miracle." I tell Doña Emma, "You were my miracle."

It's May 18th, 2005. I've made up my mind not to see her anymore. Yesterday they ran a test to see if she would breathe on her own. They disconnected her from the ventilator, and her respiration and pulse went wild. Alarms sounded, lights flashed. She can't breathe unaided. For the past eighteen days we've been hearing that the stricken Doña Emma is making progress. Nothing unexpected, no news likely to upset me, but it always does. I think it's time to release her from this pseudo life. Not everyone in the family agrees, One day there are reasons to hope; the next day there are different reasons. Every day the doctors find new emergencies that demand their attention in the indifferent body of Doña Emma. One day there's water in the pleural cavity. Another day it's swollen sinuses. Then it's blood and albumen in her urine. Too many or too few leucocytes. The doctors' midday and nightly reports tell us of the patient's progress or relapses. Their explanations of this or that indication spare them the discomfit of discussing what they can't do. They can cure anything but death. Every day there's a fresh glimmer of hope: her fever's down, the pleural membranes are less inflamed, her lungs are less congested.

Their favorite word is infection. Infected cannulas, infections of the pleural cavity, the nasal passages, the lungs, the bronchial tree—the great tree in its death throes.

We come every day, two or three times a day. We take turns with our visitor's passes and sit talking at Doña Emma's bedside in sympathy with her plight and our own. I'm hypnotized by the sight of so much tubing, of cannulas feeding blood into her arms and neck, her pallor, her furrowed brow. She`s not in pain, she's utterly unaware of her condition. Still, I'm obsessed with the thought that each drop from the drip bags brings an extra grain of physical suffering. We each follow our own solitary, futile, and slightly theatrical routines when visiting Doña Emma. My sisters pretend their mother is really listening. They speak softly to her about times gone by and the homes where they now live. Ángeles recites the events of her day. My brother Juan José prays with her, my brother Luis Miguel cries inwardly. I can't help staring as if I'd only just become aware of her fate.

When the doctors propose an operation to drain her sinuses, I announce that I'm on strike. From now on I'm keeping my opinions to myself, and I refuse to make any more decisions. My siblings' fraternal conclave decides to go along with this latest scheme. I intend to stop seeing Doña Emma. The next day, May 18th , I go to the hospital and state my intentions. In the elevator the doctor asks me if I need anything, and I tell him a miracle.

Later I go to wish Doña Emma farewell. I tell her what I said to myself in the elevator. I tell her she's the miracle. I tell her I don't know what to do with myself or with what's left of her. I don't know what to do with my memory of her. I'll write about it when I'm at least able to think about it. I say it over and over, and, finally, instead of telling her not to go, I say it's time for her to go.

On the morning of May 20th the doctors' conclave agrees

that they can do nothing more, that keeping Doña Emma alive makes no sense. They're at our service to disconnect the artificial respirator at a time of our choosing. It's our decision, which is true except that it's yet to be made. In answer to the question of how long it will take her to die once she's off life support, they reply a matter of minutes. We ask the doctors to be ready at one.

Ángeles and I go home for breakfast with Mateo and Catalina and tell them the time has come. I've stayed away in recent days, and I consider staying away for the bitter final moment. Ángeles tells me I'm crazy.

The moment is here. Doña Emma's special bed is lit up like an operating table, and around it are her children and grandchildren. The doctor disconnects the respirator and steps away on the tips of his toes, stressing the awkwardness and solemnity of the moment. It's clear to everyone that Doña Emma has felt nothing for days, but, even so, she grimaces when the respirator is taken away. She struggles when the air is gone, when the breath of life is no more. It's not much of a struggle, but it lasts an eternity. She dies step by step in imperceivable gradations. I know Doña Emma is dead when her skin changes color. It turns smooth and yellow, then white without losing its yellow cast. The scene feels slightly sinister: Emma is dead, but the disconnected respirator continues to breathe as if it were still keeping her alive. Our contemplation of Doña Emma's death comes to an indisputable end when the doctor steps in, unplugs the machine, and tells us it's all over.

I dislike the color of my mother's skin, but I'm pleased to see how clean her face looks now that the dying has passed. For a moment I see the features of the girl whose photo I keep on my desk, the face of Emma Camín, who used to sing in Cuba when she was young.

We've set a time for the wake and cremation at the French

cemetery on Legaria Street. With Ángeles I arrange for the transport of Emma's body, we select a light-colored wooden casket, choose clothes and cosmetics, pick an urn for her ashes. The plain silver vessel is free of religious embellishments and, most especially, of the cross that sticks tastelessly up from nearly all the other models on display at the funeral home. We sign the paperwork for her cremation the following day at one in the afternoon. Doña Emma's wake will take place in the *Salón Bretaña*. As soon as the body arrives, we'll be advised of its presence, and the viewing room will be open to mourners at that time. It may remain open throughout the evening and overnight. However, the family usually closes the doors at ten in the evening and returns at ten in the morning.

The customs and traditions surrounding wakes at the French Cemetery with its large visitation salons and its paths shaded by jacarandas are the least funereal in all Mexico City. While Doña Emma is in the hospital, Ángeles's cousin María Luisa Sánchez is also dying. At sixty-four Maícha is twenty years younger than Doña Emma, and she suffers from lung cancer. Her first doctor told her she had seven years to live, and her most recent one said she should have been dead five days ago. Ángeles has shuttled between visits to Doña Emma in the English Hospital and, on recent afternoons, to the apartment on Alcastre where her cousin has a small room overlooking the treetops in Chapultepec Park. Maícha may be dying, but she´s full of life; she likes to try on clothes she knows she'll never wear. He sisters bring her clothes just so they can all see how they look on her. "This green suits you, the purple not so much," Maícha tells Ángeles. "I'm quite tired, I'd like to rest. The trouble is if you leave this party, you can't come back." The family turns her viewing into a party, and Ángeles is struck by Maícha's beauty, her radiantly peaceful face, the immobile perfection of her hands. Ángeles and I see something similar when we gaze on Doña Emma in her coffin before the doors

of the viewing room are opened and the mourners stream in
with their condolences. Doña Emma is wearing dark lipstick
that clashes with her pale, slightly yellow skin. Her nose is still
wrinkled from her battle with sinusitis in her final days, but her
forehead and closed eyes preserve an air of the girl she once
was. The signs of struggle are gone.

Friends and relatives—Doña Emma's large extended
family—form a parade that lasts through the morning of the
day before the cremation. Her nephews and niece, Manuel,
Yolanda and Rodrigo Camín arrive from Chetumal that day.
We collect the ashes at three in the afternoon and carry them to
Mexico 15. My sisters have prepared a meal. We place the ashes
on a kind of altar in the dining room where they'll stay until we
take them to the nearby Church of the Coronation. We'll take
Luisa's ashes there on another day. Around the urn are candles
and photos of Doña Emma. During the dinner, conversation
remains halting and prosaic until the Camín cousins bring it
vibrantly to life. Their convoluted narratives resonate with
the same cadences as the tales told by their aunts Emma and
Luisa. They recall Doña Emma's unflappable good humor
while minding Yoli's, the dry goods store to which they gave
their niece's nickname in Chetumal. They remember how Doña
Emma described the dark fate she said awaited the cousins
for helping some Cubans accused of terrorism escape from
Mexico to Belize. They tell how Tao, the German shepherd
Doña Emma gave them, dominated other dogs and ruled the
streets of Chetumal. They recall the killing of the crocodile
famed for eating the geese Don Salvador's godfather kept on
his property at the edge of Lake Milagros. Together with friends
Don Salvador baited two meat hooks with chickens. When
the creature bit, the men were able to wedge a stake between
its jaws and walk it to the town pier like a lapdog because a
crocodile with an immobilized mouth is like Samson with no

hair. Their father, they say, taught them to swim by throwing them in Lake Milagros before they could walk. Then there was the day Don Salvador's buck was in rut and knocked down its pen. Raúl took a stick and valiantly fended off its charges until someone grabbed it by the antlers and wrestled it gently to its knees. It seems a deer in a chokehold properly applied is like a crocodile with immobilized jaws; both can be petted like lapdogs. They described how they teased their grandfather Camín, who lived alone in the back of the family store. The blind old man would flail at them with a pitchfork, and they'd dare each other to dodge its tines as if the tines were horns and they were novice bullfighters. And then there was the scandal that broke out when their Aunt Luisa couldn't stop laughing as she attempted to scold them for aiming their slingshots at the well-rounded bottom of a neighbor climbing a ladder to pick mangoes from the tree next to her house.

I thanked them for celebrating the memory of their late aunt in their own way, for paying her tribute with their eloquence, and for filling the silence that reigned in her absence.

Three days later we take Doña Emma's ashes to the Church of the Coronation. We inter them on the side of the burial ground nearest the park whose name evokes her heart's true parish, the *Parque España*. But we don't take all the ashes. Before they're moved, Ángeles and I slip into the sala at Mexico 15 and clandestinely take three spoonfuls of ashes from the urn and put them in a small silver coffer.

I have a funerary purpose for these ashes. When Héctor dies I intend to mix his ashes with Emma's and spread them under the willow Ángeles planted in a corner of our garden. I want Emma's and Héctor's remains to blend with the sap of the tree and satisfy a woodland fetish of mine. I yearn to make the tree a living urn for the two of them. As I pass by the tree each day, I'll take a childlike pleasure in greeting them. I'll suppose they're together again, that at the end of their lives they get over their estrangement, and I do, too.

November 5, 2012. My mother has visited me in my dreams. At the end of a night out with a friend, we get arrested by the police. My friend is determined to mount the balcony of his girlfriend and serenade her. The officer says if he wants to see her he'll have to enter through the door to her house. We get arrested. I realize I won't be sleeping at home, and Doña Emma will be angry. As detainees, we somehow end up in a movie theater watching a version of *Star Wars* that lasts all night. In my sleep I get the impression that, to Doña Emma's consternation, one of my brothers has stopped sleeping at home. I know I ought to go home, but I stay at the movie. I sleep, I wake up, I go back to sleep. I can't stay awake. At the end of the movie someone on the loudspeaker thanks the audience, and me in particular, for coming. My sister Emma is among the people leaving the movie, I understand that Doña Emma is in the theater, and when we leave I go with her on an errand. We go past an apartment block like the one that was across the street from the *Cine Estadio* until it was destroyed by the earthquake of 1985. We walk around the building to a sundry store where a woman with a Cuban accent waits on us. She and Doña Emma argue about an order the woman is unable to fill. Doña Emma calms her down and leaves her a roll of coins. It seems to me we can take some sandy, tree-lined paths back to the movies without retracing our steps. Through the trees I can see trucks going by on the street in front of the theater. I also see metal bars separating the park from the street. I think there's a way through them and tell Doña Emma. I guide her towards the bars, but the branches of the trees are too thick and low to the ground. Their dead limbs block the path, and Doña Emma refuses to go on. We go back the way we came. It makes me happy to hold her arm and walk with her once more. She finishes her errand and doesn't criticize me for my questionable help, my errant company. That's just the way sons are.

Mexico City, 2010

The woman who takes care of my father and stands in for the family he lost is named Rita Tenorio. In early 1998 she's out of work, and she comes to my house to ask if we know of any job openings. Ángeles refers her to a friend with whom Rita has had a recent falling out. She's serious about finding a job, but not just any job. She comes with limits and conditions. With her, minor misunderstandings can grow into major conflicts, and prolonged agreement breeds fierce loyalty. Rita comes on the scene shortly after Godot torpedoes the arrangement Ángeles made with Toña, our former cook. Toña has earned our trust over a lifetime, and strife with Godot is no reason to doubt her integrity. Ángeles gives Rita fair warning that Godot is difficult; he likes living alone, but he's no longer able to, and he won't let anybody help him. Rita gets ready to take on the minotaur. In her first weeks she hurries in and out of the apartment on Tehuantepec. She comes in early, feeds him his breakfast, cleans, shops, cooks, does the dishes. She sleeps in the room her sister Delia has on the roof of a building on Azapotzalco. Godot likes Rita's cooking. While eating, Rita recalls, he tells her strange stories of when he lived in a town called Chetumal, of lumbering in a place called Petén, and about his father Lupito who owned a movie theater and a boat. Lupe was once a very rich man, but his children squandered his fortune. He later regained his wealth and moved to Mexico City with his nurse, a lady named Flora Mayo. They married, and when Lupe died, his heirs argued with Flora, who as the widow had first rights to his estate. But there were no assets left to fight over because Godot's brothers wasted them all.

The old man I call Godot—whom Rita starts calling Hectorcito—tells the same stories over and over. When night falls, Rita pulls the shades and goes to her sister Delia's place. Hectorcito begins pleading with her not to go. He says she can sleep on the sofa-bed in the apartment's diminutive sala, and bit by bit Rita moves in. Her sister Delia is having problems with the landlord she rents from on Azacapotzalco because her room is so small and she has to share a bathroom with three families who also rent space on the roof. Rita and Godot enjoy each other's company. According to Rita, they're regular parrots. First, Hectorcito tells Rita a story, then she tells him a story, which is how Godot learns she's a single mother with two daughters ages fourteen and a year and a half. The younger one is in the care of Rita's mother in Zitácuaro, and the fourteen-year-old lives alone in a house Rita owns on the outskirts of Zitácuaro—two rooms and a toilet for the girl to live in while going to middle school. The outcome of Gabi's solitude is a pregnancy that burdens Godot in ways to be explained. Hectorcito says he wants to meet Rita's little girl and provide help for the older one. According to Rita, Hectorcito has a terrible disposition but a huge heart. What makes him difficult is his disposition, not his heart.

After six weeks of dealing with Godot, Rita has some money, and she uses it to visit her daughters in Zitácuaro. The younger one is ill, and when Rita returns to the city, the little girl is with her. She spends two weeks in the apartment on Tehuantepec and is beginning to stay there full time except for weekends. Little Lupita has barely begun to talk, but she keeps Godot entertained, and she won't let him out of her sight. She follows him around, climbs all over him, and pokes her fingers in his nose and mouth. They watch children's television programs together. Lupita becomes the child cushion that makes it easier for Rita and Godot to get along.

Godot's bouts of distemper are impossible to predict. Suddenly he gets out of his chair, goes to his room, and slams the door. At first Rita has no idea what to do. His rage can last one, two, or three hours after which he limps out of his room as if nothing happened.

Memories of his past life drive Hectorcito crazy, but they're Godot's lifeblood. He feels left out, and he's sure he's right. He gets mad at himself. He has no one else to blame, Rita says, so he blames her. He shuts himself up in his room and doesn't come out until he's over his funk. He begins to pout when Rita goes to the supermarket, does laundry on the roof, or takes Lupita for a walk: he just doesn't like it when she goes out. When Godot falls asleep in front of the television, Rita seizes the moment to wash clothes on the roof or buy groceries. She always takes Lupita with her on these outings because she refuses to leave her daughter in the care of an old man who can't even look out for himself. When she returns he's sure to make a scene. He's stuffed Rita's and Lupita's belongings into a jumble of bags and boxes, and he's waiting for her at the door. "Get out!" Godot roars as if he's banishing her from paradise. "You're not needed!" Rita's usual way of weathering these storms is to call my office and say my father has fired her. Most of the time the squall has abated before I can get to the phone.

Coping with Godot's mysterious acquaintances isn't easy. One sells scratch cards for a game of chance run by the government. They're called *Melate* cards, and Rita looks on as Hectorcito doles out bills to his friend the Melate seller when he comes to collect bets. But she never sees the cards he buys in Hectorcito's possession. A news hawker whom Godot claims to have known for years comes around every few days to collect his tip for unspecified services. A taxi driver surnamed Mondragón picks up the money Godot sends to a woman surnamed Ruelas with whom he has marathon phone conversations. Sometimes he does most of the talking, others he mainly listens because, Rita says, the Ruelas woman is quite a talker. Godot leaves the apartment for his appointments with Mr. Guerrero, the attorney who handles his lawsuits. The advice he gets may be good or may just be Guerrero's way of picking Godot's pocket. Chances are it's some of each: the lawyer listens to what the client has to say and tells him what he wants to hear. Rita discovers that Hectorcito also goes to church. He prays for hours and loses track of time in conversations with dead people. He's now a man of prayer with links to the beyond. What's odd about his absences is he's so cavalier about them. He never says a word to Rita about where he's going or how long he'll be gone. She learns of his doings in fragments Godot lets slip after he comes home. His disappearances are a source of anguish for Rita, and when they last too long, she calls my office. This leads to spats with Godot, who berates her for getting upset about nothing and making him look weak and indecisive in my eyes.

Rita's deciding battle with Godot begins when he sees my driver Lino delivering her paycheck. It's also Lino's duty to take Godot the money I promised him in a separate biweekly envelope. Some crossed wires spark Godot's sensitivity to slights. He's humiliated to see Rita being paid with money she doesn't get through him. After Lino leaves Godot vents his displeasure on Rita, and starts to play his usual number on her: he fires her. But this time Rita doesn't call me. She gathers up Lupita's and her belongings and sets out for Zitácuaro, determined never to come back, and Hectorcito's wrath costs him. In the night of the same day he dials the Zitácuaro number Rita wrote on the wall. The phone belongs to neighbors who send for Rita, but that night she refuses to answer the call from Godot. At seven the following morning the neighbor complains that Mr. Marrufo started calling at five and has yet to stop. The neighbors are no longer polite to Mr. Marrufo, and out of embarrassment for the trouble he's caused, Rita goes to the phone. Hectorcito begs her to come back. He forgives her, he hasn't eaten a thing since she left. He misses Lupita and vows that what happened yesterday won't happen again. Rita returns to the apartment on Tehuantepec, but, first, she calls me with a long list of grievances and swears that

Godot is off his rocker. In the past she's dismissed his offenses as whims, but now she says they're worse than whims. Godot offers to marry her, he makes unwelcome advances and behaves like a jealous lover.

I conclude that the time may have come to put Godot in a home. I also conclude that Rita, Godot, Hectorcito and little Guadalupe are living in quarters too small for them. Maybe we could just find an apartment where Rita and Guadalupe can have a room of their own and Godot and Hectorcito can have a room to themselves. I'll pay extra for rent and extra for Rita's patience and commitment. But Rita's stock has risen dramatically in my eyes, and she's willing to go along with option number two. This sets the stage for settling Hectorcito in a permanent home, his unlikely refuge for the rest of his days.

After scouring many areas and even after considering the purchase of a small house of the kind that once lined Tehuantepec Street in the Roma district, we find what we're looking for in a part of the city unfamiliar to Godot. It's also out of his price range and beyond his limited horizons. I come across it in my own neighborhood. The time has come, I suppose, for me to assume the expenses of Héctor's old age. He moves, along with Rita and Guadalupe, to an apartment with twice the rent but three times the space of the one on Tehuantepec. It has three bedrooms, two baths, and a dining room whose windows look out on Chapultepec Park.

Once ensconced in his new apartment two blocks from my house, time and his grasp of reality slip quickly past Godot.

He calls me on the phone:

"I'm leaving."

"Where are you going?"

"I'm told to Chetumal."

"You can't walk to the elevator in your own building, Old Man. How are you going to get to Chetumal?"

"I'll take care of everything."

Rita picks up the phone:

"That's all your father's talked about since this morning. I wanted you to hear him."

Godot calls me that evening:

"I'm calling to let you know I'm at the Posada Alcázar (where I found him eight years ago). I was at Gelati 99 for a while, but now I'm here. All my clothes are here, everything's in order. They reserved a space for me."

"You're calling from your place on Gelati, Old Man. There's no way you can be at the Alcázar."

"Then where am I?"

"At your place on Gelati. Where you live with Rita."

"Rita Tenorio?"

"That's who."

"Is she there?"

"She ought to be."

"No wonder I found my clothes where they're supposed to be. How did you know Rita's here? I don't see her."

"Call her."

He shouts at her.

"She here," he says. "I'm screwed. I'm going straight to where I belong, in the great beyond."

He calls the next day:

"How're you doing, Namesake?"

He's taken to calling me Namesake.

"Just fine, Namesake. How are you doing?"

"For my eighty years, just fine."

"Your subtracting a few years. You're not eighty."

"Of course I am. How many years is it from '17 to now? I was born on October 5, 1917, at four in the morning. A beautiful day."

"Don't tell me you remember the day."

"I remember."

"You can't remember."

"I remember the birth certificate. It says October 5, 1917. If I was born on October 5, 1917, how old am I? What year is this?"

"It's 2003. You're eighty-six."

"Exactly, eighty-six. A spotless life."

"What's spotless is your brain, Old Man."

"Remember me to your family, my daughter-in-law Angelita, and your son Mateo. How's your son related to me?"

"He's your grandson."

"That right, my grandson. If you're my son, he's my grandson. Right. Tell him I said hello."

At eleven that morning:

"Have you had breakfast already?"

"I have."

"What were you told at breakfast?"

"I don't remember."

"You're eighty-six. You've got fourteen to go, remember?"

"For what?

"To reach a hundred. You promised me you'd get to a hundred."

"What a dream. To lay a fart at a hundred."

The following Sunday while watching soccer:

"I played soccer for *Escuela Modelo* in Mérida. I played left wing. I was right-handed so I kicked with my left foot."

Then:

"How are my grandchildren? Are they going to college now?"

The following Sunday:

"How are my grandchildren? Have they finished high school? Are they already going to college?"

On June 26, 2003, forty-four years after his last conversation with her, Héctor phones Emma Camín. He tells her he loves her, that he's always loved her. I hear about it from Doña Emma herself, and she sounds less annoyed than I'd have expected. She tells

Godot she's too old for that sort of thing. Later she tells me his voice seemed very weak, "Just a whisper, the poor man."

One of the things we'd agreed to was that Godot wouldn't call Doña Emma, so it is out of a combination of curiosity and pique that I raise the subject with him:

"You called Doña Emma."

"I did?"

"You called her yesterday."

"And what did I say to her?"

"Why don't you tell me?"

"I must have said that I loved her a lot."

"That means you called her."

"Well, that's what I said."

"And what else did you say"

"I don't know what else."

I get in the habit of visiting Hectorcito early in the morning. By eight-thirty, Rita has him bathed, dressed, and sitting in his easy chair watching television.

"How are you, Old Man?"

"As old as the hills."

He focuses his watery eyes on me, rummaging through his memory in search of who I am.

"How are the properties in Chetumal getting on?"

"We don't have any properties in Chetumal."

A flicker of anguish crosses his face.

"Who's got them?"

"Goyo Marrufo's sons own the house where you and Emma Camín lived in Chetumal, and we were born in Chetumal. They also own the whole block."

This brings a look of relief.

"How's my daughter-in-law, Ángeles? How are my grandchildren? Are they going to college?"

He hands me his wallet:

"What have I got in there?"

He's got two hundred pesos to which I add another two hundred. He's also got an expired voter registration card.

"It's my proof of citizenship."

He corrects himself:

"The citizen I used to be."

His billfold is embossed with a skeleton wearing a halo and dressed as an apostle. Its face is a skull, its hands the bones of a skeleton. The bones of the right hand hold a scale of justice; the left holds a black ball to its chest. The ball could be either a heart or a bomb.

"It's the image of *Santa Muerte*," he tells me.

"And why are you carrying that around?"

"Death is avoiding me. I call her, but she doesn't come. You have to make friends with *Santa Muerte*."

On April 26, 2004, Hectorcito wakes up with a nosebleed that frightens Rita. He soaks two rags with blood. The blood trickles onto the rug and stains his shirt and sweaters. The first nosebleed is at eight-thirty, the second at ten. The doctor thinks the hemorrhage is local, the result of a ruptured vein. He takes the old man off his daily dose of aspirin because it thins the blood. He gives him Afrin drops that seem to clot the ruptured vein. He's calm once the fright has past. He's not in pain. I think he'll die a peaceful death when the time comes. Fourteen years from now.

Diego races about us. He's the delightful son of Gabi, Rita's first daughter, who's as beautiful as Rita herself and is, like Rita, a single mother. Gabi's son was born right here in Godot's apartment where Rita installed her in 2001, so she could look after her the way her mother looked after Lupíta in Zitácuaro in 1997. Within these symmetries are secrets whose depth I discern but am at a loss to understand or describe. Rita's second daughter, Lupita, is now seven and has lived with Godot practically all her life. Once Gabi is settled in, Rita brings her sister Delia to live with Godot and help her care for what remains of the minotaur.

Rita needs help. Hectorcito's aches and pains mount geometrically and silently. He falls into the limbo of old age, and little by little he loses the ability to walk and talk. He forgets who he is and forgets whom he's with. It's the sort of illness that clouds his eyes a bit more every day. You can sense it in the way he moves, his choice of words, his memories, his dreams. He suffers from terminal old age. Rita and Delia, Gabi, Guadalupe and Diego stand by Godot as his placid and implacable affliction slowly consumes him. The care he gets from his improbable family is as improbable and unlikely as the family itself.

"Dieguito was born on January 8," Godot says, "Your grandfather who so dearly loves you, was born January 16. We could be watching Lupito reappear."

"You mean to say Diego's the reincarnation of Lupito?"

"I mean, if your grandfather could do what he did with three years' schooling on Cozumel, then now, when the schools are so good, there's no end to what this child might do."

He has trouble sticking to any one subject:

"The father of your grandfather, Guadalupe Aguilar Carrasco, was named Guadalupe Aguilar Leal, and he wasn't too tall. He was on the short side, almost a dwarf. But what a set of cojones!"

He starts to chuckle:

"The man had six wives. He'd make his sons line up in front of him, then he'd grab them by the chin and say, 'All right, let's see what you've got.' He'd inspect them to make sure they really were his sons. He had no idea how many sons he had."

He loses his train of thought and ends by saying:

"My head's a blank slate."

He looks at me, and I can see he's struggling to recognize me. But, finally, he makes the connection:

"How are my grandchildren? Are they in college now?"

On Father's Day I take him old photos of Doña Emma. In

one they're together on their honeymoon, standing on the rocky beach of the Campeche Yacht Club. Héctor's wearing a white linen suit. Emma's holding onto his arm and smiling. They both look straight at the camera. It's a beautiful photo from the days of their youth, full of the promise of a bright future. Godot looks at it very carefully.

"Who's that?"

"It's you."

"I don't believe it. But if you say so."

Then his thoughts turn to his houses in Chetumal, the block where my mother's dry goods store used to be, etc.

"Who ended up with those houses?"

"Goyo Marrufo."

"I paid off Don Goyo. I donated blood for him in Mérida. What happened?"

"You used the houses to secure a loan."

"I didn't owe anybody anything in Chetumal. I repaid every last cent. But I don't remember, I don't know what happened. There's no way I can fight back."

"My left arm's useless," he says, smiling angelically.

"And the little fellow?"

"Can only make water nowadays."

I ask him for his wallet. He gives it to me, and I add four hundred pesos to the eight hundred already in it.

"You have eight hundred here," I tell him.

"I'm rolling in money."

By November 2004, Hectorcito is struggling with bouts of high fever and choking phlegm caused by pneumonia. A parallel pneumonia strikes Doña Emma. I check them into the English Hospital two days apart. They're released two days before the New Year. When Godot leaves the hospital he's a walking pharmacy.

He takes:

Añtruline, 100 milligrams, once daily

Sideral, 50 milligrams, one capsule daily.

Ortopisique, 5 milligrams, ½ tablet nightly.

Ebixa, 10 milligrams, ½ mornings and ½ at bedtime

Risperdal, 1 microgram (suspension) 0.25 of syringe daily

All the above are pyschiatric drugs to strengthen memory, combat depression, and enhance sleep.

He also takes:

Senocot (for constipation).

Adulat 20 milligrams, delayed action (for high blood pressure)

Valdure, 40 micrograms. For joint, hip and leg pain.

Asprin (to prevent heart attacks).

Life goes on adjusted according to its limits.

During my morning visits to Hectorcito in the early months of 2005, he's usually eating a breakfast of chilaquiles in the bosom of his acquired family. Sharing his table are: Rita, the head of the household; her sister Delia, acting as full-time nurse; Lupita, now eight; Gabriela, twenty-two; and her three-year-old son Dieguito, now Hectorcito's preferred companion. As always, Hectorcito is a finicky eater as he sits amidst this throng, better accompanied than ever in his waning years. The people gathered about him at the table are now his hospital and his family, the only one he's had since his father and Trinidad died. Life is prone to odd ups and downs. Godot now has the family he could never have anywhere else.

On May 20, 2005, Emma Camín dies at the English hospital. The morning of her death, Hèctor tells Rita that he's seen Emma Camín standing in the doorway to his room. Days later he begins his own downward spiral. For the first time in all the years of Godot's declining health, Rita cries into the phone. She says, "Hectorcito is fast losing ground; he's terribly depressed and thinks his children have forgotten about him."

This morning he told Delia and Rita: "Forty-eight hours from now it will seem as if I never was."

He can't sleep, he's plagued by visions. He says someone or

something is coming to get him. He tries to get out of his chair and go home. He calls for his mother, whom he claims to have seen beside him that morning. What happened to his father? Where are his brothers and sisters? He doesn't recognize Rita, and recognizing Delia, he wants to know:

"Where's that girl who treats me so well?"

The alarm in Rita's voice leads me to summon his children. Luis Miguel and his wife María Pía come to visit Godot, followed by Emma and Miguel, then Pilar and Victor. In the afternoon Juan José comes with Lucero. They don't come to see him often, a failing Godot makes them pay for. But they're all here in this moment of real emergency. Hectorcito can barely talk, he struggles to make eye contact when someone speaks to him. One eye is more open than the other, his chin droops, drool trickles down from his open mouth. Sparks of mischief or glee brighten his wandering gaze from time to time only to flicker out a moment later.

The following morning he wakes up shivering. They change his sleep medication, and we hope the change is for the better. I go to see him at breakfast time. He seems improved, and he tries to eat unassisted. It's nearly impossible to understand what he says.

"Vash eguir grethiendo?" he asks. ("Are you going to keep on growing?")

He has to repeat the question three times, a grueling effort.

His next utterance is a non sequitur:

"Titirra tirra." ("Earth, earth.")

Then:

"L stcy suv coscas a omrr." ("I'm writing Omar's things for him.")

Then:

"Viy a trbarr soli e l tiinda." ("I'm going to work in the store by myself.")

Finally:

"Ne pso den currto anyy." ("I won't get past third grade.")

I realize that, in his head, he's regressed to his childhood. He's in a dispute with his father about the store where all the brothers must work. He does his brother Omar's fourth-grade homework, and he's mad about that.

Suddenly, in the middle of his evocation of Omar, his eyes light up. He looks over my shoulder towards the wall and says with unexpected clarity:

"The Marrufos. That's where they are."

It chills my blood to think he's seeing the Marrufos, his mother's side of the family. More likely, it's his mother Juana Marrufo, who's figured in his past hallucinations. I don't turn to follow his gaze.

"Tes middo?" he then asks, stuttering once again. ("Are you afraid?")

One of my hands is between both of his, and I move it in a way that could seem like a shudder. His look is stern now, the look of a man who knows a thing or two about life.

"No," I reply.

He regards me with an old man's skepticism. The expression has less to do with his thoughts than with a wisdom imprinted deep in tissues and glands on the verge of extinction.

The doctors' offensive triumphs Napoleonically over Hectorcito's devastated body. They change his medications, control his fever, fill him with oxygen, suppress pharmaceutically induced psychoses, and, with an adequate dose of Dormecum, afford him six hours of sleep. Two weeks later, he's visibly improved. He's alert and cheerful; he speaks clearly and contributes appropriately to conversations going on around him.

His collar is turned inside out under his shirt, and Rita tries to straighten it. She slips her hand between the fabric and his skin and cautions:

"My hand is cold."

"Cold hands, cold heart," says Hectorcito.

I remind him of his past.

"These women (Rita and Delia) treat you better than anyone

past or present, knucklehead. Better than mamá Juanita, better than Mrs. Ruelas."

Mrs. Ruelas has been on my mind because she's called often in these days of crisis, and I've told Rita about the part she played in Godot's past.

"Who's Mrs. Ruelas?" Godot sneers.

"The babe that used to look after you," I tell him.

Godot looks at Rita and smiles:

"My son knows everything."

The most important thing about these precarious days is that his fever has stayed down.

"You can't imagine what Don Lupe's done to me," Rita says.

She means my grandfather Lupe, who died in 1976. A hand-colored photo makes his presence felt in Hectorcito's room.

"I moved him from where he was, in front of your dad's bed, to make room for a new clock that I bought," Rita says. "I hung the picture on the wall over the headboard next to mamá Juanita, and the next day the photos had changed places. Don Lupe was where mamá Juanita used to be and mamá Juanita where I'd put Don Lupe. I asked Gabi why she'd changed the pictures, and she said, 'I didn't change anything.' That's when I noticed that the new clock I'd hung where Don Lupe's picture used to be had stopped at three o'clock. And you know what? That night my alarm clock, which I always set for six, had gone off at three. It went off at three, the same time the new clock stopped."

I follow Rita into the bedroom, and she shows me that the framed photo of Don Lupe is back in its accustomed place next to the television. He's in his seventies, and he's wearing his horn-rimmed glasses. His wide forehead is wrinkled with age, his eyes unclouded but sad. Though his jaw is firmly set, the smile on his lips is no longer convincing. Rita has draped a wooden rosary over Don Lupe's picture. The beads pass over his nose, and the cross dangles down from the beads.

"Was Don Lupe angry, Rita?"

"I think it bothered him," Rita says. "I told América, the therapist who comes to pump the phlegm out of Don Héctor, and she says the dead often keep watch over the living. We've all felt Don Lupe tapping us on the shoulder late at night. He wants to make sure we take good care of Hectorcito."

"Was América the one who saw the ghosts?"

"She said they were watching her from the bathroom."

We return to our places at the table. Doña Leti, the new caregiver, says, "That room is full of vibrations, but they're good vibrations."

Rita says:

"I asked mamá Juanita if her son was likely to suffer. 'If he is,' I told her, 'I'd rather you come for him and get it over with. Don't let them cart him off to the hospital and abuse him.'"

Hectorcito smiles. He doesn't understand what they're talking about, but he smiles as if he did. I wonder about all the spirits and shades in his past, the battle of hexes that for a time served to explain his odd behavior. According to Luisa and Emma, he was jinxed. They had him spiritually cleansed by the witch who, Mrs. Ruelas says, kept him in her spell for twenty years.

I know nothing about Mrs. Ruelas. She used to call the apartment on Tehuantepec, and now she's begun calling here. One day she comes to visit, and she tells Rita she met Godot in 1980 when he took papers to be copied in the shop where she worked on Bucareli. He took her Arab pastries, which is how they became friends. Trinidad was very jealous, and Mrs. Ruelas had to watch her step to keep Trini from casting a spell on her since it was widely known that she could. Mrs. Ruelas says Trini took in boarders and Godot took a room in her apartment. In time they became, first, partners and then man and wife. Mrs. Ruelas says Godot was spellbound by Trini from the moment he laid eyes on her, and she made him forget about his past. Mrs. Ruelas swears that when

Trini dies, Hectorcito gets her—Mrs. Ruelas—to look after him. She makes his meals, washes his clothes, and welcomes him to her house. But Godot keeps going back to Trini's place and, for some inexplicable reason, refuses to move out. Or, Mrs. Ruelas says, for a reasons all too explicable.

Mrs. Ruelas asks Rita if I'd mind her visiting Hectorcito. I tell Rita that, far from minding, I'd be glad to have her visit and to let me know when she does.

This is how I come to meet Mrs. Ruelas, Godot's young partner at the time of Trini's death in 1980.

The day Mrs. Ruelas comes to the apartment she brings photos from her time with Godot. In the photos she's a good-looking woman of forty with big hair, a wide forehead, and a finely chiseled nose. The body of the sixtyish woman speaking into Hectorcito's ear as I arrive retains some of the firmness and agreeable proportions of years past. She rises to greet me and seems genuinely pleased to make my acquaintance. She's nervous and talks too much, but she's far from unsure of herself. Without further ado, she takes up the subject that brought her here: Godot, the Godot who lived with Nelly Mulley.

"Ms. Trini was a witch. She practiced white magic, black magic, magic of all colors," Mrs. Ruelas began. "One day she gave your father a tongue lashing aimed at the two Aguilars she knew about: the father and the son, Don Lupe and his boy Héctor: 'Just you wait,' she warned. 'The two of you are going to take a real spill from your high horses.' And she was right. From then on Héctor's businesses went from bad to worse. She just wore him out. Your father's back was all bent over, and he walked staring at the floor. Though I don't believe in witchcraft, we went somewhere or other for a cleansing. A cleansing consists of passing an egg over your whole body, your head your chest, and other parts I won't bother to mention. But, I swear to God, when the egg was passed over Héctor, he turned as red as a boiled shrimp, and when they cracked the egg, well, it's hard to explain, but a parade of clowns like the ones on Tarot cards came out, and their chests were clearly marked with the curses—the many, many curses—that weighed him down. When we got out of there, I could see Héctor was standing up straight. Though he was walking upright, he was very tired. Ms. Nelly was your dad's wife. When she died, old clients came to her house and got a lot of her photos, pictures of people linked to her in good ways and bad ways. After a while the witches came and cleansed the house with herbs. You should have heard all the screaming and squealing let loose by the cleansing. You could hear the clatter of machetes. The neighbors said at least three people died in that house."

Mrs. Ruelas speaks from a chair between Héctorcito, who's in his orthopedic chair, and me. I'm seated in my favorite black leather easy chair, the one I'd given Hectorcito in a fetishistic swap for an old watch his father gave him.

"Do you remember the cleansing Mrs. Ruelas is talking about?" I ask Godot.

He replies:

"Of course I do. On Bucareli I had a bookkeeping business. Among others, I kept books for Philco and the Enchanted Cradle."

"He doesn't remember," Ms. Ruelas says. "But I know for sure he's laughing."

She turns back to Godot:

"Go ahead and laugh, Héctor. You never told me you had children."

She turns to me:

"When I heard you'd reappeared, I said, 'You're very selfish, Hector. You never told me about your children.'"

She turns to Godot:

"You don't turn your back on your children, Héctor. A father can't just forget about his children as if they didn't exist."

She turns to me:

"When you came into the picture, I told him: 'Be grateful,

don't be angry at your son. Be good to the one who's good to you and treats you kindly.' Because your father was very angry. He has a terrible disposition, and, at the same time, I can tell you he's as good as they come. He's a good man. Nothing makes me angrier than the way people took advantage of him. Everybody wanted to get money out of him, and he let them. A worker of mine—a man called *El Acapulco*—took him to a bar and on the way out asked him for money. I never did. I disapproved of that sort of thing, I was never the kind of woman who asks for favors or tries to exploit others. My mother, bless her heart, put the fear of Almighty God in her children."

I ask her what kind of curses did Nelly Mulley lay on Godot.

Her reply:

"When Nelly Mulley died, Héctor asked me to help him with some clothes he wanted to give away. He never told me to whom. He was very mysterious, he was always very mysterious. Among the things that showed up under the clothes in one of his drawers were his picture and a dead bird. There was a cross on the photo, and the bird was pinned to the photo."

"Nelly Mulley," Godot says. "Trinidad Reséndiz, widow of Fernández. I lived in her house. I was a lodger. I had a bookkeeping business. I did the books for Philco, The Enchanted Cradle, and others."

"She was your wife, Héctor," Mrs. Ruelas tells him. "She was your wife."

She turns to me:

"When Nelly died, her two servants stole everything she had. One was tall and very homely, the other was short and even homelier. They robbed Héctor, too. The tall one said Nelly left her her bed and an armoire, she even hired a mover to take them away for her. The short one stayed behind to see if Héctor would keep her on. When I walked in, she looked at me as if to say: So what're you up to? I saw she wasn't about to go anywhere, so I went into the dining room, and there she was. The short maid was hiding behind the door. We started checking the premises, and my eyes were opened. Ms. Nelly had a dresser, and, when you opened the drawers there was a niche where she kept the money from her business in cash. When we got to the niche, there was nothing there, everything was gone. They stole it all from your father."

Ángeles, my daughter Catalina, and I pay Hectorcito a visit. He's alert and, within the parameters of his awareness, quite lucid. Catalina hasn't seen him for some time, and when she approaches him, he says, "Who am I talking to?"

Ángeles praises him to the skies. He looks so handsome, she says, so well dressed and well groomed.

"I keep up appearances," Hectorcito replies.

The two women address him with mock gravity, and he takes them absolutely seriously. He tries to maintain eye contact, and when he can't, he starts laughing.

"You're both so beautiful, I get confused," he says when they pamper him and lavish him with attention.

After the visit Ángeles tells me:

"Your father really is like a saint now. He's suffered like a dog, and all that suffering has purified him. He got his reward late in life, and he'll die in peace."

On January 4, 2007, Godot is trembling with chills and fever, and he goes to the emergency room at Mocel hospital. The crisis is neutralized in short order, and while we're waiting for the doctor to sign the release forms, I chat with Rita. She's asked me for a loan to buy a new lot on the outskirts of Zitácuaro, and I ask what happened to her old lot. It's paid off, she tells me. She's worked since she was a little girl, and she put her life's savings into the place. It now has two rooms, a bathroom, and a washtub.

"My mother put me to work when I was nine, the same age Lupita is now. She collected my pay and wouldn't let me spend it. My only clothes were the ones I was given to work in. I don't think

I ever had a house, a real home. Not ever. So I talked myself into believing the place where I worked was my home. And I still feel that way."

I'm not sure what made her tell me about her father. "He never lived with us until I was fifteen. He worked for Pemex and made good money. He wore boots and a nice jacket. He'd get out his wallet, and I'd watch him count his money. But he didn't live with us. He'd go around with someone on his arm, and my mother would say, 'There goes your dad.' And we'd chase after him like little kids shouting: 'Daddy, daddy.' And when he looked back, the woman who was with him would say, 'Are those your children?' And he'd say, 'Yes, they're mine.' He never tried to deny it. We'd ask him for money, and he'd give us twenty-centavo coins, the ones with the sun on them, enough for penny candy. Then he got laid off from Pemex. And can you imagine, the national oil company wouldn't even give him severance pay? He spent all his money on lawyers and appeals, but it didn't get him anywhere. After that he couldn't get a regular job, and the work he could get didn't pay very much. He had no savings because he always spent what he earned on women. Then, when he was flat broke, he came to live with my mother."

She finally gets around to answering my question about her new lot. "It's very pretty. It has a view. It's not too high up, but it's on a slope and looks over the highway into Zitácuaro. In the distance you can see some towns with lots of trees and sunshine. The view is very nice. I'm very happy with it, with what I've accomplished. The first time I got off the track was when I had Gabi. When she was a baby, I had to look after her and look for a job at the same time, and it got me to thinking. I said, God, what I wouldn't do for a plot of ground and a place to live. And God gave me my wish, I got what I asked for."

"You can go home now," the doctor tells Hectorcito,

"To Chetumal?" he replies.

He goes home in what for him is a party mood. You can see it in his eyes. They take him to his room to see his mamá Juanita.

"Is mamá Juanita here?" he asks, full of childish eagerness.

They tell him she is, her picture's right here. But that's not what he's asking about.

June 29, 2008:

Godot is slipping, he's in a foul mood.

"Who-o-o-r ruh, ruh yu-o-o?" ("Who are you?")

"I'm your son Héctor," I say.

"Wh-o-o?" ("Who?")

"I'm your son, yours and Emma Camín's."

"Yuh, yuh, hurrd Mmruffo?" ("You're a Marrufo?")

"Part Marrufo," I say.

He's badly disoriented, and it makes him mad. His lip is drawn back over his gum in a way that adds a cadaverous wrinkle to his face.

"I-i-iwon lul'liv tuh ano.. anoladje." ("I won't live to an old age.")

He hasn't slept well, he looks warn out. His unfocused eyes are watery and irritated. He takes a small mouthful of scrambled egg, then spits it onto his plate. Rita puts carrot juice in front of him in a plastic sippy cup with a straw. He rejects it with a gesture suggesting that he's already full. He won't look at me. His gaze wanders over the table cloth, over the dishes in front of Rita, then off to one side at Delia, at his nurse across from Delia.

"I'm sorry I couldnt brlr lo tetgo," he says, lapsing unto unintelligibility.

He's makes sounds instead of words, and the sounds make more sense than the words. He's losing both language and teeth, and his head is full of shadows shaped by random tides. He looks tired, distracted, fed up. I can't help thinking he could die at any moment. A swallow of water or a drop of wayward vomit in his windpipe is all it would take. His life hangs by a slender thread. He could die right now, this very minute, at whatever instant his mysterious inner mechanisms happen to stop. I recall a little boy with my name who lies awake at night in the stunning darkness of Chetumal, peering at the mystery of being alive, the untethered imaginings of his beating heart, the miracle of blood pumping over the pathways depicted in the anatomical drawing I saw in school that morning. I'm kept from sleeping by the mystery of my lungs inflating like balloons, by the terrifying thought that this perfect machine might suddenly stop working for the same reason that it keeps on going: for no reason whatsoever.

Advanced age is a disease in itself. It drains the body, ruins the face, gnaws at the bones, and empties the soul.

Hectorcito loses the ability to speak, then the ability to focus his eyes. He forgets how to chew, how to swallow without choking, how to lift things in his fingers. He can't sit up and must be gently tied down in his wheelchair. He still gets pleasure from the few bland morsels the doctor tells Rita he can eat and from her caress just about any time he sets eyes on her. As long as he can breathe Rita is willing to do whatever it takes to keep Hectorcito from letting go of her hand and vanishing into the ether.

On November 22 in the year 2010, at four twenty in the morning, Rita calls, sobbing into the phone: "Mister Héctor," she says. "You dad has left us."

We get up and dress knowing the evil day has begun and there's no time for us to do more than throw on the first clothes that come to hand.

Rita's house, the dwelling of Hectorcito's last family, is in a state of mourning deeper than ours. They dress him in his dark, pinstriped suit, the one he liked to put on seven or eight years ago when he could still wear a suit. I tie his tie in a windsor knot, a fashion I was taught but never used. I call my brothers and sisters and arrange another wake at the French Cemetery.

Rita doesn't take communion at the religious service. Ángeles notices and asks her why she abstains. She explains she's excommunicated for having two children out of wedlock. Ángeles has a word with the priest who said Mass. She asks him to disabuse Rita of her absurd belief. He agrees with a smile that he reinforces by hearing her confession and giving her communion himself. Rita takes the wafer for the first time in the twenty-six years since she had Gabi at the age of twenty. Through the death of Godot she gains a sense of spiritual relief tantamount to absolution.

I return from the wake with a silver urn with the ashes of Godot and Hectorcito inside. I put it on the bottom shelf of my bookcase to await the ritual I prepared for these ashes, namely: to put them together with Emma's which I preserved under the weeping willow Ángeles planted in our garden. Now I have a better option. Five years ago we planted a sequoia in the same garden, and it has flourished splendidly. It's now a giant shrub twenty meters high, a sequoia pup where I might lay Héctor's and Emma's ashes to rest and satisfy my fetishistic dream of reuniting them.

Shortly after Godot's death, Rita tells me she's decided to go back to Zitácuaro. They'll live in the house that`s built on their new lot, the one overlooking the highway and the tree-shaded towns in the distance. It's Monday, December 13th; they plan to leave on Sunday the 19th so they'll have time to settle in and celebrate Christmas. News of their departure leaves a hole in my heart. I haven't been able to speak to Rita since the death of my father. On Saturday the 18th I stop by the delicatessen that's opened on the corner for bread, butterballs, cheeses and chocolates. I find Gabi and Lupita sitting in the middle of the sala surrounded by cartons packed with their belongings. Diego's in his room watching television. Rita's on the phone with Mrs. Ruelas, and I ask to speak to her. Mrs. Ruelas reiterates that Godot never told her about us, that if Godot had mentioned us, she'd have looked us up because we were his children. "He was a good man," Mrs. Ruelas says. "I asked him to stop drinking because he drank and he didn't hold his liquor too well." I tell her Héctor was the son of a teetotaling father whose children all drank. "That's right, Perfecto was a very heavy drinker," Mrs. Ruelas says. So was Omar, I add. And Ángel, too.

The tippling offspring of a teetotaling father.

Rita says they're moving in the morning. She wants to know what they can take with them. Take everything, I tell her, except our family heirlooms. She asks me to be specific, and we review the contents of the apartment item by item. She can take the beds, including the hospital bed where Hectorcito spent his final days; her father is barely able to walk now, and she'll be needing such a bed soon enough. The same applies to the oxygen tank and, of course, the television sets as well as the furniture in the sala. Except for the lounge chair where my mother liked to sit, my sisters may want to hold onto that.

The move gets under way early on Sunday, December 19. Rita's furniture is loaded onto a small pickup. Though at first it seems as if nothing will fit in the cargo bed, it turns out to be as spacious as Noah's Ark. The owner of the pickup that takes Rita and her belongings to Zitácuaro wanted 7,500 pesos for the trip.

"But he settled for 6,500 when I started to cry."

Rita Tenorio.

All that was left in the apartment was my mother's chair, the big blue lounger of her final years that became a hand-me-down to my father. As of tomorrow, only the chair will remain in the deserted apartment. A place that grew ever more important to me in recent years, my father's final home, will have disappeared. I picture myself sitting in that chair the next day, in the empty apartment.

As I write this line, I imagine I'm still sitting there.

Epilogue

My father dies on November 22, 2010. As I leave the apartment where she's looked after him for years, Rita presses a small portfolio of imitation leather into my hand. There's a lock on it, and I leave it next to the metal urn with his ashes. In my studio the two objects sit side by side on a bookshelf that runs the length of the wall that houses my library. The portfolio stays there undisturbed until I open it on April 19, 2011, Ash Wednesday.

The first item of interest to emerge from the portfolio is a picture of my father I'd never seen before, a snapshot taken when he was six. The sepia photo dates from 1923 and is pasted to a rectangle of finely textured cardboard that serves as both backing and faux mat. For some odd reason my father held onto it through the years. The young boy has the big eyes of his father, Don Lupe. His hair is parted on the left, but no comb can subdue the cowlicks behind each ear. In no other photo does he resemble his father more. He has his father's penetrating stare, the frown and the pinched mouth that tell the world he's not about to take orders from anyone. For me he's a stranger: so similar to his imperious father and so different from the shadow father he became.

The next item I take out of Rita's portfolio is a bundle of identification cards and credentials saved since primary school. Then comes the fascinating succession of plastic envelopes with the sort of materials I'd been hoping to find: death certificates, wedding announcements, wills, the dossiers of lawsuits that track my father's doings through years of which I know next to nothing.

This is where I find the record of the crypt in the Piedad section of the French Cemetery, where Godot and Trini bury Don Lupe and where Trini had previously buried: her parents, Balbina Vega y Remigio Reséndiz; her older sister, María Ciriaca Rosaura (Zulema Moraima); and her daughter Nellina, who died prematurely. Here I find Don Lupe's 1976 death certificate and the 1980 bills for burying Trini in a different section of the French Cemetery, away from her family. One document is a receipt made out to Héctor Aguilar Marrufo in the amount of thirty-thousand pesos for a "white gravestone in the Italian style for my wife."

I begin going through the portfolio on Ash Wednesday, 2011. On Easter Sunday I go to the Piedad section of the French Cemetery to locate the graves. The cemetery is on the corner of Cuauhtémoc and the viaduct beside the Piedad River. There's a sentence in French on the arch over the entrance: *Here lie those who are with the Lord.* The outer fence opens onto a beautiful avenue with elegant mausoleums on either side. Once inside the fence, I find one of the sextons who maintain the place and ask where to park my car. He points to a space just inside the fence and in front of the offices. My question tells him I'm new to the cemetery. He asks what he can do for me in a voice that manages to seem both forbidding and accommodating. I tell him I'm looking for my grandparents' graves. I show him the sketch of plot locations that I found in Rita's portfolio.

"I'm looking for tomb 201 on Avenue 6," I say.

"This way," he replies.

He quickly starts left along the main avenue.

The avenues are set two or three meters apart from one another, and it doesn't take long to reach Avenue 6. Grave numbers are carved on the bases of the crypts. We walk some 200 meters to tomb 201, The sexton sweeps the dirt off a base and shows me the number I'm looking for. The flat stone is covered with leaves and dirt. On each corner there's a marble vase and flowers. There's a crack in one of them.

"What's the name you're looking for?" the sexton asks.

"Trinidad," I reply.

He dislodges the caked mud from the epitaph with his hands, and the name appears.

"Trinidad," he says.

Leaves and dirt make the epitaph hard to decipher. I hesitate to disturb a grave, but the full inscription can't be read unless it's cleaned off, and I can't clean it from a distance. I step forward and crouch down on the gravestone. The message that appears in low relief against a fading gold background isn't what I expected. It stands the saga of my long-missing father on its head.

I take some photos with my cell phone. I clean some more and read some more. I take more photos from the sidewalk, from under the scrawny privet tree to one side of the plot.

"Would you like me to help you find another grave?" the sexton says.

"Yes, please."

"Which one?"

"Two-sixty-eight, Avenue 19."

"That's another section."

We walk back towards the main avenue, retracing our steps.

The sexton explains that the cemetery is divided into 25 avenues and seven streets. The avenues go the width of the cemetery, the streets go its length. The avenues are longer, the streets shorter. The chapel and the main avenue are between Avenues 13 and 14. Thirteen goes all the way down to First, and 14 goes up to 25. We quickly reach Avenue 18, then we walk sixty tombs to 268.

"Here's 268," he says. "What's the name you're looking for?"

"José G. Aguilar."

A similar carpet of mud and leaves covers this grave. Once again the sexton dispatches the patina over the name with his hand. This time the letters set in low relief against a fading gold background read:

José G. Aguilar C.
Your wife Flora
And your children Trini and Héctor
Thank you for your goodness
Ω 23 IV 1976

I position myself to record the inscription on my cell phone, but the sexton says:

"No photos. You took the others before I noticed, so I let it go. But it's against the rules to take pictures."

I copy the inscription by hand and don't insist on photos. On my way out I say to the sexton:

"This cemetery doesn't get many visitors. Today's Easter Sunday, there ought to be lots of people here."

"There used to be, but not anymore."

"How come?"

"Not many people remember their dead."

I have lunch in an Arab restaurant. When I get home, Ángeles is on her way out to buy fruit. I take her in the car.

"Did you find the graves?"

"Both of them."

"And what did you see?"

"Undying love."

"Tell me what you saw."

First I read her the inscription on Don Lupe's grave, the one signed, "*Your children Trini and Héctor.*"

"So they were in love with each other. They were a couple, a family," Ángeles said. "Don't make me angry. Tell me what did he put on the witch's grave?"

I find the photo in my cell phone and set it between us for her to read. The inscription reads:

My darling Trinidad, my one true love,
whom I remember for the beauty and sweetness
of our life together, I adore you heart and soul
                              Héctor

"He never talked about that," Ángeles says. "He never spoke of his love for Trini."

"No, but that's what the epitaph says."

2

I wake up with a sore neck, and I feel faint climbing out of bed. I think, as my brother Luis Miguel writes of himself in a poem: I'll be annoyed when it's my turn to die. I pick up my iPad and use it to light my way. The sun isn't up yet, and the room is dark as pitch. I shuffle around the bed and go to the sink for the analgesic I use every morning for my sore muscles, then I go to the next room where the bathtub is, where I raise my feet and fold my arms each morning to ease the pain that accumulates in my shoulders overnight.

The bathroom has a gray stone floor with heating coils underneath that make it deliciously warm in winter. The pain in my back dissipates when I stretch out on the floor. With the pain come visions of the face of Emma Camín. How can Emma Camín be dead? How strange it is that she and Luisa are dead and I'll never see them again.

I leave the bathroom in semi-darkness, guided by the iPad. When I go down the stairs to the ground floor I feel the winter chill of the morning. I can see my breath as I cross the yard to my studio; water droplets form in each breath I take of the damp air. The sunrise is a mix of red and grime. I see the sequoia that's grown up in the yard over the past five years. It's little more than a shrub, the trunk has yet to take shape, but it's already twenty meters high. I remember it was just a shoot of fifty centimeters when Luis de Pablo gave it to me in a pot I could carry under my arm like a baby.

To fulfill my childish dream of reuniting them, I'd planned to bury Emma's and Héctor's ashes at the foot of that tree. The success of the tree adds to my melancholy. I turn to look up at its green branches. The tree takes pleasure from the morning cold that diminishes the pleasure I get from looking up at it too long. It aggravates the soreness in my neck and forces me to lower my head. I proceed to my studio with my head down. I don't know why I go to the studio when it's so cold, but I do. It's a daily routine that entails booting up the computer and checking my mail. I don't check the mail. I open the files where I keep the materials for this book, among them the transcriptions from the seven days when I recorded Luisa and Emma Camín in April and May of the year Luisa died. I've transcribed and edited these conversations. I jump from the files with the transcripts to the recordings themselves. I click on the first one. I dislike having to fiddle with the sound and rein in the decibels captured in the original recording. Having adjusted the volume, I hear the alien sound of my own voice explaining why I want to preserve the ensuing conversation. Then I hear Luisa and Emma start to laugh and wonder if what we're doing is really worthwhile. It's a kind of flirtation that soon gives way to reminiscence. They begin telling stories and butting in on each other. They're oblivious to the telephone when its ring echoes through the house. They correct each other and step on eachothers' words. The clock strikes in the breakfast nook, tolling the irrelevant hours as Emma and Luisa continue on under full sail. Before seven minutes go by they've told: how Don Lupe landed in Chetumal; how he left home with help from a black woman who "cast out spells" and showed him how to get rich; how he broke away from his father.

It's a familiar story, one I've heard a thousand times, and there are many more that I recorded and draw on in the writing of this book. But the stories and the voices feel different to me now. They're less a narrative challenge than something like a salve. They catch hold of me like old songs on the radio. Their voices are old, they flow, they stop and start, but the exuberance of the stories they tell is inexhaustible. It fills my ears, soothes my sore neck, and straightens my posture. My backache disappears along with the chill of morning, the sadness of night, the demise of these women and the certainty of my own. Their words are like caresses from two elderly ladies not much given to caressing.

They tell and retell their stories with the mix of facts, idioms and dialogues characteristic of good narrators. I stretch my legs and settle back in my chair. I slip into a dreamworld where my grandfather and father tramp through the forests of the Petén and Quintana Roo, an inchoate world with the voices of Emma and Luisa in the background. The voices literally jump out at me. They take me back to childhood dreams of striding across a plain free from the bonds of gravity, as omnipotent as the little boy dreaming in a place called Chetumal where there was a hurricane and two sisters who talked endlessly into the night. I'm no dreamer, but these imaginings free me from myself, from my sore neck, from the cold of a dreary morning. I'm snapped out of my revery by Luisa's laugh near the end of our first recording on April 16, 1991, an awakening that tells me I've dozed off for an hour and a half since Luisa is now describing the booty Don Lupe stole from his son in 1957 and took to Cuba in 1960 only to lose it in the island's Revolution. I've heard her laugh at the end of the first tape any number of times, but I hear it now as if for the first time. Luisa's laugh mocks the chicanery in the tales she tells, and Emma joins in her mirth. For the first time I'm moved to listen to this tape in a different way, to share her pleasure upon reaching a stage in her life when she can find more humor than remorse in the losses of the past. It strikes me that this book should leave the sisters at their best, laughing at their own stories. That morning they're in high spirits, and though death is creeping up on them, it hasn't caught them yet, not while they can still talk and laugh as they do that morning. Not yet.

The dilemma of Emma's and Héctor's ashes remains unsolved. I haven't decided where to put them. More to the point, I've decided not to put them together. They'll stay where they were: Héctor's in his silver-plated urn on the bookshelf in my studio; Emma's in her small silver jewelry box in a drawer of my night table.

HÉCTOR AGUILAR CAMÍN

HÉCTOR AGUILAR CAMÍN (born July 9, 1946 in Chetumal) is a Mexican writer, journalist and historian. As a journalist, he has written for *Unomásuno* and *La Jornada*, the magazine *Proceso*, and currently for *Milenio*. He founded and is the editor of *Nexos*, one of the leading Mexican cultural magazines. In 2017, he received a lifetime achievement award from Mexico's Instituto de Bellas Artes, the country's top cultural institution. *Adiós To My Parents* (which as *Adiós a los padres* was shortlisted for the 2016 Mario Vargas Llosa Prize) is his third book to be published by Schaffner Press.

CHANDLER THOMPSON

Chandler Thompson acquired his translating chops in the 1960s as a Peace Corps Volunteer, then while writing news stories in English from raw copy in Spanish and French. He's covered Mexico as a stringer for *The Christian Science Monitor* and as reporter for *The El Paso Times*. In addition to *Adiós To My Parents*, he has translated two novels by Héctor Aguilar Camín for Schaffner Press: *Death In Veracruz* and *Day In, Day Out*.